Death of a Plantation

by

Sherman Briscoe

RoseDog ❧ Books

PITTSBURGH, PENNSYLVANIA 15222

ISBN: 978-1-4349-9257-4
Library of Congress Control Number: 2008934283

Printed in the United States of America

First Printing

For more information or to order additional books, please contact:
RoseDog Books
701 Smithfield Street
Pittsburgh, Pennsylvania 15222
U.S.A.
1-800-834-1803
www.rosedogbookstore.com

This Book Is Dedicated to My Beloved Family

To my mother, Addie Marsaw; my wife, Revella C. Briscoe; my daughter, Marion Finley; my son and daughter-in-law, Percy W. Briscoe and Jeanette Briscoe; my grandsons, Sherman Briscoe II and John K. Briscoe; my granddaughter and my grandson-in-law, Karen A. Briscoe-Reed and Eric D. Reed; and most especially, to my beloved great-grandson, Eric Jacob Briscoe-Reed.

Also to all of the disadvantaged farmers and sharecroppers I had the privilege to serve.

Contents

Autobiography of Sherman Briscoe

Sherman Briscoe, the author of this book, *Death of a Plantation,* was born on a farm in Brunswich, Mississippi, on December 15, 1908. He was fatherless at the age of seven, to be reared to manhood and indoctrinated in the value of education by a beautiful, strong black mother, the late Addle Peters Briscoe Marsaw, whom he passionately loved all his life. From Greenville, Mississippi, whose quiet streets and railroad tracks he explored as a child, he was sent to boarding school at what is now Alcorn A&M College, in Lorman, Mississippi. He graduated from Southern University, Baton Rouge, Louisiana, to become a high school teacher of science and mathematics in Monroe, Louisiana, and publisher of his own newspaper, the weekly *Monroe Broadcast,* from 1932 to 1938.

Going North, embittered but unbowed by the mounting conflicts that killed his newspaper and threatened his own life, he became Assistant City Editor of the *Chicago Defender* in 1939, then National News Editor, and then Director of Circulation and Public Relations.

He was appointed in 1941 through the vigorous efforts of the late Claude A. Barnett, founder of the Associated Negro Press, and his own "credentials" as Information Specialist, U.S. Department of Agriculture. He served there until his retirement in 1968 and earned a master of arts degree in public administration at the American University, where he completed all required courses for the doctorate degree. He earned honors that included agriculture's second-highest tribute, the Superior Service Award, and the Tuskegee Institute of Alabama's "Man of the Year in Agriculture Award," and he covered assignments that included coordinating the department's press activities for its exhibit at the 1961 World Agriculture Fair in Cairo, Egypt.

He came out of retirement to become Executive Director of the National Newspaper Publishers Association in 1970, where he coordinated the organization's national activities from its office in Washington, D.C.; helped enlarge its scholarship fund to train black journalists; initiated publication of the Black Press Handbook and Directory; and contributed to the establishment of the Black Press Archives at Howard University.

He co-founded in 1943, The Capital Press Club, the nation's oldest predominantly black organization of the professional working journalists and creator of its "IN BOOK," a directory of Washington clubs and other organizations. He is a life member of the NAACP and long-time officer of the D.C. Branch and Board of Directors of the Twelfth Street YMCA, the National Press Club, and the Phi Beta Sigma Fraternity of the Southern University Alumni Club of Washington, D.C.

Foreword
by
Percy W. Briscoe

I am the son of the author, Sherman Briscoe, and am uniquely qualified to give an overview and attest to the customs, ways of life, and dialects of the black sharecroppers in the Mississippi Delta, as depicted in this book, entitled *Death of a Plantation*. This Book covers the periods of the 1940's through the 1950's, more or less. I was actually raised and lived as a cotton sharecropper in the Mississippi Delta during that era until the age of eighteen in the same counties of the State of Mississippi and in similar families, as are depicted in this book. I chopped, pick cotton and corns, and plowed mules, among other things. Most of the language in this book is done in an uneducated dialect and in a different world than were other people in much of America at a time and place where black people getting an education was not allowed. Yet in spite of their isolation in the world, it is clear they had the same underlying good common sense, judgment, and deeply seated religious beliefs in Christianity and God as other Americans, all of which are explicitly exhibited throughout this book.

Death of a Plantation starts out by telling how the main characters and a black cotton sharecropper family lived in Chicago after having lived on plantations all of their lives. After the family moved to Chicago, the men had to live separately from the women and children in order for the women and their children to remain on welfare while the men with no skills were working low-paying manual jobs and pretending to live elsewhere.

The book closely follows the lives of the members of one cotton sharecropper family who lived on the Bend Plantation: Silas Henry, the father with jet-black skin, as head of household; Becky Mae, the yellow-skinned spouse; the mother; Naomi, the very black teenage daughter who didn't like her color; River, a six-year-old son with yellow skin and curly hair, named for the nearby Mississippi River because he was born while the family was crossing it and who is the perceived narrator of the story in the book; Robert, the youngest child, who was left behind and was never found after the white men burned their house down; and Ms. Carrie Mae, the maternal grandmother who exclaimed that she would never leave the plantation because people in the cities freeze to death or die from starvation; and all the other black sharecroppers who lived on the Bend Plantation and the plantation owners, among others.

This book also goes on to explain the religious revival services on the plantation, such as young black children sitting on the mourner benches in churches during the autumn of the year to get born again. The ministers would explain that the children must have an unusual experience to be converted to religion and to become members of the churches, such as experiencing unusual signs and revelations from God so as to validate their conversions and exclaim how devastating failure would be.

Moreover, the book describes the day-to-day toils of chopping, picking, and plowing cotton in the hot sun, among other things, by black sharecroppers to eke out the very modicum of food, clothing, and shelter that others took for granted. It tells how the sharecroppers, who provided all of the services in exchange for the use of the equipment, land, shelter, and credit, provided by the plantation owners. Some of the sharecroppers had their own mules, and just as other Americans save for the future, they had been trying for years to save from their meager income to buy their own land. For many years, they would work for an entire year, only to find out that the plantation owners would not settle with them and when they did, the sharecroppers would receive very little or come out in debt, which they could not oppose for fear of physical harm or even losing their lives. Thus, on many occasions, they had to depend on their food from their vegetable gardens, milk cows, barter systems, and credit at a rate of 25 percent or more on the dollar from the plantation owners, thus usually resulting in insurmountable debt yearly while having no choice but to stay on the plantations in the hopes that the next year would be better.

The black sharecroppers lived in fear that white people would attack them and their families without provocation, for which there was no protection. Thus they had to be careful not to offend or appear to offend white people because the white people were always right. Moreover, the black sharecroppers had difficulties with plantation owners making unwanted sexual advances upon the wives and daughters, wherein rejections could result in assaults or even deaths.

There came a time that the sharecroppers were very worried about the possibility that the new machines and chemicals would discontinue the needs for their labor. Moreover, the Bend Plantation owner had notified them that he may lose the farm because the government refused to help him and he could not acquire credit elsewhere because it was well known that he testified truthfully at his brother's murder trial. By doing so, he did not implicate his brother's black girlfriend, who accidentally shot him, as his murderer. As is the case, there are many good white people in America, the Bend Plantation owner and spouse, after realizing that the farm may be lost, started training the men and women on the plantation to read, write, and do other skills other than those on the plantation.

After the Bend Plantation owner lost the farm, he told the sharecroppers another person had become the owner, who had promised him that he would allow the sharecroppers time to move. But the new owner notified the sharecroppers they had to move within days of his taking over the plantation. The sharecroppers could not find work or housing elsewhere either because the chemicals and new farm implements had mechanized the farming industry forever. Thus the black poor sharecroppers, being without funds, had to rely on their children, who had moved to various towns throughout the country, to pay their fares on the Greyhound buses and trains to join them. The maternal grandmother of the Silas family refused to leave their house, even though the new plantation owner was tearing the house down on them. She held onto the door jamb, eventually giving in, only to die holding onto her lifelong beliefs that people in town freeze to death or die from starvation. Shortly after her funeral, the family boarded a Greyhound bus for Chicago. Thus the era of mechanization caused the death of the plantations.

I

Cotton Sharecroppers, Silas's Family, Living in Chicago

It's been almost twelve years since Mr. Holly put us off his place. I realize now, mean as he was, he didn't do it all by himself. Weed killers, mechanical cotton pickers, beef cattle, and the government helped. Yes, the government helped a lot.

Being put off the plantation with no place to go but to town killed Grandma, who was afraid of the city, and finished breaking Papa's heart. I'm surprised he lived this long. Wish he could have lived until I graduated so I could have made things easier for him and Mama and Naomi.

Here in Chicago, Papa seemed lost, especially after he couldn't find steady work anymore, and Mama and my sister, Naomi, took most of the responsibility of providing a home for us, that is, until Papa and I moved so they could get on welfare.

Sometimes Papa would try to rescue his pride by talking about how straight a furrow he could plow on the plantation, how much cotton he raised the years the boll weevils didn't take it, how large a garden he grew, and the meals Mama used to cook: fried corn and okra, snap beans, black-eyed peas, greens, sweet potatoes, hot cornbread with butter oozing out of it, salt meat or fried chicken, and cool buttermilk. Then he would swallow hard and wipe his mouth with his hands while a broad smile spread over his black face. But his dream of long ago was usually short-lived. Soon he would come to himself with a complaint about surplus commodities we stood in line to get. "I'm so damn sick o' cheese 'n' peanut," he would say butter, "I don' know whut to do," he would say.

Often after he and I moved, he would recall the sixty acres he thought he was going to get out back of Red Wood near Vicksburg and have a farm of his own. Then he would look around our small room as if comparing it with sixty acres, and then he would jump up and start cursing Mr. Warrenton, the Farmers Home man, calling him everything he could think of.

If Mama were visiting us, she would say, "Now, now, Silas, that's all over 'n' done with. Jes' thank the Lawd things ain't no worser."

And Papa would grunt and look at her with all the love of all the years in his eyes. But his eyes were duller now. There seemed to be shame in them for not being able to provide for his family, and most of all for having to live apart from Mama and my sister and her children. The caseworker had explained that the women and children could not get on welfare as long as there was an able-bodied man in the apartment, whether he could find a job or not.

Mama and Naomi had been working at a laundry in the neighborhood until laundromats and home washing machines forced them to shift to laundering only work clothes. Most of the women were laid off. Mama and Naomi worked on for a few weeks, and then they were laid off, too. But they got the man to give me a part-time job after classes. I still have it, helping to load and unload trucks.

Papa had been working full-time up to about four years ago. When we first arrived here, he got a job at the stockyards loading boxes of meat into refrigerated trailers and freight cars, but the weight of the boxes and the coldness of the trailers and cars got to his knees and they began to swell. He worked on for months with swollen knees until he could find another job. He finally landed one helping the janitor at an apartment building, where he worked for six years, shoveling coal into the stoker and helping to clean the halls. Four years ago, the owner switched from coal to oil and no longer needed a second man.

Since then, Papa had been working a day at a time, loading trucks, helping deliver furniture, and doing odd jobs. But more and more, those in charge at the hiring hall passed over him for younger men. For the next three years, he had worked only one or two days a week, and this wasn't enough to keep things going, even with my part-time job and Naomi and Mama's day's work cleaning when they could find it. Papa kept looking for a full-time job but never found one. He had lost the battle of the city as well as the battle of the plantation. Welfare was the only way left.

So Papa and I took a room a few blocks away on Hoyne Street, right around the corner from the laundry on Madison, where I work. Part of whatever Papa and I earned went to Mama and Naomi and her children. Besides Carrie Mae, whose father was Mr. Win on the plantation, there were now Robert and little River, named after me, and Becky Mae, named after Mama. My sister wanted to name one of the boys after Papa, but he said he didn't want any of her children named after him until she got married. Naomi cried and Mama stopped speaking to Papa for nearly a week.

Roosevelt, who worked at the laundry with Naomi, was the father of both of the boys, but he never married her. When the first boy came, Papa got out his pistol and told Roosevelt, "You half-white sonofabitch, ef you don' marry my daughter, I'm gon' kill you sho' as hell."

Instead of marrying, Roosevelt disappeared for almost a year. I don't think Papa ever saw him again. But I saw him and Mama did, too, when he used to sneak by while Papa was at work. After little River was born, he stopped coming altogether.

Naomi grieved about him for years, and then Jesse, another half-white fellow, started stopping by. My sister likes them light with good hair. She says he's Becky Mae's papa, but no wedding is in sight. Mama told me the other day that Jesse had to climb out of the window one night last week to keep from being caught by the caseworker.

We never told Papa, who sat in our room most of the time when he wasn't working, waiting for Mama's daily visit. He took no chances of causing them to be put off welfare by visiting. My sister came by occasionally, and Carrie Mae and the other children visited sometimes, mostly when they wanted something.

This evening when Mama came, she and Papa sat on the side of the bed because we had only one chair. She leaned over and rested her head in his lap. A smile of satisfaction settled over his face as he ran his knobby fingers through her soft straight hair and caressed her light yellow face. These were at the center of his pride and happiness, although he would never admit it, claiming always, "Color don' make no diff'ence." Mama would usually smile with a glassy twinkle in her eyes because she knew so well all the difference color had made in our family.

I went for a walk while they visited. When I returned, Mama was standing in the doorway, screaming and crying, and all the folks in the apartment building had come to see what had happened. Papa was dead.

I had been gone only a little over an hour. It was the edge of winter, and the wind blowing off the lake came down West Madison cold and searching. I turned my coat collar up close about my neck and rammed my hands into my pockets as I walked. I stayed on Madison, where the lights were bright and police cars passed frequently. Many of the buildings were gone and others were boarded up as a result of the burning and looting last spring following the assassination of Dr. King.

I recalled grabbing a television set out of a window myself and rushing to our room with it, only to be told by Papa to take it back. When I was halfway to the store, I saw a policeman and set the TV down on the street. It barely touched the pavement before a boy ran by and picked it up on the fly.

That was months ago, but Madison was still in shambles. As I walked, I thought of how book-keeping had looted us on the plantation. I was nine when Mr. Holly put us off his place, so I remember about the plantation. From what I remember, and from what Papa and Mama and Grandma told me, life on the plantation was mostly disappointments. But Papa loved farming; he wanted a little piece of land of his own more than anything else in the world.

II

Fears and Intimidation of the Sharecroppers on Plantation

The only plantation I remember was Williamson Bend. All I can remember before the Bend was riding in a wagon in the dark with unshucked corn and a lot of quilts. And that is about how it was, I learned later from Papa and Mama, who said they had lived on four plantations before going to the Bend.

The first place they said they lived was in Sunflower County, where Papa was born and raised. They left there in 1935, Papa said, when the man with whom they were sharecropping refused to give them their share of the cotton parity check. They left in the middle of the night, Papa explained, because the landlord sent some men out to his house to kill him, he thought, after the man found out he had reported him to the government.

Mama said the men drove up yelling and shooting. They called to Silas to come out, she said. But instead of going out, he aimed his shotgun out of the window, over her protest, and fired on the car. One of the men cried out as if he had been hit, she said, and the car took off.

Mama and Papa said they knew the men had only gone to get help and would return. So they loaded a few things into their wagon, drove into a nearby skirt of woods behind their house, and hid there. They said they had barely reached the woods when three carloads of men drove up to their house and opened fire. In the midst of the shooting, they saw a blaze rise from their house and consume it.

While the house was still burning, Mama said she reached out in the darkness for little Silas, their two-year-old son, whom she had placed in the wagon, but he was not there. Then she and Papa searched the woods around the wagon but could not find him. The awful thought then struck Mama, Papa said, that little Silas may have returned to the house, and Mama called out for the child in the loudest, saddest scream he said he had ever heard. But he quickly put his hand over Mama's mouth so the men wouldn't hear her. They were still there, he said, watching the flames as if waiting to hear their bodies frying.

When the cars left, Papa said they crept back near the spot where their house had stood and searched everywhere for their son but did not find him. Then they returned to the woods and searched there for hours. Finally, Papa said they gave up and drove southward along the edge of the woods until daybreak. Then they pulled into the woods again and hid there all day.

"Us was too sad, too numb, and too scared," Papa recalled, "to be sleepy or hungry."

After two more nights of driving southward by night and hiding in the woods during the day, they said they made their way to the first farm shack they saw and asked for help. The family took them in and helped them hide their mules in the woods and bury their wagon. It turned out they were near

Belzoni in the next county. For weeks they and the family talked in a whisper about a family being burned to death on Mr. Dobbs Johnson's plantation near Inverness and the overseer, Mr. Henderson Oliver, being shot in the shoulder in a hunting accident. But Papa said Mama's eyes were seldom dry for months to come.

The plantation on which they found themselves was owned by Mr. Bob Wilson. They share-cropped with him eleven years mostly because they were afraid to leave. Year after year, they either came out in debt or just broke even, although they raised most of their own food. Papa said he had a feeling that Mr. Bob knew they were the ones who were supposed to have burned to death on the Dobbs Johnson plantation and was going to turn them over to the sheriff if they tried to move.

Scared every day and tired of coming out in debt, Papa said he finally made arrangements secretly to move to a plantation near Hollandale in Washington County. "Us moved during the night 'n' us put a county line 'tween us 'n' Mr. Bob," Papa said to stall the sheriff.

I was born en route to that plantation, Mr. Jim Yancy's place. Mama said it was the first year Grandma Carrie came to live with us after her husband died of sunstroke on a plantation up around Clarksdale.

"You was born jes' as us crossed the bridge over the Sunflower River," Grandma used to recall. "Yo' sister, Naomi, was 'bout nine 'n' her helped carry water outa the river that night 'n' her started callin' you Little River. That's how come you named River," she would explain.

But things didn't work out on that plantation, either. Papa didn't explain to me why until a couple of years ago, shortly after we moved out of the Project with Mama and Naomi, all during the years, he would merely say, "Things jes' didn't work out."

Then one day as we sat in our room looking out of the window, Papa came to that plantation in his mental wandering. "You know," he said, "Mr. Jim Yancy was a sonofabitch."

"Who is Mr. Jim Yancy?" I asked.

Then he reminded me that I was born the year we had moved to Mr. Jim Yancy's place, near Hollandale. "Mr. Jim was a bachelor and a bastard," Papa said. "He went with evvy good-lookin' woman on his place, 'specially ef they was yaller."

Papa said that when Mr. Jim saw Mama with her straight hair and half-white skin, he came right out and told him he didn't have a wife, and so he went with the women on the place.

"When I come to yo' house," that sonofabitch said, "all you got to do is take yo' chillun out in the yard or in the field or to a neighbor's fer a little while 'n' come back when you see my car is gone."

Papa said he forgot himself and all he and Mama had been through, and how close the sheriff of Humphreys County might even now be on his tail. "I tol' that sonofabitch, 'Nawsuh, ain't nobody gon' top my woman but me, long as I live.'" Then Papa stomped around the room for quite a while before he settled down and continued the story.

"To my surprise, he didn't tell me to git off his place. He jes' said, 'That's all right; that's all right, Silas, I understand.'"

Papa said he thought Mr. Jim was willing to bide his time and wait because he knew how desperate families on his plantation got when their rations ran out. "But us rations didn't run out," Papa recalled. "Us carried some chickers, two three hams 'n' shoulders, a couple o' side o' salt meat, 'n' some cabbage, mustard, okra 'n' tomato seeds. 'N' there was a neighbor with a cow who let us have a little buttermilk from time to time. So us ain't never had to go to the sto' fer nothin' but salt 'n' pepper 'n' coffee 'n' a little tobacco."

Papa said he knew Mr. Jim was just waiting until settlement time, when they would need shoes and clothes for winter. But long before that, while most of his cotton was still in the field, he had made arrangements to move to Mr. Addison's place at Nitta Yuma in Sharkey County. He said they moved one Saturday night in early October, a few days after the first frost, carrying along a hog, some corn and sweet potatoes, and a few heads of cabbage.

"Me 'n' Becky 'n' Naomi 'n' Miz Carrie picked cotton by the hundud clear up 'tel Christmas to git money for shoes 'n' clothes 'n' a big sack o' flour," Papa said.

As Papa remembered it, we stayed on Mr. Addison's place three years: cleared eighty-eight dollars the first year, came out thirty-nine dollars in debt the second, and was twenty-two dollars behind the third year. It was moving time again.

III

Old-Time Religious Services and Conversion to Christianity

Papa said this time we moved to Williamson Bend in Warren County, right on the Mississippi River. It was our second year at the Bend when I first remember the place. I was six years old, out in our cornfield praying to get religion. Revival had started at our church late that summer after cotton was laid by. The corn was tall and green, and I was near the back of our field, where I could pray loudly so the Lord could hear me and show me a sign before Friday night, when the revival was to close. I had just three more days, including that day to get religion. I had been on the mourners' bench for almost two weeks, but I hadn't come through. The night before, I had stood up as a convert, but when Reverend Fisher demanded to know what sign I had seen, I had to admit I had seen no sign.

"He'll show you a sign," Reverend Fisher had said. "You jes' keep on prayin'. Go down in the cornfield by yo'self 'n' pray hard 'n' the Lewd will sho' show you a sign. Yes, He will."

And everybody in the church said, "Yes, He will. Amen, yessuh, Jesus."

So I was down in the cornfield praying. I prayed so hard that I fell asleep. When I awoke, I heard a moaning and a groaning and a grunting and a scuffling a few rows away. I got up and saw a white man fighting Lilly Mae, the preacher's daughter. He had her down on the ground, and she was bucking like a young colt and calling on the Lord. But when I rushed through the corn to help her fight off the white man, she hollered, "Go away, boy, go away!"

And the white man, who was losing his pants in the fight, pulled them up enough to reach into a pocket and hand me a dime. "Go get some candy, boy," he said in a fading voice as if he was out of breath.

I backed away a few steps as Lilly Mae and the white man kept on fighting, then I turned and ran through the corn to pray some more, "to save my soul from burning hell," like Reverend Fisher said. But I couldn't keep my mind on the Lord while thinking about that white man fighting Lilly Mae. So I moved a few rows farther back and got down on my knees again.

The night before, when Reverend Fisher sent me back to the mourners' bench because I hadn't seen a sign, I sat there and cried with envy and shame when Pleas Miller and Silvester Robinson and General Lee's little sister, Laura, told how they had come through. Each had seen a sign, mostly a man riding across the sky on a white horse. But Pleas had also crossed over hell on a spider's web, and Laura had seen the sun shout and the moon drip blood.

Reverend Fisher said, "Thank You, Lawd, thank You, Jesus, fer these three fine chillun who done come to yo' throne of grace."

And the folks all said, "Hallalujah, Jesus! Thank You, Lawd."

And General Lee's mama, Mrs. Luiza, shouted, slinging her handbag all the way up into the pulpit. Then everyone came up and shook the children's hands. When Mama and Papa and Naomi and Grandma Carrie came up and shook their hands, passing by me almost as if they didn't know me, my heart broke and the tears came. As soon as Mama took her seat, I was there, placing my face in her lap and crying her dress wet.

Mama patted my head softly and ran her fingers through my hair. "He'll show you a sign, River; the Lawd will show you a sign, baby," she said quietly.

While Mama was patting my head, Reverend Fisher prayed a short prayer and then dismissed the congregation. He stood at the door as the folks passed out, shaking hands with everyone. "Keep on praying, River," he said to me as he grasped my small hand.

"Yessuh," I said in a timid voice. "I sho' will."

On our way home in our wagon, Grandma said, "Wasn't it wonderful how Silvester and little Laura and Pleas done come through?"

"It sho' was, Miz Carrie," Papa agreed.

And my sister added, "They sho' done seen signs."

Mama patted my leg and said, "My baby gon' see a sign; he gon' come through; you jes' wait 'n' see."

I trembled a little in fear and doubt as Mama spoke, but I trembled more when Grandma said, "'Course he is," she said firmly, "'cause he got to save his soul from hell 'n' damnation."

Then Grandma went on to describe how she had come through more than fifty years ago. "I wasn't no older'n River here when the Lawd washed my soul as white as a newborn lamb," she said. "Us was livin' up at Friars Point on Mr. Robertson's place. It's a place jes' like the Bend, right on the river with plenty o' good fishin'. I come through 'n' was baptized right in the river. I was so little I slipped right through the preacher's hands when he took me under. 'N' I 'spect I woulda drowned ef Mr. Robertson's boy, Mr. Hood, hadn't jumped in 'n' save me."

There was a long pause. And until the day she died, I never heard Grandma call Mr. Hood's name, but what she didn't pause a long time. "Somethin' happened 'tween me 'n' Mr. Hood when he save me from drownin', although I was jes' a chile, 'n' he was no mo'n leben or twelve hisself," Grandma said.

Nobody said a word except Naomi, who twittered and asked, "Was he good-lookin', Grandma?"

There was a smile in Grandma's voice when she said, "You see yo' ma, don't you? Well, her jes' the spittin' image o' him. I sho' wish you was good-lookin' like her, stid o' bein' so black."

"Oh, Ma, don' say that! " Mama said quietly, knowing how Papa felt about being called black or hearing Naomi called black.

After that not a word was spoken all the way home. There was only the sound of crickets and katydids mixed with the squeak of the wagon as it rocked along the ruts. The only thing that was on my mind was praying some more in the cornfield so that I could see a sign.

It was now mid-morning that day I saw Lilly Mae and the white man fighting. I had prayed a long time but had stopped now, and I wondered if they were still fighting. I listened and heard corn being torn from the stalk, and then I saw Lilly Mae walk casually out of our cornfield, through a patch of cotton, and through her own sickly, grassy corn toward her house, which stood in hollering distance of ours. She held her dress to form a bag for the roasting ears she was carrying. On the other end of our small cornfield, I heard a car start up and drive away. I walked to the edge of the field and saw a white car racing down the road with a trail of dust behind it.

By now Lilly Mae was in her yard with the corn. It was not unusual for her to pull roasting ears out of our field. Papa and Mama had told Reverend Fisher to help himself. Papa always said the preacher could pray the longest prayers and grow the shortest cotton and corn of anybody he had ever seen. So I thought nothing about her taking our corn, but I couldn't understand the way she and the white man had fought and parted so quietly. When Mama and Papa fought, and it was usually Mama striking Papa and him defending himself, there was a lot of loud name-calling and sulking. And sometimes Mama even refused to cook, leaving it up to Grandma and Naomi to get the meal together.

But with Lilly Mae and the white man, it was different. There was just a quiet parting, no chasing, no running to get a stick, no loud name-calling, only the crack of corn stalks as they gave up roasting ears, and the noise of a motor starting up, and a white man driving away in a white car. Still pondering this kind of fighting, I knelt again to pray for a sign that my soul had been saved. Then it struck me. This was the sign the Lord was giving me. Lilly Mae was my sins; the white man in the white car was my forgiveness, and he had given me a dime to boot.

I ran home, screaming, "Mama! Mama! The Lord done showed me a sign."

Mama and Naomi were in the kitchen, canning corn and okra, and Grandma was sitting nearby, giving unneeded directions.

"I done seen a sign! I got religion!" I yelled with joy as I ran into the kitchen.

"Bless the Lawd, bless the Lawd!" Grandma said, almost in her shouting voice.

Mama dried her hands on her apron, stooped, reached out, and folded me in her arms. "Praise the Lawd, praise the Lawd!" she said. "My baby done come through." Her eyes were moist as she sat down and took me on her knee.

"Lawd, thank You, Jesus," Grandma added. "Us been lookin' fer this day. Whut sign did you see, River? Tell us 'bout it."

"Yes, baby, tell us 'bout it," Mama asked.

Naomi stood behind Mama's chair, looking down at me and smiling with admiration. Grandma moved her chair closer.

As I told them what I had seen and heard, their enthusiasm seemed to die. Naomi ran into the front room, laughing her fool head off, and Mama and Grandma just looked at each other in the strangest way. I paused, looking from one to the other, hoping for encouragement and assurance that the Lord had shown me a sign after all my praying in the cornfield. But they were quiet as if they knew no words and looked down at the floor in distress. I was confused. Tears gathered in my eyes, and I was about to bury my face in Mama's breast when I heard Papa open the back gate to come into the kitchen for water as he always did when he was working near the house.

New hope sprang into my heart. I ran to Papa as he entered the door. "I done seen a sign, Papa! I got religion! The Lawd done showed me a sign, but ole black Naomi laffed."

That's as far as I got. Papa slapped me so hard, my head rang for hours. "Ain't I done tol' you 'bout callin' yo' sister black," he stormed. "Jes' 'cause you got a little yaller smeared on you, don' git sides yo'self, boy."

Mama and Grandma tried to explain that I was excited and hadn't meant to call Naomi black, but Papa turned and walked out of the door without saying another word. He didn't even get the water he had come for. I had bruised the vitals of his spirit. Better to spit in his face than to call him or Naomi black. But it was the one sure way I knew how to get back at Naomi whenever she hit me or poked fun at me. I am sure I learned it from Grandma, who hated "black" worse than sin, although she herself was as black as our skillet. Ever since I can remember, she had been greasing my sister's face and arms and legs with hog lard and homemade ointments and rubbing her with all her might over Mama's protests. Every Saturday afternoon, after we came from the field and every day it rained, she spent hours greasing and rubbing Naomi as if she could rub the black off as if it were soot or paint. And whenever she paused from her rubbing to rest and survey her work, she usually said, "Jes' the spittin' image o' ole black Silas. How come you couldn't be bright 'n' have good hair like River 'n' yo' ma? How come you had to be so black?" If Mama or Papa came in while she was making her comment, she quickly lowered her voice or spoke under her breath.

Grandma hated Papa for marrying Mama; she never forgave him. But Papa didn't seem to mind much so long as he had Mama. He loved her with all his heart, and most of all he loved her bright skin and straight hair like white folks', but he wouldn't let it touch him. He lied to us about it, and I think he even lied to himself, saying he was proud of his black skin and his bad hair, "proud as any man." Yet I think he knew deep in his heart that he wasn't altogether honest about it, or how else could he explain to himself the anger that rose within him when anyone called him or Naomi black?

When Papa came to the house at noon, after another hour in the field picking boll weevils out of cotton squares and turning watermelons so they would ripen evenly, he had cooled off. He said nothing to me about Naomi when he passed me sitting under the tree in our yard. And he or no one else mentioned my conversion as we ate dinner. I was puzzled and hurt. Everyone was happy about the conversions of Pleas and Silvester and Laura; no one appreciated mine. They seemed to doubt the sign I had seen. I had prayed as hard as I could for two weeks, and Lilly Mae and the white man fighting in that strange way in the cornfield was the only sign the Lord had shown me. But what was wrong with the sign that made Naomi laugh and Mama and Grandma act so queer? If I could just ask my sister about it, but she was still mad because I had called her black. Maybe I ought to talk with Lilly Mae about it. Except for a glass of buttermilk stiff with crumbled cornbread, I had no appetite. I wanted to find out what was wrong with the sign I had seen, and Lilly Mae would certainly know. Being the preacher's daughter, she would know all about signs and getting religion.

Before going over to Reverend Fisher's, I decided to pull some chinaberries out of our tree for my popgun and take it along to shoot at birds. While in the tree near the kitchen window, I heard Papa laugh so loud he started coughing. He was laughing the way Naomi had laughed. And Mama and Grandma were laughing, too. Naomi was still in her room pouting. I felt that their laughter had something to do with my conversion, so I climbed down out of the tree and crept close to the kitchen door to try to find out for sure what they were laughing at.

"Wait 'tel I tell Ben 'bout this," Papa was saying. Then he laughed again. "Ain't that somethin', ain't that somethin'," he chuckled.

"Be careful, Silas," Mama warned, "'cause us don' want no trouble. Mr. Win done give him a dime to buy some candy, 'n' I'm sho' it was so he wouldn't tell nobody."

I was right. They were laughing at my conversion. After all that praying, the Lord hadn't shown me a sign. That was Mr. Win, and he and Lilly Mae were really fighting, only white folks don't fight like colored folks.

Still I thought I ought to run over to Lilly Mae's and find out for sure before going back to the cornfield to pray some more. Between my house and hers, I met her brother, Willie, standing in our sweet potato patch, getting ready to dig a potato. Willie was about my size but nearly twice my age. Mama and Papa said the preacher's children never got enough to eat and that stunted them.

"I'm gon' see yo' sister, Lilly Mae," I said.

"Her ain't home," Willie replied.

"Where is her at?"

"Gone to the sto' to git somethin' t'eat."

"Gone to the sto'?"

"Yes, Mr. Win done give her a note this mornin' so us can take up some mo' rations."

"Mr. Win give her a note to take up some rations, after the way they was fightin' this mornin'?" I asked, puzzled.

"Fightin'?"

"Yes, I saw 'em fightin' in us cornfield. He had her down on the ground, 'n' her was buckin' 'n' kickin' 'n' mournin' somethin' awful," I said. "Then her pulled some o' us roastin' ears, 'n' he drove off in his car. I ain't never seen nobody fight like that 'n' I thought it was a sign I done got religion."

Willie laughed more than Naomi or Papa. He fell down in the potato patch and rolled and laughed and laughed. He finally paused in his laughter and asked, "River, ain't you got no sense a'tall, boy?" Then he pointed at me and began laughing again.

As I started to return home, feeling silly and knowing there was no use waiting for Lilly Mae, Willie yelled, "Wait a minute, River! I'm gon' 'splain it to you!"

I turned and walked back to where he was sitting in the sweet potato vines. Tears of laughter were still running from his eyes, which always seemed to me to be too big for his thin, hungry face. Mama sent some of our milk over to the preacher's house almost every day, but it was never really enough to meet the needs of Willie, Lillie Mae, and their papa and four brothers and sisters.

Willie looked up at me quizzically and asked, "Don' you know nothin' 'bout fonkin'?"

I stared at him, digging one of my big toes into the soft black earth, and asked, "Fonkin'?"

"Yes, fonkin', fonkin', fonkin'," he said impatiently, "like roosters 'n' hens 'n' boars 'n' sows."

I still stared at him, not quite certain what he meant, and more uncertain about the connection between fonking and my conversion. "Whut that gotta do with my religion? I been converted, ain't I?"

Willie laughed again and then asked, "How old is you, River?"

"I'm six goin' on seven," I said shyly, ashamed that I wasn't older.

"That all?" he asked disappointedly. Then he got up out of the vines, came over close to me, and said, "I'm gon' 'splain to you 'bout fonkin' 'n' it ain't got nothin to do with no religion."

Within the next few minutes, Willie told me all about fonking and also about seeing signs and being converted. Then he and I went down in the cornfield and I rehearsed the new sign I was supposed to have seen. It was part of the same one he told his papa he had seen a few years ago. I went over it until I knew it by heart. Willie said it sounded fine the way I told it, except I would need to whine and cry a little as I told it in church.

But the more I rehearsed my conversion story, the more afraid I became. "Is you sho' the Lawd ain't gon' strike me dead fer tellin' a story in church?" I asked fearfully.

"Naw, boy, didn't I tell you I done tol' this same story when I was converted, 'n' Lilly Mae tol' one jes' 'bout like it, too, 'n' us ain't dead, is us?" Willie said.

"But y'all the preacher's chillun? Maybe that's how come the Lawd ain't struck you dead," I said, still afraid.

"Well, General Lee's papa ain't no preacher, 'n' he ain't dead, 'n' he done tol' a bigger tale 'n us tol'. Talkin' 'bout the Lawd done come down from heaben 'n' done picked him up in His arms 'n' took him way up in the air 'n' set him on a pretty cloud where he could see evvything in the world, 'n' then he said the Lawd done tol' him this his sign he done got religion."

"General tol' that in church?" I asked, trying to make sure Willie wasn't telling me a tale.

"He sho' did; I clare fo' Gawd he did," Willie replied, crossing his heart and holding up his hand as if to take an oath.

I started to run home when Willie and I parted and tell Mama about my new sign, but the closer I got to the house, the more ashamed I was of the old sign I thought I had seen. And I didn't feel I could bear in one day to go over all that again with Mama and Papa and Naomi and Grandma. So I said nothing about praying or my new conversion when I got home, and nobody asked me about it or where I had been.

But that night at the revival meeting, when Reverend Fisher went up and down the mourners' bench, asking who had been saved, I stood up and said, "I is, Reverend Fisher, 'cause I done seen a sign this time."

The words were barely out of my mouth when Mama yelled, "Naw, naw, that boy ain't seen no sign! You come here, boy, 'n' set by me." Mama was standing now.

"But I is seen a sign, Mama," I insisted.

"Naw, naw, boy, you ain't seen no sign. You come here," she ordered, starting down toward the mourners' bench to get me.

Reluctantly I went to her and she and Grandma shook their fingers in my face and told me to keep quiet.

Two children told about their conversions, and then there was more praying and shouting and hand shaking. On our way home, I related my conversion story after saying that I had been back down in the cornfield that afternoon praying. My folks seemed pleased and relieved by the new sign I had seen, but they weren't overly enthusiastic. Perhaps two signs in one day was too much for them.

The next night in church, I stood up and told Reverend Fisher the sign I had seen. Like most of the other converts, I said I had seen a white man on a white horse, but I didn't say he was riding across the sky or across hell on a spider's web. I said the white man was riding just above the top of our corn-field. I could have said it was a white man in a white car on the ground with a trail of dust behind him. But I wanted to be converted so that Mama and Papa and Grandma could be proud of me. So I related the story Willie had told me. I said the tail of the white horse knocked tassels off the corn and all these fell down in the middle of the row and the wind blew the tassels into a big pile, which burst into flames. Then I said the white man on the horse said, "Them is yo' sins; they all been burnt up 'n' yo' soul is done been saved."

Reverend Fisher said, "Amen, amen, Lawd, bless this boy." He said it hastily as if he had heard this unusual conversion story before.

Then all the folks said, "Amen, hallalujah, Jesus."

Mama and Papa and Naomi rushed up and crushed me in their arms. Grandma was not there. She had said her knees were aching and had stayed home. Everybody in the church praised me and shook my hand. I had tasted my first victory; it was not sweet.

IV

Plantation Owner's Relations with Girls on the Plantation

Although Mama and Papa never asked me about the first sign I thought I had seen, I soon found out it was never off their minds. Not because I had seen Mr. Win and Lilly Mae together in the cornfield, but because they were afraid Mr. Win might visit Naomi in the cornfield, too. My sister, however, was flattered by the thought. It was she who told me what Papa and Mama were thinking.

"Papa keep warning me 'bout Mr. Win," she said the next Sunday as we walked toward Sunday school.

"How come he warned you?" I asked.

"It's 'bout whut you seen him 'n' Lilly Mae doin' in us cornfield. Course, Mr. Win ain't thinkin' 'bout me."

"They wasn't fightin', they was fonkin'," I said.

"Yes, that's whut I'm talkin' 'bout," Naomi replied and broke into loud laughter. "But how did you find out? Come runnin' home talkin' 'bout you done seen a sign that you been converted." She laughed again, running in a zigzag movement along the road for a short distance. Then she stopped, turned to me, and asked, "How did you find out whut they was doin', River?"

"Willie Fisher tol' me."

"He tol' you yo' new sign, too, didn't he? Papa 'n' them been wonderin' who tol' you that sign."

"Yes, Willie said it was whut he tol' his papa he seen when he got religion."

"I thought so," she chuckled. "Now you stay 'way from Willie, 'cause he too old fer you. Next thing you know he'll have you fonkin' us hens 'n' us sow. They say he killed the last two hens his papa had, fonkin' 'em, 'n' folks say he fonks his sisters, too."

"I don' want to fonk no chickens 'n' git chicken shit on me. Is you gon' fonk Mr. Win?"

"Mr. Win don' want me," my sister said with a tinge of regret in her voice. "Evvybody on the plantation know he like yaller gals like Lilly Mae 'n' Sally Hawkins. That's whut Grandma tol' Papa when he come talkin' 'bout he'd kill the sonofabitch 'n' whup me in a inch o' my life, ef he ever caught me in the cornfield or any other place with Mr. Win. Since yo' conversion, that's all Papa 'n' Mama been talkin' 'bout evvy time you sleep or is out the house."

"It is? They scared, ain't they? Scared you gon' be with Mr Win. But you ain't, is you?"

"I jes' tol' you Mr. Win don' like no black gals. I sho' wish I was yaller 'n' had good hair like you 'n' Mama."

We had almost reached the main road, which wraps around three sides of the plantation. It's almost like a twin to the levee, which loops the Bend to keep the river out. Standing in the main road waiting for us were Della and Mary Lou Woodson. They live along the main road on the side of the plantation where the church sat. We lived on the other side of the u-shaped plantation and had to take the road across it to get to the church or go all the way around the main road, past the store and the nice houses where Mr. Win and Mr. Walter, Doc Boyd, and Mr. Lige lived.

Mary Lou was yellow like me and was about my age. Della and Naomi were chocolate brown and near the same age. But Della's eyes were a kind of sleepy gray, and in the front of her mouth was a gold tooth. She got it after settlement time last year, Naomi said. It was the talk of the plantation and ranked her along with Mrs. Mary Moses and Mrs. Luiza Lee, who were the first to go to a dentist in Vicksburg and get gold teeth. These were not only supposed to add to the beauty of the possessor, but they also were the new signs of success on the plantation. They and used cars and new stoves and washing machines had replaced the status of the traditional whole barrel of flour instead of only a half or even a tall wardrobe with mirrors on the doors. Della had used her gold tooth to cut into Naomi's courtship with Roscoe Jackson. Of course, it didn't last because Roscoe left for the levee camp in the spring and hadn't come back.

Naomi and Della greeted each other like the best of friends, but I knew all the things my sister said about Della when she was talking with Grandma or me. And I knew how she envied Della's gold tooth. She wanted a gold tooth, too, more than anything, except bright skin and straight hair. For all Grandma's greasing and rubbing of her, Naomi knew her black skin was here to stay.

"I can't change my color," she would say, "but a gold tooth right in front o' my mouth where it would show evvy time I smiled would sho' make a heap o' difference."

A new option had begun to be heard in the levee camp song about a yaller women. The new version indicated that black hadn't gone altogether out of style, if a black woman had a gold tooth in her mouth when she smiled.

Naomi and Della walked on ahead talking while Mary Lou and I trailed behind. She caught my hand and told me how glad she was that I had come through, and she related how she had prayed for a sign last year before she came through.

"I'm gon' be baptized next Sunday," I told her, "then I'm gon' be a member o' the church."

She seemed impressed and told me that she and Della and their folks were going to be there. I felt important, but I also felt hollow and empty, too. I really didn't have any religion; I was only pretending. I was sorry now that Willie had told me about seeing signs. Maybe if I had kept on praying, I might have really seen a sign. We were near the church now, and Mary Lou and I ran to catch up with Naomi and Della.

Two weeks after my baptism, it was cotton-picking time and school closed again. Of course, I hadn't started to school yet; I was supposed to start right after cotton picking was finished. When we began picking, our field was white with the biggest bolls Papa said he had ever seen. "Us sho' gon' make a good crop," he said, looking across our eleven-acre patch as far as he could see. "I wouldn't be surprised ef us made twelve bales—fo' fer Mr. Walter 'n' Mr. Win 'n' eight fer us."

Our good crop didn't just happen. Of course the weather helped, and Papa said the weather and the Lord seemed to be against us two years in a row. But mostly it was Papa's determination to kill "them damned boll weevils."

All of us pitched in to help, fighting boll weevils and grass from sunup to sundown. In addition to Papa's hand poisoner, which he cranked up and down the rows once every week and twice if it rained to wash the poison off the leaves, all of us walked through the field every day we weren't chopping, looking into cotton squares for the snout-nosed insect. Every one we found we put it into a bottle and capped it with a rag or a piece of corncob. And sometimes we put a little coal oil in the bottle first to kill the boll weevils.

Not only did we pick the insect out of squares on the stalk, but we also carried along flour sacks into which we put any squares that had fallen on the ground. In this way we tried to keep our field free of boll weevils and boll weevil eggs. All the boll weevils and squares we collected were burned when we got back to the house. Some folks said, "Ole Silas got his wife 'n' chillun in the field picking boll weevils like they cotton."

But every time we went through our field, we found fewer and fewer of those ole bugs. And of course, a weed or a sprig of grass had practically no chance of surviving in our cotton. As we chopped, Papa and Mama carried two rows each, Naomi carried one, and Grandma and I carried one together. But even so, Grandma and I often got behind, and my sister or Papa or Mama would reach over and do a little chopping on our row to help us catch up.

Grandma often complained of her back or her knees, and sometimes she would bank her hoe upright under a mound of dirt so that she could find it easily and then go off and sit under one of the nearby trees. Mama said Grandma had earned a rest because she had been chopping and picking cotton on plantations for more than fifty years.

Even before we lay by, Papa had begun talking about how good our cotton looked. He could size up cotton the way Mama could tell a good piece of cloth in a store for a dress. Papa knew when cotton was tall, but not all stalk and few bolls, and when the leaves were plump and dark green, that meant a good crop because the plants had had plenty of sunshine, enough rain but not too much, and just about the right amount of fertilizer.

When we began picking, the stalks were loaded from top to bottom, and Papa started saying, "Us might go to Vicksburg, with the Lawd's help, ef us comes out all right."

He was cautious like all farmers are cautious, especially sharecroppers, because they know there can be many a mishap between the time the crop matures in the field and the time they come home with the settlement money in their pockets. They know a week's rain can wipe out a crop or lower its value, a storm blowing up out of the Gulf or out of nowhere can carry their crop away, and if they escape these, there is always the landlord with his sharp pencil who can figure them out of more cotton in a minute than they can plow and chop and pick in a year. And so in their calculations, they always say "might" and add "with the Lawd's help."

But as the weeks passed and our black hands sweep through our field, leaving the bolls clean and empty, Papa changed his promise to: "I think us gon' go to Vicksburg, ef it's the Lawd's will." He dared to leave out "might."

And Mama, who had been disappointed so many times, began to listen and hope. "You think so, Silas?" she would ask in wary anticipation.

"I'm sho', ef it's the Lawd's will," he would answer.

As we neared the end of the picking, Mama took courage and began asking, "Think us might have enough to buy us a new stove, Silas?"

"Ef us come out all right, Becky, you sho' gon' git a new stove," Papa would say.

Still wary, still uncertain, Mama would add, "Silas, you know us been needin' a stove fer a long time. Us had us old stove since us firs' moved to Mr. Bob's place up in Humphreys County. Naomi was a baby when us got it."

I think Mama was pleading because she thought the money might go for something else, like another mule, a new shotgun, or maybe a used car. Papa had been saying how nice it would be if we had a car. To which Mama kept replying, "Where us goin'? 'N' where you gon' git the money fer gas? 'N' when us gon' start saving fer a farm o' us own?"

Although our stove looked its age, standing in our kitchen on one leg and three stacks of bricks, Mama could conjure out of it the best meals, especially biscuits and ten-layer jelly cakes with each layer so thin and light and fluffy it would melt in your mouth. "Ef a new stove gon' make Mama's cookin' better than it already is, Papa, you sho' oughta git her one," I said one day as Mama continued her plea.

Naomi hadn't said what she wanted if we went to Vicksburg. I think she was too afraid of being disappointed. But late one afternoon, she slowed down her picking little by little so that I could catch up with her. Papa and Mama were well ahead, and Grandma had dragged her sack under a tree and was lying on it, resting.

"River," my sister whispered, "do you think Papa'll buy me a gold tooth?"

"I don' know, he might," I said.

"He might be willin' to git me one," Naomi agreed, "but Mama might not let him. You know how her is; her think only fast women gits 'em."

"Yes, I know how her is," I replied, "but ef her think you needs it, her might let Papa git it."

"You right, River," my sister said. "Little boy, how did you git so much sense?"

After that day in the field, Naomi began to complain about her teeth. Every time she bit into a bone or tried to crack pecans with her teeth, or took a drink of cool water or hot coffee— and she drank coffee sparingly because Grandma said it would make her black—she would complain that her tooth hurt. She always pointed to one of her teeth right in front, and Mama tried to find a cavity in it so that she could apply turpentine or a little antiseptic, but she could never find one.

Before long, I think both Mama and Papa were on to her game, but they didn't let on. And Grandma had been for a gold tooth ever since Naomi mentioned her tooth hurting. Grandma was for anything that might detract from my sister's blackness.

"When y'all go to Vicksburg," Grandma suggested, "how come you don' git the tooth man to put a gold tooth in that gal's mouth so her teeth won't hurt her so?"

Naomi almost smiled—her mouth was open for a big grin—then she caught herself and converted what could have been a happy smile into a painful scowl. "A pain jes' shot through my tooth," she said, slowing her picking a bit.

The sun was out almost every day during cotton-picking time. Sometimes it seemed to shine so bright and hot that the air stood still. Perspiration ran down our faces and necks and backs and stomachs and legs, transforming our clothing into a soggy mass and chafing our shoulders over where the shoulder-strap went.

Our bodies stayed wet and our throats stayed dry. It was my job to go and get the bucket of water every hour or so. We kept a water of bucket water sitting under a tree or a bush in the field with a bunch of leaves spread over it to help keep it cool. Before drinking, I would dip out the trash or insects that might have fallen into the bucket; then I would stir the water with the dipper, which somehow made it seem cooler. Sometimes my throat was so dry and hot and the water so refreshing that I would try to hold it in my mouth and chew it. I would pass the bucket around so that everyone could have a drink. Papa and Mama always poured dippers full of water over their heads to cool them off after they had drunk. But Naomi and Grandma never did this because it would make their hair kinkier than it already was, they said.

Back of our cornfield the turn row between our farm and Reverend Fisher's ran on an angle, giving us about a dozen rows that became shorter and shorter. I liked picking or chopping these rows because it made it seem that you were working faster.

As the second and final picking neared an end, there was more and more talk about going to Vicksburg. We had already ginned eight bales, and what we had still in the field, plus what was on our porch at home and in the wagon, Papa said, was bound to make three or four more bales. "Eight fer us after Mr. Walter 'n' Mr. Win git their fo'," he estimated.

"There gon' be nuff fer my new stove, ain't it, Silas?" Mama asked for the hundredth time.

"Yes, Becky, honey, you sho' gon' have a new stove," Papa assured her again and again.

I don't really think Mama was afraid Papa wouldn't get the stove if we came out all right, but I think she enjoyed the anticipation and this was the way she showed it. Mama knew if it came to a showdown between a stove and mule or a shotgun or a used car, she would win out because Papa loved her more than anything else in this world. He not only loved her color and soft straight hair, but he also loved the kind of woman these helped her to be. She was sure of herself and sure of him and didn't ask for proof every day of the week, or even every year.

And Mama could work from sunup until sundown in the field with Papa, or in the house sewing or cooking or canning or cleaning, and she didn't feel she was getting the short end of the stick. She worked fast and walked fast and fished with a restless pole.

"I got to keep busy," Mama would say sometimes. "I guess it's the white blood in me."

This comment about her white blood would always cause Papa's rancor to rise. "Always talkin' 'bout that little speck o' white blood you got," he would say. "But you jes' like any other nigger on this plantation. Whut it done got you anyhow, nothin'."

Sometimes Mama would pout for a while, but at other times, she would jump into Papa's lap and say, "It got me you, ain't it?" And Papa would smile as if his lips would go all the way back to his neck, and he would lock his arms around Mama and bury his head in her breast and rock her like a baby.

Out in the field the last day of picking, the sun was beginning to set over the levee. There were just two more rows and all of us got on them. We were determined to finish before the day ended. Mama didn't say anything about getting a new stove, but Naomi continued to complain about her tooth hurting. Grandma put in no request. Said all she needed was a little money for her snuff and tobacco and for her church and burial society.

My list was long. It included a suit and hat and shoes and socks and an automatic cap pistol.

V

Silas Family's Settlement for Cotton Picked on the Plantation

After settlement with Mr. Walter and Mr. Win, Papa walked into the house like a king. His overall pockets were bulging. "Us goin' to Vicksburg," he yelled, "'cause us done cleared five hundred 'n' ten dollars 'n' fifty-five cents!"

This was the most money he had ever cleared, and he spread in out on the bed. It was mostly one-dollar and five-dollar bills and looked like all the money in the world. Papa and Mama counted it over and over, feeling each bill and each coin with a tenderness that gave the money new value.

Papa said there was one thing about the Williamsons; they always settled with their tenants. This had been a policy handed down by old Captain Winfield Scott Williamson, who fought with General Pemberton against Grant and Sherman at Vicksburg. After the war, he had come back to this place, twenty to thirty miles north of Vicksburg, where the river makes a sharp left turn, loops Eagle Lake, and provides some of the best fishing in the world.

Old Captain Williamson and some of his men had provided fish for the people in the town during the siege until patrolling gunboats made it impossible to deliver the fish. But after the war, Captain Williamson had left his native Alabama and returned to this bend in the Mississippi River, bought the land for next to nothing, named it Williamson Bend, and added cotton land year after year until he had more than three thousand acres. He never had any trouble keeping families on his place because he always settled with them.

"The Williamsons sho' gon' settle with you," everybody on the plantation said over and over again as they recalled the story of the plantation as told by their parents and grandparents.

Most people who had been on the plantation for a while knew that when old Captain Williamson died in 1905, his son, Mr. Winfield, Jr., took over and ran the plantation until he was drowned during the 1927 flood, trying to help get all his workstock to the levee.

Mrs. Mary Moses's mama, Mrs. Caline Johnson, got misty-eyed whenever she recalled the flood and how Mr. Winfield and her husband, Israel, drowned together as they neared the levee with the mules and horses when a big wave as high as a house rolled right over them.

"They found Mr. Winfield right away," she would say, "'n' they took his body to Vicksburg, where they 'balmed it 'n' kept it 'tell the water went down 'n' they could bury him on the place. But po' Israel, they ain't found him fer three days. Then they chained his body to a tree so it wouldn't float away. 'N' they buried him 'n' Mr. Winfield on the same day."

Practically everybody remembered that Mr. Winfield's son, Mr. Scott, had charge of the place after that until he was thrown by a horse in 1940. "He lived 'bout two years," they would say, "but he wasn't no 'count, 'n' his sons, Mr. Walter 'n' Mr. Win, started runnin' the place."

Mr. Walter had graduated from the University of Virginia, where he met and married Mrs. Rhoda, a student at nearby Sweet Briar College. Folks said Mr. Walter had met Mrs. Rhoda one weekend when she had come up to the school to accompany her fiancé to a dance and found him protesting the seating of a black singer in the university dining room. Mr. Walter, they said, was standing on a table, pleading with the students to be reasonable, and Mrs. Rhoda jumped up on the table beside him and joined him in his plea.

They said Mrs. Rhoda came from Georgia, where her mama was a teacher at a school for colored girls. She was a kind and gentle woman whose eyes always seemed a little sad, as if they had seen a great tragedy. Some said it was because she didn't have any children; others said it was because she was sorry for the colored folks on the place.

Mr. Win, the folks said, had attended a half-dozen colleges and finished from none, mainly because he was so crazy about women and whiskey. His wife, Mrs. Susie, was as cute as a pin. She had been homecoming queen at Rolling Fork High School the year before Mr. Win married her. After her second child, Miss Millie, was born, they said her back wasn't any good, and that was why Mr. Win fooled around with the girls on the plantation. But both Mr. Win and Mr. Walter believed in settling with the folks, everybody said, and in never putting anybody off the place unless they had to. "You can stay here long as you live," they said, and they meant it.

After Papa and Mama had counted their money for the last time, Papa divided it up. "This is yo'n, Becky, fer a new stove 'n' some new clothes." It was two hundred dollars.

Mama picked up the stack of bills and press it against her heart. "All this fer me?" she asked, blinking back tears. Then she ran into the kitchen with the hem of her apron up to her eyes.

Papa stopped counting out Grandma's money for church and snuff and burial society, and rushed into the kitchen and put his arms around Mama. "You is got yo' stove at last, honey," he said, and then they each mumbled something and remained in the kitchen for a long time. It may have seemed longer to me because I was waiting to see what Papa was going to give me. In the past, I remembered him giving me fifty cents one time and a quarter another.

When Papa returned to the bed and resumed counting, he handed Grandma forty dollars. "This oughta buy you a whole lot o' snuff, Miz Carrie."

"Thanky, Silas. I'm much obliged to you; this is plenty," she said with a big smile and then turned aside and raised her dress far enough to reach her sack into which she placed the money. It was a coarse cotton bag attached to a string, which she tied around her waist. The sack was never entirely empty from the day she first put money into it. Sometimes it may have been down to a nickel, but it was never empty.

Naomi received twenty dollars and I, two. Papa said he had more for us to buy clothes and shoes and other things.

Out of the rest of the money, Papa set aside sixty dollars toward a farm of our own, fifty as a down-payment on another mule, and forty for a new shotgun.

"Do you have to have a new gun, Silas?" Mama asked. She had returned to the room after her little cry.

"You know I needs a new gun; had this one goin' on nineteen years, 'n' it ain't nomo' good fer huntin'."

"You might need a new one, but I'm jes' scared o' you gittin' it. Might git us in trouble like that time up in Sunflower County," she argued.

"Ef us hadn't had a gun, us wouldn't be here now to talk 'bout it."

"Maybe they wouldn'ta killed us, Silas."

"To hell they wouldn't; them bastards was after us, 'n' that's fer sho'," Papa said.

"Well, all right, go 'head 'n' git yo' gun," Mama said in doubtful agreement. "When is us goin' to Vicksburg?"

"Sadday, Sadday," Papa replied.

There was little sleep in our house during the next two nights. We all were busy getting ready to go to Vicksburg. It was going to be our first trip to a big town. The biggest towns Mama and Papa had ever been to were Indianola, up in Sunflower County, and Rolling Fork, near Nitta Yuma, where we lived before coming to the Bend. Grandma had been to Clarksdale, though, and she said that was enough town for her. "I ain't lost a thing in Vicksburg," she would say when Mama tried to persuade her to go with us.

Getting ready to go to Vicksburg for Mama meant taking our clothes out of the trunk every day and hanging them on the line to sun; for Naomi, it was greasing her face and straightening her hair and smiling before the mirror for hours, imagining how she was going to look when she got her gold tooth. For me, it was telling the children at school over and over again that I was going to town. For Papa, it was visiting all over the plantation, telling everybody how he had come out and that he and his family were going to Vicksburg.

Early Saturday morning, all of us, except Grandma, got into Mr. Willie Woods' car and headed for town. He had picked up the mail when he came for us, so we didn't get to go by the store and tell everybody there that we were going to town. We waved at every house we passed, however, as if we going to be gone for a month instead of half a day. In Vicksburg, Mr. Willie put us out at the post office, where he took the mail and said for us to meet him there at two o'clock.

Mama bought her stove at the first furniture store we came to. The man was standing out front, saying, "Come on in, folks; I got jes' what you want and I treat you right; come on in."

Papa and Mama paused undecidedly, as if they were afraid to pass the store without the white man's permission, although Mr. Willie had suggested the Valley Store. I think the salesman knew we were from the country by the way we stared at the buildings and the cars and the way we were dressed in homemade clothes, except Papa, whose store-bought suit was old and rumpled and several shades of brown.

"Come on in," he said more boldly as we paused. "I got nice furniture—beds, dressers, stoves, refrigerators—cheap, too."

"I want a stove," Mama said hurridly, involuntarily, and yet somewhat uncertainly, as if she was afraid Papa was going to object.

"I got plenty stoves—all kinds. Come on in, come on in."

Our feet followed the man into the small store and when we came out, Mama had bought her stove and a broad smile lit up her face. The store was going to ship the stove up to the Bend by truck within a week.

Up the street loomed a tall store with the word "Valley" hanging upright in front of it.

"That's the sto' Willie was talkin' 'bout," Papa said, and we headed straight there for our shoes and clothes and Papa's shotgun.

There were so many toys in the large store: tricycles and bicycles and toy guns and pistols and army trucks and tanks, and navy boats and airplanes and cowboy suits. But what I liked most was a pretty blue tricycle. I caressed the handlebar, touched the rubber wheels and, upon invitation of the salesman, sat on the tricycle and put my feet on the pedals and moved forward a few feet. It seemed like the best ride I had ever had.

Papa who, along with Mama and Naomi, had walked on through the toy department after he had bought me a cap pistol, came back looking for me and found me seated on the vehicle. "Us been lookin' fer you to try on yo' new suit; come on," he ordered.

"This whut I want, Papa," I said.

"You want this mo'n you want a new suit?"

"Yessuh," I said slowly, knowing how all year I had been talking about a new suit for Christmas.

"How much is it, mister?" Papa asked hesitantly as if he was afraid it would be too much.

"Nineteen ninety-five," the salesman said casually.

"Nineteen dollars 'n' ninety-five cents?" Papa wanted to know.

"That's right. You see, this is one of our deluxe models."

"Ain't you got no cheaper ones?"

"Yes, I have one right over here; it's thirteen ninety- five."

"Nothin' cheaper'n that?" Papa asked in a kind of pleading voice.

"No, this is the cheapest," the salesman said.

"But I want this one over here, Papa, this blue one," I explained.

Papa stood there scratching his head. I knew he had allocated every penny of the money he had cleared at settlement, except the money for our clothes, and both of us needed suits, and the whole family needed shoes, and Naomi was counting on a gold tooth. I knew he was figuring all this in his mind as he scratched his head, looking first at me, then at the salesman, and then at the floor. Suddenly with a big grin, he turned to me and said, "Man, I thought you wanted a hoss; that's whut mens want, not a little ole toy thing like this. You a man, ain't you?"

"Yessuh," I said, and with that I knew I was trapped because I wanted to be a man more than anything else in the world.

I slowly slid down off the tricycle, trying to hold back the tears that I felt burning in my eyes. I held on to the handlebar for a long time, and then I let it go and caught Papa's hand and walked on into the clothing department, still looking back at the blue tricycle.

I had no taste for a suit after that. I tried on the first one he showed me and said I liked it. Papa also got a suit and we all got shoes. I don't recall what else we bought, but I do remember Naomi complaining about her tooth hurting all the time we were shopping. As Papa paid the man, he asked where he could get a man to fix a tooth for his daughter.

"There's a dentist," the salesman said, "right down the street about two blocks; he's upstairs; anybody will show you."

I saw my sister twisting her face up tightly to keep from smiling while the man was telling us where to find a dentist. Going to the dentist's office was an uphill walk, but nobody complained, and there was even a spring in Naomi's step.

"What's the trouble?" the dentist asked when our turn came, and Papa explained that his daughter's tooth was hurting. "Come on in," he said, holding the door open for my sister.

When the door opened again, Naomi walked out with a smile on her face, such as I had never seen there before. There in the front of her mouth was a shining gold tooth. I don't know whether it was the tooth or the smile that made her seem so different, so proud, so self-assured, so thoughtless of her blackness that had made her shy all her life. My sister paid the dentist out of the twenty dollars Papa had given her, and we left.

Outside, Mama said, "I hopes you satisfied now; you got that gold tooth."

"Well, ef it make her happy, Becky," Papa said, "ain't that whut us been plowin' 'n' choppin' 'n' pickin' cotton all year fer?" And that's about all that was ever said in the family about my sister's gold tooth.

But later at home, Naomi told me how at first the dentist frightened her, talking about a jaw tooth that needed capping instead of the one right in front. "I don' want no gold wasted in the back of my mouth," she said she told him. "I want it in front where evvybody can see it."

Reluctantly, she said, he ground away the good enamel of one of her front teeth and capped it with gold. "The grinding sho' hurt, but Lawd, it was sho' worth it, wasn't it, River?"

"It sho' was," I said, "'cause it make you look pretty."

Word about Naomi's gold tooth spread over the plantation like a grass fire. That Sunday at church, every girl asked to see it, and some of the boys gathered around, too. But they didn't really have to ask to see it because my sister was smiling all the time, not a silly, giggling grin, but a studied, poised smile that parted her lips just enough to let the tooth peep out, and she captured every eye. No matter how much I limped to call attention to my new shoes, nobody noticed. them or my new suit.

When church let out, both Richard Noses and Elijah Hawkins walked Naomi home. All before, only Richard walked with us. But Naomi had her heart set on Luke Robinson. She had been sparking at him ever since Roscoe shifted his affections to Della. That Sunday my sister had showed him her gold tooth twice and sat next to him during the services, but he had chosen to walk home with Jo Anna David, one of Mr. Tobe's girls.

"Ef ole black Richard 'n' Elijah hadn't come jumpin' 'side me to walk me home, Luke mighta," Naomi said late that afternoon.

"How come you so crazy 'bout Luke?" I asked.

"'Cause he bright 'n' good looking 'n' got good hair."

"Do he like you?"

"I think he would ef he didn't think I was stuck on ole black Richard."

"How come you don' like Richard?

"'Cause he so black 'n' ugly; he blacker'n me."

"Whut black got to do with it?" I asked.

"A heap," my sister said and wrinkled her nose up as if she had got a quick whiff of something that smelled bad.

"I can't see nothin' color got to do with it."

"That's 'cause you a boy 'n' you ain't black. But I'm a girl 'n' I'm black 'n' I know the difference color make. 'N' ain't none o' my chillun gon' be black," Naomi said firmly as she finished milking and picked up the bucket and went into the kitchen.

As the weeks went by, my sister saw less and less of Richard and Elijah, and Luke not at all. Sometimes I came up on her in her room crying; at other times I would find her sitting by the window, staring out into space. And almost every night, she stared out toward the lane. One night I stood by her knee to try to see what she was looking at. After a while a car drove up near the tree by the lane in front of Reverend Fisher's house and blinked its lights.

"That must be Mr. Willie," I said. "Maybe he wants Papa."

"That ain't Mr. Willie!"

"How you know?" I asked.

"I jes' know, that's all," she replied as we went to bed.

It was weeks before I found out what she was watching for and who was in the car that blinked its lights. Willie told me, and Lilly Mae hinted something about it every time she came to our house to get the milk, or a little flour, or a piece of salt meat. And it seemed she came to our house for something more often than ever.

Sometimes Lilly Mae would holler to Naomi, "Been riding lately?" or "You had to git that white meat, didn't you?" or "You cuttin' in, hanh, Naomi?"

Mama didn't seem to pay any attention to Lilly Mae's remarks, but my sister would quiver every time the preacher's daughter spoke out, and she seemed to have been on pins and needles until she left.

Then one day while Willie and I were walking home from school, he stopped in the middle of the road and said, "Yo' sister's been fonkin' Mr. Win."

I looked at him in disbelief. "You jes' tellin' a tale," I said.

"Ef you don' b'lieve me, you ast Lilly Mae."

"How her know?"

"Her seen 'em?"

"Where her seen 'em?"

"In the back o' Mr. Win's car, that's where," Willie shot back.

"You jes' tellin' a tale, Willie," I said strongly. "Where was her to see 'em?"

"Her was standin' right by the car. I swear fo' Gawd her was," he insisted.

"How come her standin' by the car?"

"Her seen Naomi hop in Mr. Win's car one night week fo' last right in front o' us house before my sister count get there, 'n' Mr. Win drove off down the road 'n' Lilly Mae followed 'em."

"Oh, go on, Willie, Lilly Mae ain't seen my sister hop in no car with Mr. Win."

"Her did, too; her tol' me yistiddy. Said her followed 'em 'n' found 'em under that clump o' trees over by the levee across from Mr. Ben Moses," he explained.

Recalling now how funny my sister had acted a few nights after she was sitting by the window watching a car drive up and wink its lights, I asked weakly, "Is you sho'?"

"Yes, I'm sho'; Lilly Mae seen 'em. Her said Mr. Win was drunk as a piss ant 'n' they was in the back seat. Her said her stood by the car 'n' watched 'em. Her said Mr. Win was so drunk he didn't even know who she was. Her said after he buried hisself in yo' sister, he turned at look at her 'n' ast her who her was. 'N' when her tol' him her was Lilly Mae, then he ast her who this was he was with in the car ef it wasn't her. 'N' when her tol' him it was Silas Henry's gal, he come to his senses 'n' jumped up. But he had already finished, Lilly Mae said, 'n' was jes' layin' there. When Mr. Win jumped up, my sister said he ast, 'How did Silas' gal git here?' 'N' Naomi hopped outa the car 'n' run, Lilly Mae said."

"Lilly Mae jes' tellin' a tale," I said with tears gathering in my eyes.

"My sister don' have to lie on ole black Naomi," Willie replied and ran on down the road.

I stood there crying for a while, and then I walked on toward home slowly, recalling again how funny my sister had acted several nights in a row a week or two ago. Instead of using the slop jar, she had got out of the window to go to the privy, she said. And after a while each night, she came back through the window, claiming she didn't want to wake up Mama and Papa by opening the door. Although I still doubted that Willie was telling the truth, I wanted to get home as quickly as I could and find out for sure.

As I ran, I recalled something else. The last night Naomi said she had gone to the privy out of window, she was trembling a little when she got into bed with me, and she seemed colder than usual, but she seemed happy. She put her arms around me and snuggled up to me, and I could feel her smiling.

VI

Sharecroppers and Daughter's Pregnancy by Plantation Owner

I rushed into the house to confront my sister with the story Willie had told me, but she was sitting by the churning fireplace and Mama and Grandma were sitting nearby, piecing a quilt. So I knew I would have to wait until I had Naomi by herself. It was a cool day and the butter was slow coming. I begged Mama to let Naomi pour a little hot water into the churn so the butter would come faster and I could have good, fresh buttermilk with my cornbread and baked sweet potato. She reluctantly agreed and I got the teakettle and put it on the fire. When it began steaming, my sister poured a little of the hot water down by the side of the dasher. In a little while, the butter came and Naomi poured me a big cup of buttermilk.

When I had finished eating, it was time to go and get the cow and bring her up for Mama to milk. I tried to get my sister to go with me, but she refused, saying she had to peel some potatoes and help Mama get supper ready.

After supper we gathered around the fireplace as usual, but I was so anxious to ask Naomi about what Willie had said that I decided not to roast any peanuts or sweet potatoes in the ashes. I merely sat in my corner under the mantelpiece in my little shuck-bottomed chair. Naomi sat opposite me with her feet tucked under her chair; Papa sat directly in front of the fire with his long legs stretched out as usual halfway over the hearth. Mama sat on one side of him, sewing pieces together for a quilt, and Grandma sat on the other side of him, smoking her pipe. The drier logs on the fire were cracking in the blaze like a whip while the wet ones sizzled and oozed steam. Our cat, Albert, weaved in and out of my legs when he was not sitting with his head against my knee.

As usual Papa talked about crop prospects. He wondered if Mr. Win was going to give him a larger cotton allotment this year. Said he could use three or four more acres with the big tractors doing all the breaking. I didn't like to hear about more acres because it meant more chopping and picking. As if hearing my mind at work, Papa said Mr. Win had told him our farm might be one of those selected for a test of weed killer that would reduce our chopping to almost nothing if it worked.

"Whut is a weed killer, Papa?" I asked.

"Mr. Win say it's some stuff that you put down like fertilizer 'n' it keep weeds 'n' grass from growin'; he tol' me 'bout it this evenin'," Papa replied.

"Shonuff?" I asked in puzzled delight.

"That whut he say."

"I'll b'lieve that when I see it," said Grandma, emphasizing her doubt with a spew of snuff juice into the center of the fire.

"Well, I jes' don' know, Miz Carrie,"Papa replied. "So much is happenin' now."

"Them's the Lewd's weed 'n' grass," Grandma said firmly, "'n' He know whut he doin'."

"But Ma, like Silas say, there could be something that'd kill the weeds 'n' grass," Mama said.

Grandma only grunted and Papa dropped any further talk about weed killers. Instead, he turned back to the outcome of our crop:whether we would make as many bales as we made last year, how much more we would make if we got two or three extra acres, andwhether we would be able to put aside sixty more dollars, or maybe one hundred or two hundred dollars to buy a farm of our own.

"These white folks ain't gon' sell you no land, Silas, don't you know that?" Grandma cut in.

"Maybe they would, Ma," Mama said.

"I hear folks is buyin' forty 'n' eighty-acre cuts out 'yond Rollin' Fork," Papa explained.

"Well, they mus' be different white folks from any I ever knowed," Grandma said.

"Ef us could git a piece o' land over 'round Rollin' Fork, that'd be fine with me, 'cause I'm sick o this place," Naomi out in.

"How come you sick o' it so all of a sudden?" Mama asked.

"Oh, I don' know," my sister replied. "I'm jes' sick o' it."

Grandma Carrie repeated her doubts about white folks selling land to colored folks out beyond Rollin' Fork or any place else.

Papa said no more about saving to buy a farm. He never liked to argue with Grandma because they didn't get along anyhow, and their arguments usually ended in name-calling with "black" somehow dragged in. And any mention of "black" just set him off.

But Grandma persisted, recalling how a colored farmer up around Friars Point had tried to buy a piece of land from the white folks once and then drove him off the place. "I think he went to Memphis," she said.

"Times is different, Miz Carrie," Papa said.

"Different my foot; these white folks ain't gon' never change."

When no one challenged her, she began talking about her favorite subject: ghosts. Told about passing a ghost in the road last fall on her way down to Mrs. Mary Moses one night. Said she saw him coming, but when she got to him she didn't see a thing, just felt some hot air. Then she told about ghosts in the graveyard.

I was so frightened when we went to bed that I really wanted to sleep with Grandma so she could keep the ghosts off me, but I decided to sleep with Naomi as I had planned so that I could find out about what Willie had told me. Naomi had heated four smoothing irons in the fireplace and wrapped each in a piece of an old torn sheet and placed them in the beds. One for everybody except me.

I crawled into bed close to my sister. It was an unusually chilly night, but her body was warm. She pressed her feet against the iron and got them warm, then she folded her legs back against her thighs so that my feet could reach hers and absorb their warmth.

"Naomi, Willie say," I began uncertainly, "Lilly Mae tol' him you been goin' with Mr. Win, but that ain't so, is it, 'cause you tol' me Mr. Win didn't want you?" I felt her body jump a little like the bobbing of a cork on a fishing line when a small perch nibbles at the bait.

But my sister did not answer right away, not, I think, because she did not have an answer, or because she was ashamed of what she had done, but because she did not quite know how to explain it to a boy of six. When she did speak, she admitted to my great disappointment that she had waited behind that tree out by the lane several nights when she had told me she was going to the privy and had watched Mr. Win drive up and wink his headlights and wait for Lilly Mae to run out of the dark up by her house and jump into the car with him. Then one night about two weeks ago, she said she run and jumped into the car with Mr. Win before Lilly Mae could get there.

She said Mr. Win had driven over by the levee by that clump of willows, just as Willie had said. And then my sister said Mr. Win had taken a big drink out of his bottle and had passed it to her. She said she pretended to take a drink and handed the bottle back to him. Then she told me Mr. Win had ordered her into the back seat, asking her "why in the hell" she was so slow about it and why was she so quiet. After taking another drink, she said Mr. Win got into the back seat with her, leaving the door open so their feet could hang out.

From the way my sister explained what she had done, not so much what she said but how she said it, it seemed to me the night with Mr. Win had fulfilled a long, aching desire.

"River," she whispered, "you don' know whut it's like to be a girl 'n' be black 'n' ugly 'n' have kinky hair, 'n' to have someone to be scrubbin' 'n' greasin' 'n' rubbin' you, tryin' to git some o' the black off; 'n' to have the good-looking boys pass you by for gals like Lilly Mae 'n' Della 'n' Sadie."

Naomi was crying now. Her body heaved in anguish as the tears came "'N' River, you don' know whut it's like to want to be bright and pretty when you ain't, 'n' to have soft straight hair like Mama, when yo' own is hard 'n' knotty. Maybe I wouldn't feel like this so much," she added, "ef you 'n' Mama I wasn't bright 'n' didn't have good hair, 'n' ef evvybody wasn't always comparin' me 'n' Mama, 'n' ef Grandma did hate black so much.

"I hates black, too, River, 'n' I don' want no black baby. I want my baby to be bright like you 'n' Mama 'n' have good hair 'n' I seen my chance. It was with Mr. Win, ef I could jes' beat Lilly Mae to his car one night, I figgered in the dark he wouldn't know no difference, being drunk, too. He didn't neither, 'cep'n he thought I smelt cleaner'n usual, he said."

Naomi had been whispering through her tears. Then she paused for a long time, as if to recollect, to search her soul for answers she herself did not know. I lay quiet, pressed close against her warm cotton flannel nightgown. I wanted to say something to make her feel better, but I didn't know what to say. So I put my arms around her as far as they would go and just lay there.

After a while, my sister sat up in the bed and placed her pillow at her back between her and the iron frame. Tears no longer came, and she was calm and poised. "I'm sorry I hates black, River, but I do," she whispered. "Do you reckon 'n' the way Grandma do? All niggers hates black the way I do 'n' the way Papa. Do you reckon, River?"

"I 'spect so, but I don' know," I answered, "but Papa 'n' Grandma Carrie sho' hates black. Ef all niggers is like them, I reckon they do, Naomi."

"Well, Papa 'n' Grandma gon' like my baby 'cause it gon' be bright 'n' bear good hair," my sister whispered proudly. Then she broke into quiet laughter with her hand over her mouth. Still laughing, she slid down under the quilts and went to sleep.

Although I ducked Willie for the next several days because I didn't want to admit to him that he was right about my sister and Mr. Win, he didn't forget about it, neither did his sister, who continued her snide remarks every time she came to our house, and later on, long before school was out for cotton chopping, all the girls at school seemed to know about it. Some giggled in my face and asked me if Naomi was getting fat or why she didn't come to Sunday school anymore.

And there was whispering at home by Mama and Papa and my Grandma. One day when I came home from school, I found Papa and Mama questioning my sister in loud, angry voices. I stopped by the steps to listen.

"I'm gon' ast you again who did it, Gawddamit, 'cause he gon' marry you or I'm gon' kill the sonofabitch," Papa said.

"I jes' can't tell you, Papa," Naomi answered, "not right now, Papa."

"Don' try to hide the boy, Naomi, 'cause us gon' find out anyhow," Mama added, "'n' us gon' make him marry you."

Naomi was silent for a long time, then she said again, "I jes' can't tell y'all right now, Mama."

"Well, Gawddamit, us gon' find out, ef I have to beat you 'n' a inch o' yo' life," Papa stormed.

"Now, you ain't gon' beat her in this condishon, Silas," Mama spoke up.

"All right, Becky, you jes' let her keep on bein' stubbo'n 'n' you gon' see. I ain't been workin' my ass off 'n' givin' her money fer a gold tooth fer her to start droppin' no bastards 'round here," Papa said in a voice that grew thinner, indicating how angry he was becoming.

"All I got to say, Silas, you ain't gon' whup her," Mama said firmly.

"Naw, Silas, don' whup her, not in her condishon," Grandma asserted in her own defiant way.

"Now, Miz Carrie, you stay outa this."

"Stay outa it nothin', you big black knotty-headed fool," Grandma replied.

"Hush, Ma, now I ain't gon' have you callin' my Silas no names, do you hear?" Mama ordered.

"I don' give a Gawddam whut none o' y'all say, this gal gon' tell me who done it or I'm gon' whup her so help me Gawd."

I didn't hear my sister say a word.

"Well, you jes' set there!" Papa shouted. "I'm gon' git my whip 'n' I'm gon' show you, gal." A moment later, the door opened and Papa rushed out, heading for the barn. "Whut you doin' ease-droppin', boy?"

I did not answer. Instead, I grabbed his arm. "You ain't gon' whup Naomi, is you, Papa?" I pleaded.

"I sho' is," he said and snatched away from me.

But by this time, Mama had his other arm, pleading, "Please, Silas, please wait a while 'tel you cool off some. Don' beat Naomi now."

Papa tried to snatch away, but Mama held on and I caught his other arm again.

"Please, please, Papa, don' whup Naomi," I begged, letting his arm go and grabbing his leg.

"Wait 'n' think 'bout it, Silas, don't you whup Naomi in her condishun," Mama said with more firmness and less begging.

Papa's steps slowed. Mama's words had reduced the determination in him.

"Please, please, Papa," I said again, dragging back on his leg.

"Naw, Silas, don' whup Naomi now while you so mad. Wait a while 'n' think 'bout it, Silas," Mama said, this time with less firmness and more pleading.

Papa stopped and stood still for a moment. I could feel the muscles in his leg jumping. Then Mama put her arms around him and he walked on a step or two and stopped again. Then he stooped down and picked me up in his arms, something he hadn't done in two or three months. I put my arms around his neck and hugged him as he walked out of the yard and out across our cotton field, where the young shoots stood three or four inches above the ground. Mama did not follow us. She went back into the house when Papa started walking across the field.

VII

Sharecroppers and Use of Chemicals as Weed and Grass Killers

As we walked up and down the rows looking at the young cotton, there were no weeds or grass racing with it. I had gotten down out of his arms and was walking by his side so that I could get a close look at the small plants. The cotton had the whole field to itself. "Look like that weed killer stuff gon' work," Papa said, talking partly to me but mostly to himself.

One of the Williamsons' tractor drivers had put down the weed killer along with the fertilizer on part of our cotton and most of Reverend Fisher's as an experiment. "Course, puttin' this stuff down gon' cost somethin'," Papa said, "but it sho' look like us ain't gon' have to do much choppin' this year 'n' you 'n' yo' mama can fish, too, 'n' Miz Carrie can set at the house most all the time now."

Papa omitted Naomi. I knew it was on purpose because he had to think hard not to include her. I think she had been included in all his thoughts and plans all her life. He and she were entwined like morning-glory vines. And separating Naomi from himself must have taken a lot of effort and hurt an awful lot. But whether he mentioned my sister or not, she wasn't going to have to do much chopping, either.

The thought of not having to do much chopping sent a feeling of pleasure through me. Jumping up and down, I said gleefully, "Us ain't gon' have to chop much, is us, Papa?"

"Well, maybe a weed here 'n' there, no real choppin' on this part o' us farm, ef the stuff work," Papa explained, "least that whut them folks from the Fitlers say."

He was referring to ole Mr. Gus Hawkins and his family and ole Mr. Sidney Jones and his who moved to the Bend last year, I had heard Papa and Mama say, after they were put off one of the plantations up there. They said Mr. Win and Mr. Walter took them in because they didn't have any place to go. They had moved in the houses where Mrs. Mead and Mrs. Shannon had lived before they died, Mama had said.

"They gittin' lot o' machinery up 'round Fitlers, 'n' this is cuttin' down on the people. Don' need so many people on a plantation when you got machinery 'n' got this weed killer stuff," Papa said. "They say there jes' 'bout ain't no choppin' up there 'n' there won't be much pickin', they say, ef they git one o' them machines they say that can pick cotton."

"A machine that can pick cotton, Papa?" I asked in wonderment. "You is jokin', Papa; I know you is jokin', 'cause they can't make no machine pick cotton. How it gon' find all them bolls?"

"Well, that's whut they say, River. Course I ain't seen one," he replied.

"Ef they do make a machine that can pick cotton, Papa," I said, "then us won't have to work nomo', jes' fish 'n' hunt pecans 'n' go church."

"Man, you don' think Mr. Win 'n' them gon' keep all us folks on the plantation jes' to fish 'n' hunt pecans 'n' go to church, do you?" Papa asked.

"Well, whut is the folks go do, Papa?"

"I don' know." Then he said nothing for a long time as we walked randomly across our field, hoping in a way to confirm our doubts about weed killers. Finally he said again, "I don't know." But this time he said it as if his admission that he did not know the answer to my question came not merely from his lips, but deep inside his head, where he was beginning to realize he did not know the answer.

We had walked over most of our field where the weed killer had been applied without seeing a weed. Then suddenly there stood a dandelion. "Well, that stuff sho' don' git 'em all," Papa said half in boast and half in doubt.

But a closer look told us the dandelion was dying. Its jagged, tooth-like leaves were beginning to curl like sick collard greens, the stem was leaning, and the flower, more brown than yellow, was bowed as if in prayer. The center of the flower, out of which comes a mosquito net-like growth of tiny seed to form a ball that looks like cotton's first cousin, was dark and dead-looking. Papa and I knew no ball of feather-light seeds would ever form on this plant, and none would blow from it across the field, as in the past, to give cotton choppers trouble trying to dig up the long roots without disturbing the cotton.

Papa and I sat down in the middle of the row and stared at the dying dandelion. To me, its death signaled the end of backbreaking cotton chopping. All I would need my short-handled hoe for in the future was to dig bait, and this gave me a good feeling. Lay-by time would come early and last most of the year, except during poisoning and cotton-picking time.

I jumped up to chase a butterfly, but Papa still sat there. When I came back to his side, he said, "Ef this stuff shonuff do kill all the weeds, 'n' ef they is got a machine that can pick cotton shonuff, whut is us gon' be doin'?"

After a while, he stood up and we started back toward the house. He had made only three or four steps when he turned back and raised his foot to stomp the dandelion. But his foot stopped in mid air and he turned away from the weed. Perhaps the thought ran through his mind that the dandelion was dying fast enough, and with it the plantation itself and our future on it.

On our way back to the house, we walked close to the turnrow between our farm and Reverend Fisher's to see how free his cotton was of grass and weeds. Like our own, there wasn't a weed to be seen in his field, and he usually had the grassiest cotton on the plantation.

When we got back to our house, we got some corn out of the crib and fed our two mules. Mama had fed and milked the cow; we saw her returning to the house from the lane with the pail of milk. Our new mule, Salt, was big and speckled and as scary as a rabbit. I think the day hands on the place, who had driven the mules before the Williamsons got tractors, must have been mean to him. But little by little he was learning from Miss Lady, who had been with Papa since Humphreys County, that Papa wasn't mean to his stock. He worked them hard, but he seldom struck them. After I primed the pump and pumped water for the animals, we went into the house for supper. Papa didn't say anything to Naomi. I think he was too concerned at the moment about our future on the plantation.

In an effort to keep Papa's mind off my sister, I think, Mama asked, "Silas, how is the crop?"

"It's comin' 'long fine; that weed killer stuff is sho' workin', hardly a weed a'tall on that part o' us cotton where the stuff was spread, or in Reverend Fisher's, either."

"You mean there ain't no weeds in Reverend Fisher's cotton?" Mama asked in surprise.

"Maybe one or two here 'n' there, but nomo'," Papa replied.

"Yessum," I added, "jes' one or two maybe."

"Well, ef that stuff can keep the weeds 'n' grass outa Reverend Fisher's cotton, it'll keep 'em out anywhere," Mama said.

"Course," Papa said, "this gon' mean mo' time fer you to fish this year, Becky, but after the 'sper'ment's over 'n' the Williamsons start using that stuff on the whole place, I don' know whut's gon' happen to sharecroppin'."

"Reckon they gon' start puttin' folks off the place like they doin' up at Fitlers 'n' Babylon?" Mama asked fearfully.

"They might; I jes' don' know," Papa replied in a slow, worried voice.

"Where us goin', Silas? I'm so tired o' movin', I don' know whut to do," Mama said, not really expecting an answer but expressing her fears.

"Whut that y'all sayin' 'bout movin'?" Grandma asked, limping a little as she walked into the kitchen because her arthritis was bothering her knees.

"Ma, Silas was jes' sayin' ef that weed killer stuff work fer sho', Mr. Walter 'n' Mr. Win might not need no sharecroppers after while," Mama explained.

"Whut weed killer stuff?"

"You know, the stuff whut's suppose to kill weeds in the cotton that us was talkin' 'bout few weeks ago. 'N' the tractor drivers done put it down on part o' us cotton 'n' all o' Reverend Fisher's, 'n' Silas say the stuff is workin'."

"It sho' is, Grandma," I said. "Us ain't seen nothin' but one little ole dandelion in that part o' us field where they put the stuff down 'n' it was dyin'. But in the rest o' us field us seen a lot o' weeds 'n' Johnsongrass."

"'N' you didn't think it was gon' work, Miz Carrie, but it sho' workin'," Papa said, glad to reproach her for being wrong.

"I said them's the Lawd's weeds 'n' He knowed whut He was doin' when He put 'em here,"Grandma came back. "Now whut this I hear 'bout movin'?"

"Silas say, Ma, ef that stuff shonuff kill all the weeds in the cotton, there ain't gon' be no need to chop 'n' Mr. Win 'n' Mr. Walter ain't gon' need no sharecroppers."

"Didn't I tell you, Mr. Smartaleck, that them was the Lawd's weeds, 'n' He knowed whut He was doin' when He put 'em here?" Grandma asked, shaking her finger in Papa's face.

"Well, the weed killer sho' workin', Miz Carrie," Papa said. "Do that mean the Lawd's gon' let the white folks git rid o' weeds 'n' niggers, too?"

"But evvybody say the Williamsons don' never put nobody," Grandma said. "They say they done tol' all the ole folks they can stay here 'tel they die."

"They is, Miz Carrie; you know Mr. Win done tol' you that," Papa recalled. "But that was 'cause he was countin' on us 'n' us chillun bein' here to chop 'n' pick cotton. Whut ef there ain't no choppin' to do 'cause o' this weed killer stuff?" Whut he gon' say then?"

"Maybe there ain't gon' be no choppin' to do, 'n' that's you saying that, Silas, there always gon' be a heap o' pickin' to do," Grandma asserted.

"Right now it is, Miz Carrie, but they say they got a machine whut can pick cotton. Suppose to be gittin' one up at Fitlers this year," Papa said with the smug satisfaction of knowing something Grandma knew nothing about.

"A machine whut can pick cotton? Have mercy, Jesus. Is you sho', Silas?" Grandma asked.

"I ain't seen one, Miz Carrie, but they say they sho' got ' em."

"Well, ef the white folks got stuff whut kill the weeds 'n' grass so they don' need no cotton choppers, 'n' ef they shohuff got machines whut can pick cotton, like you say, Silas, whut is us po' colored folks gon' do? Is the Lawd done 'bandoned us?" Grandma asked and then limped back to her rocking chair, where she sat shaking her head and poking in the dying embers of the fire while Mama finished cooking supper.

VIII

Silas's Anger and Physical Threats to Pregnant Daughter

My sister began staying close to her room in our four-room shack, especially when Papa was home. And after a while, she stopped going to Sunday school with me and never went to church except at night. "Goin' to Sunday school with her stomach sticking out like that?" Mama would say.

But Mama regretted very much that Naomi couldn't go to Sunday school anymore, not only because she knew the folks on the plantation were whispering about it, but also because my sister couldn't go and win another Bible illustration to paste over one a mouse had eaten through.

Our home was papered with old newspapers and magazines Mrs. Paralee, Mr. Win and Mrs. Susie's cook, had given us, and with Bible illustrations Naomi had won by answering Sunday school questions put by Mr. Hamp, the superintendent. Flour paste was used to glue the paper to the walls, and the mice loved it. They crawled around under the paper eating the paste. There were three illustrations on the walls of the room where Mama and Papa slept. There was one of the Last Supper with Judas sopping out of the plate with Jesus. I often wondered if he was sopping molasses with a biscuit. If he was, I knew it was good, because next to cornbread and buttermilk and my Christmas apples, I thought biscuits and molasses were the best eating in the whole world.

Another illustration showed Saul on the road to Damascus. And the third one was of Christ with some sheep. But this one had been marred by an ole mouse that had gnawed off the crook of Jesus' staff and part of His hand. I wondered how Jesus could stand there and let a little ole mouse chew part of His hand off. I would have slapped that little ole mouse all the way across the plantation.

Mama complained every few days about the ugly hole in the illustration and about Naomi not being able to go to Sunday school and win another one to paste over it. So the next Sunday, when I went to Sunday school, I thought I would try to win an illustration for Mama.

I stood in line with several other children. Most of them were bigger than me, and I was afraid. It was the first time I had tried to win a Bible picture. As the questions went around, the line kept getting shorter and shorter. I had answered two questions with a tremulous voice. Now the third was coming and my stomach was quivering with fear. Somehow I answered it. Finally, only Emma Lou, General Lee's big sister, and I were still standing. I was more afraid than ever, feeling sure I was going to lose and then I wouldn't have the pretty Bible picture to take home to Mama for her wall. I regretted I had ever gotten into the contest. As tears seeped into my eyes,

Mr. Hamp was ready with the next question.

"Where was Paul goin' when he fell off his hoss?" he asked Emma Lou.

She fidgeted with the belt on her pretty dress, looked up in the ceiling of the church from which hung three naked bulbs, and said, "Jerusalem."

Mr. Hamp shook his head slowly as if to give Emma Lou more time. I was so excited I was afraid to move a muscle, but my stomach seemed to turn, and my penis began stinging, and I felt a little water rolling down my leg. It couldn't be true, there was something wrong, Emma Lou wasn't going to miss the question.

Then I heard Emma Lou stammer, "Er er er, wasn't it Jerusalem?"

Mr. Hamp turn to me. "Whut do you say, River?"

"Damascus! Damascus!" I shouted in anxiety, knowing I was right because we had a picture Naomi had won of Paul lying on the ground in front of his horse, shielding his eyes from the sun. And the printing said, "Paul on the Road to Damascus"; my sister had read it to me a hundred times.

"That's right, River," Mr. Hamp said. "You done win the picture fer today's lesson." Then he walked over to the alter rail, tore off the picture from the rest of the illustrations, and handed it to me with a pat on my head. "That's a good boy, River," he said.

As I look back, I haven't won many victories in my life, but that crowning moment of triumph in Sunday school on the plantation years ago I think thrilled me more than any of the rest, although it turned out to be short-lived.

I had won a picture of Paul and Silas in jail with the door shook open and the guard standing with his sword drawn as if he were going to kill himself. "Paul 'n' Silas—Silas—Silas," I kept saying to myself. "Papa gon' sho' like this picture 'n' Mama will be glad to have it fer her wall."

It was a beautiful picture in bright colors. I was so proud of it, I kept holding it up for all to see, as if it had not been on display all morning in Sunday school. Even as I started for home, I was still holding it open, rejecting all suggestions that I roll it up. I was still standing at the church gate proudly holding up my picture when Willie Fisher ran up to me.

"You think you somethin', don't you, jes' 'cause you done win a little ole pitchur?" he said, grabbing for it and adding, "How come yo' sister, Big Belly, wasn't here to win it?"

I snatched the picture almost out of his reach and struck him hard in the face. He stumbled back, and the force from my second swing, which missed, toppled me over, but somehow I released the picture before I fell and it glided away several feet unharmed, except for the small tear Willie had put in it.

I had barely struck the ground when Willie jumped on top of me and began pummeling me with his fists. But I fought him off, rolled over on top of him, and was about to give it to him good when Lilly Mae pulled me off him and told me to go home before she called her papa.

"Willie done started it," I said as I got to my feet. "He sho' done started it," I repeated with tears in my eyes.

"I don' care who done started it," Lilly Mae said firmly. "You go on home."

As I tried to brush off my clothes, tears still in my eyes, Mary Lou brought my picture to me and helped me brush at the mud and grass stains on my suit. "You sho' beat him good, River," she whispered.

I did not reply, but what she had said made me feel better. I took my picture, still holding it open, and we walked on quietly up the lane from the church. When we came to the fork in the road where she was supposed to turn off, she kept right on walking at my side. "Beinst I'm so fer ahead o' Della, I'm gon' walk piece-ways with you," she said. Della and the rest of the children were barely out of the church yard.

Although I said nothing, I was happy that she had not turned off. Having her at my side kept my mind off the mud on my suit and the tear in the picture and what Papa was going to say when I got home. She continued with me almost to Mr. Riley Jones' house before she turned back, kissing me quickly on the cheek as she did. "Goodbye!" she hollered as she ran.

Della, who was standing at the fork, yelled, "How come Naomi don' come to church nomo'?"

I did not answer. I merely held my picture high as if to say, "This is all I know." Then I turned and ran toward home.

The picture fared all right until I reached the top of a knoll near Mr. Albert Moore's and in sight of my house over the top of the corn. Of course, the sweat from my hands had soiled the picture a little, and there was the small tear Willie had made, but otherwise it was fine and I was counting on it saving me from Papa for the mud on my clothes. Then a little whirlwind came dancing across Mr. Albert's cotton field right straight at me and my picture. They say the devil travels in whirlwinds, and I believe it now, because the wind snatched the picture out of my hands, almost tearing off the head of the guard who was about to kill himself with his sword. The picture sailed through the air as the whirlwind swirled in a wigwam of dust.

I ran across the field to where the ole whirlwind left the picture lying in the middle of a row. I picked it up slowly as if to delay my knowing that it was torn almost in two. I tried to pull the picture together and roll it up, but the wind kept tugging at the corners. So I started home again, holding part of the picture in one hand and part in the other. The tears, which had dried as Mary Lou and I walked along, began to flow again. My steps became shorter and shorter and slower and slower. I wished I would never reach home. Then suddenly I found myself walking into our yard. Although my head was down and my eyes were full of water, I know I was home because the skirt of grass between our house and the road ended, and I was walking on hard, bare ground, which had been swept clean.

As I came around to the front of the house, I heard Papa and Mama and Grandma Carrie talking. I could feel their eyes upon me as I crept toward the steps. The tears increased, my heart was broken; my day of triumph was ending in tragedy. The porch was quiet, too quiet. It was at a time like this when I welcomed Grandma's presence the most because she usually spoke up for me. But this time she said nothing. Then if only Mama would say something, but she was silent, too. Instead, I heard my father clear his throat like the sound of doom.

"Whut in the world done happen to you, boy? You come on in this house 'n' git outa yo' Sunday clothes," Papa said gruffly.

"Yessuh, yessuh," I said quickly without moving because I felt sure he was going to slap me as I approached.

"Whut that you got in yo' hands?" he asked. "It ain't no Bible pitchur, I know, 'cause wouldn't nobody tear up a Bible pitchur like that."

I fumbled for a safe reply. "The ole devil in the win' done tore it, Papa," I explained sadly, hoping to hear Mama's voice. But she must have wanted the picture awful bad because when she did speak, it was in an accusing voice.

"How come you ain't rolled it up like you got some sense?"

"I don' no'am," I said, wondering why she couldn't understand how badly I wanted to carry the picture open in complete triumph.

"'N' whut done happen to yo' clothes?" she asked.

It took me a long time to answer. I stood there on the bottom step, trying to hold time under my feet. Finally I said weakly, "Willie Fisher done jumped on me."

"Whut did he do that fer?" Papa asked pointedly.

"I don' know, suh, 'cause I win the pitchur, I guess, 'n' 'cause he say Naomi got a big belly," I replied fearfully.

"He said that 'bout yo' sister?"

"Yessuh, he sho' did, Papa, 'n' he done tried to snatch my pitchur 'n' us got in a fight," I explained, gaining courage as I went along.

"How come he say Naomi got a big belly?" Mama asked in a voice edged with anger.

"I don' no'am, 'cause he seen her, I reckon, goin' to the pump or to the privy. 'N' some o' the girls like Della done ast how come her don' come to Sunday school 'n' church nomo'," I replied, still standing on the bottom step.

"Have mercy, Jesus!" Grandma intoned.

And Papa and Mama looked at one another in a funny kind of way.

"Well, you come on in the house 'n' git them clothes off," Papa said roughly.

Although I felt the interest shift from me and my soiled clothes and torn illustration to my sister's belly, I was still afraid that Papa was going to slap me. So I scooted by him as fast as I could. Inside, I talked with Naomi while I changed my clothes. "Ole Willie Fisher tried to snatch my pitchur, 'n' he say you got a big belly, 'n' I whupped him good."

Naomi, who was leaning in the window, looking out across the field when I came into the room, looked around at me and grunted, and then turned back to the window. "I don' care whut that ole fool Willie Fisher say," she said with her back turned to me.

"'N' Della 'n' them ast how come you don' come to Sunday school 'n' church nomo'," I told her.

"That all they got to say?" my sister asked without turning around.

When I had pulled my suit off and was about to hang it behind the door out of sight, Naomi looked around.

"Don' hang yo' muddy clothes back there with my good dresses; why don't you hang yo' suit on the line out in the back where the mud will dry 'n' us can brush it off?" She took the suit and hung it on the line and then came back and sat on the side of the bed silently.

Since my sister was so quiet, I wanted to go out on the porch where Papa and Mama and Grandma were, but I was afraid they might be reminded of my muddy suit and the torn picture. So I went to the kitchen and got a cold biscuit and some buttermilk. As I passed the door, I heard Mama talking low, almost in a whisper. Curious, I decided to go out on the porch when I had finished the snack. Immediately, Grandma said, "River, go play."

No matter how much Mama and Papa and Grandma whispered at home about Naomi's belly, the folks on the plantation weren't whispering; they were talking out loud and staring. At school, at church, at the store, there were the same knowing stares, as if to say, "You think I don' know 'bout Naomi, but I do." You could hear the talk, which stopped abruptly as you approached, and you could feel the stares even when you weren't looking, and you could feel, too, your place in the community slipping down day by day like an unshod mule slipping down the side of the levee in front of a heavily loaded wagon to which he was harnessed.

I knew it was bound to get under Papa skin sooner or later and he was going to explode. It happened the next Saturday at the store when Della's mama, Mrs. Nettie, greeted Mama on the porch with a big hug and a big question: "When is Naomi gon' git married?"

Before Mama could find a good answer, Papa shouted, "Whose damned bizness is it?" Papa spoke before he thought. I could tell by the way he lowered his head. "I mean, I mean," he added but did not finish because he had no answer. But the implications of the question cut him to the quick.

Mrs. Nettie backed away with a loud, "'Scuse me, Mr. Henry, I don' care ef her never git married."

The store porch fell silent, and Papa turned around and headed for the wagon with Mama and me following him. He unhitched the mule and we got into the wagon and he drove straight home. All the way he fussed and fumed. "Now this jes' done gone too fer," he said. "Evvybody on the place laffin' at us 'n' pokin' fun, 'n' all 'cause o' that gal. Her gon' tell us who the papa is 'n' all 'bout this thing, or her gon' git outa my house."

"Now, Silas," Mama said.

"Now, Silas, nothin', that gal gon' tell me or her gon' git out, 'n' that's that," Papa stormed.

"Where her goin'?" Mama wanted to know.

"I don' care where her go, jes' so her git outa my house," my father insisted.

"Now, Silas," Mama pleaded, "Naomi ain't the firs' gal whut been spoilt 'n' her ain't gon' be the las'."

"I don' give a damn whut you say, Becky. I done spoke. Either that gal gon' come clean with us or her gon' git out."

"Papa, Papa," I begged, "please don' put Naomi out, please don' put Naomi out." Tears gathered in my eyes and I found myself crying and screaming, "Please, Papa, please."

"Now you got this chile all worked up!" Mama yelled.

"I don't care. That gal gon' talk."

"Silas, don' be too hard on Naomi; 'n' don't you fergit, her yo' daughter, too, 'n' her jes' the spittin' image o' you in her looks 'n' in her stubbo'nness," Mama continued pleading.

"You can talk all you want to, Becky, but that gal's gon' talk. Got this chile fingtin' at church 'n' got us bein' insulted 'n' laffed at at the sto'. Naw-naw, he gon' talk."

"I'm sho' her'll talk, Silas, when her ain't so frightened. Jes' give her mo' time, Silas."

"Her done had all the time her gon' git, 'cep'n 'tel Monday mornin'; leas' I won' put her out on Sunday."

"Well, I sho' hopes you knows whut you is doin', Silas," Mama said as the wagon rolled up the gate where it opened to the road that led from the lane past our house. I hopped down to open the gate; Papa was saying something to Mama, but the spring breeze blew it away before I could hear.

At home, Papa and Mama had it all over again with Grandma joining in as Papa tried to get Naomi to tell him who the baby's papa was. He ran down the list of just about every boy on the plantation, but my sister did not answer. Then Papa started cursing and ran out to the barn to get his whip, yelling, "Gawddamit, gal, you gon' tell me tonight, or I'm gon' give you a whuppin' you ain't gon' never fergit!"

Mama was standing in the kitchen door when he came back with the whip. "Now, you wait a minute, Silas," Mama said firmly with no pleading in her voice. "You ain't gon' whup that gal in her condishon, less'n you whup me firs'."

"Woman, you git outa my way," Papa raged, shoving her aside and proceeding toward Naomi's room, dragging part of the long whip on the floor.

Mama grabbed it and tried to snatch it away from him, but he was too strong. He jerked it away from her and, in his anger, came down with a lash of the whip that sent her to the floor.

Mama screamed in pain and yelled, "Gawddamn you, Silas! Whut did you do that fer?" Grandma and I rushed to her, but Papa was already there.

"Baby, baby," he pleaded, "I didn't mean to do it. I sware to Gawd, I didn't mean to do it, baby."

"Don't you baby me, you Gawddamn black nigger, you! Let go o' me."

But Papa did not let go. Although I know the words "black" and "nigger" stabbed him like a butcher knife, he did not cease pleading. Despite Mama's twisting and turning on the floor, he kept one arm around her gently, his face pressed to hers, and the hand of his other arm gliding tenderly over her long, straight hair. "Becky, baby, you got to believe me, honey, I didn't go to do it."

Papa was still repeating these words when Naomi grabbed my arm and rushed me to the door, pushing me out of it ahead of her. Out in the lane we trotted toward the store in the twilight. I wondered where we were going, but I did not ask because I knew my sister was troubled. Her face was twisted up in fear and tears ran down her cheeks.

As we neared the store, Naomi stopped, sat down under a tree with some effort, and scribbled a note on a piece of paper she had in her pocketbook, which she had been holding with one hand along with a bulging pillowslip. "Take this to the sto' like a big boy 'n' give it to Mr. Win," she said, handing me the note. "Nobody but Mr. Win. Ef he ain't there, you bring it back, do you hear?" she warned.

"How come I got to take it to Mr. Win?" I asked.

"Nevermin', you jes' do like I say, 'n' don' give it to nobody but Mr. Win."

"You ain't gon' git Mr. Win to come to us house 'n' jump on Papa, is you?"

"Naw, naw, you know I wouldn't try to put the white folks on Papa."

But I was still slow about going.

"Don't you worry 'bout Papa; this note ain't got nothin' to do with him."

I pressed the note in my sweaty, dusty hand and trotted off to the store right up the road. As I walked up the steps and all the way inside, folks said, "Howdy, River." "Hi, River." "Hey, River." "Ain't he cute?" "Where yo' pa?" The store was crowded.

I replied, "Howdy, Mr. Jones. Howdy, Miz Hawkins. Good-edenin', Miz Lee." But I did not tarry. I looked around store for Mr. Win; there were three white men there. I wasn't sure which one was he. I had seen him only a few times, mostly at a distance. I looked first at Mr. Lige, who I later learned was the store manager, but he looked fatter and older than the man I had seen in our cornfield that day with Lilly Mae. Mr. Walter's rimless glasses told me he wasn't Mr. Win. Then the other man had to be Mr. Win. As I approached him, he smiled friendly-like, and I felt sure that was he. So I handed him the note and ran out the store and back down the road to where Naomi was waiting. "I give it to him," I told her, standing by her side as she sat there on the ground.

"You sho' it wasn't nobody but Mr. Win?"

"It was him; I 'member from that time I seen him in us cornfield when I thought I done got religion."

"That's a good boy," Naomi said and wrapped her arms around my legs and hugged them. "Now run on home to Mama 'n' Papa fo' they miss you. Ef they ast you 'bout me, tell 'em you ain't seen me. Do you hear? Tell 'em you ain't seen me."

I stooped down, put my arms around her neck, and pressed my face against hers. It felt wet; I knew she was crying again, and I started crying, too. We cried quietly in the gathering dusk, hugging each other tightly, and I realized for the first time how much I loved my sister.

I suppose all before we had been too busy to show our love—too busy chopping and picking cotton, toting water, feeding and watering the stock, milking the cow, churning butter, rounding up the animals when they got into the fields; too busy worrying about getting religion and saving our souls from hell; too busy worrying about boll weevils and Johnson grass and Jimson weeds, about ducking Papa and pleasing Mama and Grandma.

Or maybe it was the wide gap in our ages—eleven years—or her concern about her blackness or her hair, and her desire for a gold tooth, or mine for Christmas shoes, a cap pistol, and all the apples and oranges I could eat. Or maybe there was some hidden fear that blocked the free flow of our love. A fear that lurks on every plantation—a fear that children absorb from their parents about settlement time and coming out in debt, about arguing with the white man and moving in the night, about enough to eat and a shack to live in, about living and dying.

And so it was not until this night when Mama and Papa were fighting and Naomi was in trouble with no place to turn, except to the white folks, that our real love for each other showed itself.

"Now you be a good boy 'n' run on home fo' Papa miss you," my sister ordered. "'N' ef they ast you 'bout me, tell 'em you ain't seen me. Now don' fergit, hear?"

"Where you goin', Naomi?" I asked with fresh tears in my eyes.

"I don' know fer sho', but I ain't goin' back home fer Papa to beat me."

"But where is you goin'?" I insisted.

"I don' know, River, but I'm gon' be all right. Now you run on home 'n' don' fergit whut I tol' you. Tell Papa 'n' them you ain't seen me, ef they ast you, do you hear?" my sister said and squeezed me tight for just a moment with a big grunt. "Now you run on home," she repeated.

I turned away from her slowly with both my hands trying desperately to stem the tears. Then I ran all the way home. As I neared our house, I got out of the lane, cut through the field between our house and Reverend Fisher's, and came around past the privy and the barn and up by the side of the porch so that Papa and Mama wouldn't see me if they were sitting there cooling off. When I came around the house, only Grandma was sitting on the porch. She was rocking slowly. Inside was quiet; Mama had won the battle.

"Where you been, boy?" Grandma asked.

"To the privy, Grandma."

Then I sat on the edge of the porch with my back against a post while Grandma rocked and talked about the stars and the new moon and about Halley's Comet, which she said she had seen years ago. Said it had a tail that reached away across the skies. I liked to heard Grandma talk about the stars and the moon when it was planting time, but that night my mind was on Naomi, and I really wasn't listening to what Grandma was saying. But I didn't want to go into the house because I didn't want to be the one who found out that my sister wasn't home.

Naomi didn't return home that night, but her absence wasn't discovered until the next morning. I had slept with Grandma so that Mama and Papa wouldn't think I knew anything about her disappearance and, therefore, not be questioned too closely about it. I knew if they questioned me much about Naomi, my eyes would give me away. Because I could not look them in the eye and tell them a lie. So I knew the best thing for me to do was to appear to know nothing about my sister's leaving and lie through my actions but not with my lips.

"Naomi mighty quiet in there," Grandma said.

I pretended to be asleep and did not reply. She rose up in the bed on her elbows and listened for Naomi's snoring. Then she lay back down.

But I was too scared and too worried abut my sister to sleep anymore. I lay there wondering where she was, what she had written to Mr. Win, whether he had come outside the store and helped her, where he took her, when he would bring her back. I was so engrossed in my thoughts that I was not aware that Grandma had got up to make her coffee.

"Where Naomi?" I heard her asking in a loud voice. "Her ain't in here."

Mama yelled, "Whut you say, Ma?"

"I say Naomi ain't here," Grandma replied.

"Ain't here? Where is her?" Mama asked, running through Grandma's room and into Naomi's in her bare feet.

The noise awoke Papa. "Whut's goin' on?" he wanted to know.

"Naomi ain't in her room," Mama said, returning to confront Papa, who was standing in the middle of the floor trying to get his eyes open. "Naomi ain't in her room," Mama repeated.

"Where is her?" he asked.

"I don' know."

"Maybe her out in the privy," Papa said, jumping into his overalls and shoes and running out the back door. In a few seconds, he was back at the kitchen door, saying, "Her ain't out there!" Then he trotted around the house, looking across the field as far as he could see. "I don' see her nowhere," he said excitedly as he came back inside.

"Ma say her ain't heard her all night," Mama told him.

"Reckon her been gone all night?" he asked.

"Ain't no tellin'," Grandma replied.

"'N' all 'cause o' you, Silas," Mama charged, "talkin' 'bout whuppin' that chile in her condishun."

"Maybe ef you hadn't stopped me from whuppin' her, her would still be here 'stid o' Gawdknoswhere."

"All I got to say, Silas, is you better find my chile," Mama warned.

"Whut you think I'm gon' do, woman, 'cep'n look fer her? I'm gon' ride over evvy inch o' this plantation 'tel I finds her."

"'N' don't you touch her when you do, do you hear me, Silas?" Mama ordered coldly.

"I hear you, woman," Papa replied with anger in his voice as he went out to the barn. So sure was he that he was going to find my sister that he didn't saddle ole Salt, but hitched him to the wagon so that he could bring her back.

Mama and Grandma went back into Naomi's room and looked again, as if they might have overlooked her in the small room with an iron bed and a homemade dressing table. Then Mama sat on the side of the bed and mourned, "My po' baby, my po' baby, Oh, Lawd, where is my po' baby?" As tears came, she stretched out on the bed and sobbed. One of her hands hung limp toward the floor.

Feeling helpless by the side of the bed and a little guilty, too, I slumped to the floor and caught her hand and rubbed and patted it. Her nails were hard and broken, and her hand was rough and calloused from the hoe, the pump handle, the broom, the reins to our mule, cotton bolls, her fishing pole, and dozens of other chores she put her hands to. I had never studied her hands before. I pressed the one I was holding to my face; I was crying now.

When Papa had finished hitching up the mule and putting on his Sunday clothes, he yelled, "I'm goin'!"

"Wait," Mama said, "I'm goin' with you."

"Well, hurry up 'n' git yo' clothes on," he replied.

When Papa and Mama had gone on a house-to-house search for my sister, Grandma turned to me and asked, "'How come you ain't slept with Naomi las' night, boy? It's the firs' night you ain't slept with her in a week. How come you ain't slept with her las' night?"

"'Cause I wanted to sleep with you some," I lied, feeling like a rabbit must feel when he is being scented by a hound.

"Is that so?" Grandma said in a doubtful tone.

"Yessum," I replied and shut my mouth tight as if to keep the truth from spilling out.

"Was you in the privy las' night like you said? You sho' stayed a long time. Is you runnin' off at the bowles?"

"No'am," I replied and kept my eyes focused downward so that Grandma couldn't look into them.

"Look at me, boy."

I raised my eyes slowly with water gathering in them.

"Where is Naomi at?" Grandma demanded. There was certainty in her voice; she knew she had treed a coon. "Where is Naomi at, boy?" she repeated.

"I don' no'am," I said as innocently as I could.

"Don't you lie to me, boy. Where is yo' sister at?"

"I don' no 'am, I left her by the road near the sto'."

"When was this?"

"Yistiddy 'bout dus' dark."

"Whut her doin' by the side o' the road?"

"Waitin'."

"Waitin' fer whut?"

I was now in full retreat from the promise I had made Naomi, and tears began to flow. "Her was waitin' fer Mr. Win to answer her note," I said between gasp for breath.

"Have mercy, Jesus. Mr. Win?"

"Yessum, her done wrote him a note."

"Done wrote Mr. Win a note?"

"Yessum, I took it to him."

"Lawd, have mercy," Grandma mourned. "Whut her write Mr. Win fer?" Sweat stood out on her face and there was a quiver of fear in her voice.

"I don' no'am, I didn't read the note," I said in a tone that asked her not to question me anymore.

"Whut Mr. Win say when you done give him the note?"

"He didn't say nothin, jes' smiled a little at me."

"Lawd, Jesus! 'N' you don' know whut her was writin' him fer?"

"No'am, 'cep'n maybe her was tellin' him her done had to run 'way from home 'cause her gon' have a baby fer him."

"Whut you say, boy? You mean Mr. Win is the papa o' that baby Naomi gon' have?"

"Yessum, that whut her say."

"Lawd, Gawd, have mercy, Jesus!" Grandma screamed as she got down on her knees.

This was old territory for Grandma. She had traveled over it before, long years before at Friars Point when she was carrying Mama for a white man. But Mr. Hood was a bachelor and she was a girl of fifteen whom he had at one time saved from drowning when she was baptized. I had heard her tell of it many times as I sat under the house when she thought I was off playing.

She would recall the loneliness and the emptiness until Mama was born, and then she said she had a pretty baby to play with. "The prettiest baby in this world," she would say. Soon after that she married Cleve Johnson, but they had to leave that plantation because of Mr. Hood and move down almost to Clarksdale. Sometimes Grandma mentioned it boastfully when she was admiring Mama's color and her soft straight hair; at other times she brought it up to prove the meanness of white folks, and occasionally she recalled Friars Point and Mr. Hood with a fondness the years had not dimmed.

As Grandma began to pray, her thoughts seemed to center less on the loneliness and lovelessness and fearfulness she knew Naomi was going through and more on the meanness of white folks and the hard reality that her granddaughter was going to have a baby for a white plantation owner who had a wife and two children and a brother and a sister-in-law right on the place. This made all the difference in the world between her own case years ago and that of Naomi's right now, and she made this plain to the Lord in her prayer.

And then there was Papa, whom she referred to as ole hot-headed black Silas as she talked with her God. And she wondered in her conversation with the Lord what Silas might do if he found out that Mr. Win was the father of Naomi's unborn child. Grandma was still on her knees praying when Papa and Mama returned. They had found out from Mr. Miller Jackson, at the second house where they had stopped, that I had been to the store last night and took a note or something and gave it to Mr. Win.

"Boy, how come you ain't tol' us you done went to the sto' las' night? 'N' whut was you doin' at the sto' anyhow?" Papa asked.

"It was yistiddy edenin' late," Grandma said before I could open my mouth. "I couldn't find my snuff, 'n' I sent him to git me 'nother box."

"Well, whut was that note you give Mr. Win, boy?" Mama wanted to know.

Again Grandma answered. "It wasn't no note. Las' time this boy brought me Scott's 'n' you know I don' dip nothin' but Garrett's. So I found one o' the old Garrett cans 'n' I tore the label off 'n' give it to River 'n' tol' him to give it to Mr. Win when he ast him fer the snuff. Y'all hear anything 'bout Naomi?" Grandma asked calmly, still on her knees.

"No'am, us ain't got no further'n Miller Jackson's 'n' he tol' us 'bout seein' River in the sto' las' night," Mama replied.

"It was yistiddy edenin' 'bout dus'," Grandma repeated.

Disappointment showed on Mama and Papa's faces as they left again to look for Naomi, but there was a kind of relief, too, especially in Mama's eyes and around her mouth.

Only when Papa and Mama were well down the road did Grandma get up off her knees. "River, I'm so glad you didn't say nothin', boy," she said almost prayerfully and patted me on the head. "You coulda give the whole thing away, 'n' you know how crazy yo' pa is. That fool mighta got his gun 'n' gone lookin' fer Mr. Win."

"Yessum," I said in gratitude for her praise and in admiration and wonderment at the way she had handled Mama and Papa.

"But us got to do somethin' right away, 'cause yo' ma 'n' pa sho' to find out you ain't bought no snuff las' night 'cause Mr. Win ain't done give you nothin' when you give him the note. Soon as they finds out, they gon' be back here astin' mo 'n' mo questions."

"Whut can us do, Grandma?"

"I don' know yet, but the Lawd, He gon' help us."

"Reckon Mr. Win know where Naomi is, Grandma? Reckon he done hid her somewhere?" I asked.

"That's it! That's it! River, you a smart boy. Us got to find Mr. Win 'n' see ef he know where Naomi is."

"Wan' me to go 'n' ast him, Grandma?"

"Yes, you run up the lane as fas' as you can 'n' go to Mr. Win's house. You know where he live, don' you? It's the firs' o' them three pretty white houses jes' 'yond the sto'. Mr. Walter he live in the second one, 'n' Doc Boyd lire in the other'n, the smaller one over next to the levee."

"I know, Grandma. They sho' pretty white houses, ain't they with red chimneys?"

"They sho' is, boy. Now you run to the firs' house, where Mr. Win 'n' Miz Susie lives. 'N' you go 'round to the back do', not the front do', the back do' 'n' you ast fer Mr. Win 'n' you tell him yo' sister done runned off 'n' us can't find her. Then ef he know where her is, he gon' come down the steps 'n' whisper it to you. 'N' don' you tell nobody whut he said 'tel you get back here 'n' tell me."

Grandma repeated the message in puzzlement, looking up in the ceiling, as if it was written there, and slowing down more and more as she went along. Then suddenly she stopped and said, "Naw, naw, I'm gon' go with you." She had decided this was too important a mission to trust to a child.

We put our clothes on hurriedly and walked up the road. Grandma carried her stick to help take some of the pressure off her knees and ease her limp. It was Sunday morning, and the bells of Mt. Olive and Moses Chapel were ringing for Sunday school. Along the way, we passed two or three cows with yokes on grazing in the lane. The yokes kept them from getting through the fence and into the fields where cotton and corn were growing. When we left the plantation a few years later, pastures with hundreds of cattle grazing in them had replaced more than half the cotton, and the people were in the lanes. You couldn't see the yokes, which kept them out of the cotton fields, but they were there.

When we got to Mr. Win's back door, Grandma tapped on the steps with her stick and called to Miz Paralee, the cook, and asked if Mr. Win was up yet, and told her to ask him to come to the door, please. Instead, Mrs. Susie came to the door after we had waited a long time.

"Whut y'all want, Antie?" she asked in a cold voice.

"Mornin', Miz Susie," Grandma said wearily. "I was jes' hopin', Miz Susie ma'am, that Mr. Win might go over to the sto', ma'am, 'n' let me have some black draught, please, ma'am. I'm in misery, ma'am."

"How come you didn't git yo' medicine yesterday? That's whut's wrong with you folks; you never think o' nothin' 'tel the las' minute, 'n' then you come botherin' evvybody. I don' know ef Mr. Win can go to the sto' or not; I'll ask him."

"Thanky, ma'am," Grandma said with a wrinkled smile.

Black draught, I thought to myself. *Us ain't come fer no black draught; us is lookin' fer Naomi. Whut is wrong with Grandma? Maybe this mean ole white woman done scared her.* But I was sure glad Grandma had come herself instead of sending me.

I had heard Mama and Papa say that Mrs. Susie had come from over around Rolling Fork, where her father owned a big plantation and was as mean as a dog to niggers. Folks said Mrs. Susie was just like him, not like Mrs. Rhoda at all. They said that although Mrs. Rhoda was from Georgia, she was real white folks.

Finally, Mr. Win came to the door. "Whut you want, Ant Carrie, on a pretty, bright Sunday mornin' like this?"

"Thanky, suh, Mr. Win. I jes' want some black draught, please, suh," Grandma replied.

"Oh, all right, this time I'm gon' git it fer you, but in the future, please try to think o' yo' medicine befo' Sunday, hear?"

"Yessuh, Mr. Win, I sho' will, I sho' will."

When we got to the store, Grandma told me to wait on the steps while she and Mr. Win went inside to get the black draught. *Black draught,* I thought to myself again as I stood on the steps. *Us ain't come fer no black draught; us lookin' fer Naomi. Grandma musta fergot.* I decided to remind her and ran up to the door and opened it and started in, hollering, "Grandma, you ain't!"

She cut me off right there. "Didn't I tell you to stay on the steps while Mr. Win git the medicine fer me? Now you do like I say, River."

They both looked at me while I backed out of the store.

After a while, Grandma and Mr. Win came out of the store. She was carrying her black draught and looking very grave. Mr. Win was looking solemn, too, but his face soon broke into a smile. Then he walked up, put both his hands on my shoulders, stooped down, and looked at me intently as if he had never seen a boy before. But he was smiling all the time.

"This is a fine boy, Ant Carrie," he said and stood up with one hand still on my shoulder.

With his other hand, he shaded his eyes as he scanned the plantation. Then he pressed on my shoulder lightly and walked off. When he was at the gate leading through the fence to his house, which sat back quite a distance from the road, he turned and hollered to Grandma, "Now you make that clear to Silas 'n' Becky, Ant Carrie!"

"Yessuh, Mr. Win, I sho' will, suh," she replied.

When Grandma and I started back down the road to our house, I asked her, "How come you ast fer black draught, Grandma, 'stid o' ast 'n' where Naomi at?"

"Course, you jes' a chile 'n' you don' understan', 'specially white folks. But in this world, River, you can't always go straight to whut you wants; sometimes you have to zigzag."

I did not fully understand what she meant for many years, but I did suddenly realize how quickly she had thought of black draught when Mrs. Susie came to the door, like she had thought of snuff when Papa and Mama began questioning me about taking a note to the store to Mr. Win. Looking at her as she limped along on her stick, I wondered if she always anticipated questions and carried the answers with her. *Maybe all black people do when they are grown up,* I thought. *Maybe that's how they get by.*

"Did Mr. Win tell you where Naomi is, Grandma?"

"Yes, Mr. Win done sent her to Vicksburg 'tel Silas cool off, or 'tel her have her baby. He done got Willie Woods to take her."

"Her in Vicksburg, her in Vicksburg," I said. "Then Papa can't find her 'n' whup her, can he, Grandma?"

"Naw, he sho' can't, boy."

"Whut is you gon' tell him?"

"Well, fer one thing, Mr. Win want me to tell him he ain't took advantage o' Naomi. He say he was in his car in front o' the preacher's house waitin' fer Lilly Mae when Naomi jumped in his car. He say it was dark 'n' he was kinda drunk 'n' didn't know the difference."

"That's whut Willie Fisher say his sister tol' him, 'n' that's whut Naomi say, too."

"When Naomi tell you that?"

"A long time ago, befo' us planted us cotton."

"Boy, is you been knowin' this all that time?"

"Yessum."

"'N' ain't breathed a word about it?"

"No'am."

"Boy, you is a old man; I b'lieve you jes' pretendin' to be a chile, but you is a old man. Been keepin' this to yo'self all that time. Whut else do you know?"

"Nothin'."

"You sho', boy?"

"Yessum, I'm sho'."

"Well, you keep on keepin' it to yo'self, 'cause I don' when I'm gon tell know yo ma and yo' crazy pa."

IX

Owner Sends Pregnant Daughter to Vicksberg as Rumors Spread

It was late in the afternoon when Mama and Papa returned. They had been all over the plantation looking for Naomi and had come back empty-handed. It hurt their pride to admit to all the families they visited that their daughter had run off. But their desire to have her back outweighed all other considerations.

"I done cooked y'all a good supper, 'cause I know y'all hongry. Find out anything 'bout where that fool gal might be?" Grandma asked as she put the food on the kitchen table.

"No'am, not a thing," Mama replied, "'n' me 'n' Silas done been all over the place. Us stopped at evvy house, 'cep'n right next do' at the preacher's. 'N' us know her couldn't stay in that filthy house."

"You know, I keep thinkin' 'bout Willie Woods 'n' how funny he acted," Papa said, reaching for the fried chicken and gravy after saying the blessing.

"He sho' did; made like at firs' that he did even know Naomi," Mama added. "'N' he jes' took us to Vicksburg las' fall, 'n' 'member how he carr'ed on so 'bout Naomi's gold tooth?"

"Well, maybe he jes' fergot her with so much on his min', carr'in' the mail 'n' all," Grandma said, busying herself with the table with butterbeans, rice, okra, buttermilk, and more hot biscuits. She outdid herself trying to make Mama and Papa forget Naomi for a while, since she knew where she was. But the meal proved no substitute for the whereabouts of my sister.

Papa and Mama sat quietly as they ate. Then Papa recalled again their stop at Mr. Willie's. "He sho' did laff a heap. Course, he always laff a lot, but not this much," Papa said. "'N' I don' trus' nobody whut laff so much. Whut he got to be laffin' 'bout?"

"Folks say he make his way by laffin', 'specially when he 'round white folks," Mama explained. "They say that's how he got his job carr'in' the mail, showin' his snaggle teeth to Mr. Win 'n' them's daddy."

"Well, Becky, I don' min' him laffin' 'round white folks, ef he can fool 'em that way 'n' use 'em," Papa said. "But I don' want him laffin' 'round me when I'm astin' him where my gal at."

"Silas, you might not min' him laffin' 'round white folks, easin' they conscience 'n' makin' 'em feel us is happy, but I do, I sho' do," Mama complained.

"I guess you right, Becky, 'bout him laffin' 'round white folks," Papa admitted. "I hadn't thought 'bout it that way. 'N' you know, Miz Woods, who ain' never laffed befo', her laffed a heap today, too."

"Her sho' did," Mama agreed, "but her didn't laff when us firs' got there. Her jes' stood on the porch while Willie laffed his fool head off."

"Maybe her jes' natch'ly got excited when y'all tol' 'em Naomi done run off," Grandma said calmly. "Now eat yo' supper 'n' stop worryin' fer a while; that gal gon' turn up sooner or later right here in the plantation."

"I hope so, Ma, but Silas ain't had no bizness talkin' 'bout whuppin' that chile," Mama said accusingly. "Whut good whuppin' gon' do now?"

"Well, I don' know, Becky; maybe I was too hasty; maybe I shoulda give her mo' time, but how come her got to be so stubbo'n 'bout tellin' us who the papa is?" my father asked, pushing his chair back from the table and getting up. I knew it was to avoid another losing argument, as well as his temper, because he usually remained at the supper table a while, smoking his pipe or putting a fresh chew of tobacco in his mouth and just talking with Mama and us.

Of course, he often took his breakfast on the fly, finishing his bacon and bread and grits and coffee standing up. And he never tarried at noontime, unless it was raining or we had laid-by. Usually as soon as he had finished his meal, he was out in the lot hitching up the mule again. And if he wasn't plowing, he was hunting weeds with a hoe, or looking in cotton squares for boll weevils, or turning watermelons or cantaloupes so they will ripen faster, or sharpening our hoes, or taking a plow point to the blacksmith shop, or greasing the axles and tongue of our wagon, or going to the store for more poison, or hauling wood for winter. Like Mama, he was always busy, except at night.

Papa walked out on the porch and stood leaning against a post for a while. Then he drifted out of the yard and down to the gate at the lane and just stood there, looking up and down the road as if he expected Naomi to come walking up any minute. I wanted to join him, but two things held me back: I knew he wanted to be alone, and also I was afraid if I went to him, he might pick me up and pat my back, and I would hug his neck and find myself overcome with sorrow for him, telling him that Mr. Win had sent Naomi to Vicksburg and that the white man was the father of her baby. So I went around to the back of the house and sat on the steps playing mumble-typed with the old knife Papa had given me after he bought a new one in Vicksburg.

A week went by, and Papa and Mama had no word from Naomi. I wanted to tell them and ease their sorrow, but I was afraid of what Grandma said Papa might do. Grandma believed in time and in waiting when she had no sure answer to a problem. "Problems can work they ownselves out better," she would say, "ef you give 'em time 'n' don'try to force 'em." So she didn't breathe a word about my sister being in Vicksburg, and neither did I, but I had a hard time pretending to be worried about Naomi.

Papa and Mama went through the motions of living, moving like mummies in a fairytale. You could tell them anything, but they didn't hear you, and you could ask them something, but there was seldom any reply. In the field sometimes in the half where chemicals had not been out down to kill the weeds and grass, Papa would attack the harmful plants with his hoe as if they were snakes, while Mama would be chopping them as gently as if they were roses she regretted to destroy. And on other days it would Papa, who calmly dug at the roots of Johnson grass while Mama struck the weeds with hard blows.

And sometimes Mama would stand in the field a long time leaning on her hoe handle and looking into the empty distance with tears in her eyes. And Papa would come over and put his arms around her and say, "Don' cry, honey; us gon' find Naomi." And Grandma would raise a song. Usually it was "His Eye Is on the Sparrow." She would sing it loud and strong in her cracking old voice. Sometimes Mama dried her eyes on the corner of her apron and joined in; sometimes she remained silent but resumed her chopping.

Papa was strong and silent. When sorrow struck him, he would bank his hoe under a pile of dirt and walk off across the field with one of the gallouses of his overalls down as if he were going to the toilet behind a big bush. There he would sit as I found him one day gathering up handful after handful of the black soil and letting it pour through his fingers like an hourglass back to the ground. At such times, his eyes were moist and his mouth stood open and twisted in helplessness.

Then one day, he stood for a long time with his hoe held in mid-air as if he had forgotten how to bring it down against a weed. Suddenly he dropped his hoe with no thought of banking it upright so that he would know exactly where it was when he returned. Instead, with a wild look in his eyes, he ran off across the field with both of his gallouses up.

Mama hollered, "Silas, where you goin'?"

He didn't reply but ran on headlong.

I took out after him, calling, "Papa, Papa, Papa!" but he neither looked back nor answered.

At the turnrow where our farm ended and Mr. Ben Moses's began, he kept right on running. By some instinct, his feet seemed to know the cotton from the weeds. And although he was running wildly, he was not trampling any cotton. I am not sure about my own feet because I was not watching where I was stepping. My eyes were on Papa and I kept them there, although he continued to gain on me.

Papa ran on toward Mr. Willie's as unerringly as fish-bait earthworms seek damp ground or wriggle their blind way to the underside of a fresh-turned clod. He slowed down only along the muddy rim of Mr. Miller Jackson's cornfield, where a few stalks of sickly yellow corn stood slender and stunted from too much water.

As Papa sank his feet into the mud and pulled them up again and again like a dasher in a churn, he looked back for the first time and saw me following him. He paused and yelled, "Go back, boy!"

But I kept on coming.

"Don' you hear me, boy? I say go back, do you hear me?"

"Yessuh, Papa," I said weakly and stood in my tracks as he turned and kept on going.

In a few moments, he was beyond the muddy edge of the field and on solid ground again between the rows of corn that got taller and taller. I looked back toward where I had left Mama and Grandma chopping, but I could not see them; too much cotton and corn stood in between. I felt a sense of panic; I wasn't sure about how to get back to our farm, and I was afraid to go ahead against Papa's orders. But I knew he was more bluff than bite when it came to me and Mama. There was something about our bright skin and soft straight hair that diffused his anger and weakened his resolve. I think it was because these things gave him so much pleasure and so much pride as well as reduced somehow the black in his own blackness that he didn't ever want to lose them.

I knew that if I could reach Papa and put my arms around one of his legs and hug it, he would soon be running his knobby fingers through my hair, and finally he might pick me up and hold me in his arms as a sign of ownership. So I decided to keep on following him. I ran through Mr. Miller's taller corn, not the sickly rows that stood in the mud. Beyond the cornfield, I saw Papa running through Mr. Gus Hawkins' place, looking back occasionally to see if I was following him. He did not even wave or reply to Mr. Gus when he yelled, "Where you goin', Silas?" and he and his family waved at him.

I ran along the edge of the cornfield where Papa would have difficulty seeing me, until he was well over in Mr. Willie's field. The cotton there was taller because the seepage water from the river receded earlier from his farm and all the others nearby, permitting them to plant sooner than the folks who lived nearer the levee. I was not much taller than the cotton, so it was not easy for Papa to see me following him.

He had barely reach Mr. Willie and his family chopping in the field and was just beginning to ask Mr. Willie if he knew anything at all about where Naomi might be, when I caught up with him and attempted to put my arms around one of his legs. He jumped in surprise and grabbed at my arms. "Boy, whut you doin' here? Ain't I tol' you to go back?" he asked angrily.

"Yessuh, Papa," I replied, still holding his leg firmly.

"Go 'way, boy; do you hear me?"

"Yessuh, Papa," I said, beginning to cry. "Please, please, Papa, don' make me go back." I could feel some of the tenseness going out of his leg, and his voice was quieter and calmer when he spoke again.

Disregarding me, and yet not quite, because my presence was changing him all the time, Papa said to Mr. Willie, "I come to talk with you again 'bout my daughter, Naomi, Willie."

Like Papa and Mama had said, Mr. Willie did laugh or grin a lot. I didn't remember him grinning this much when he took us to Vicksburg. As he talked with Papa, there was always a fixed smile on his face as if it were painted there. And he never completely closed his mouth; it always hung open like a gate you forgot to shut.

"Let's walk down to the end of the row, where us can talk to usselves," Mr. Willie suggested.

They walked to the turnrow with me following them.

"Now, Willie," Papa said calmly, "somehow I don' b'lieve you tol' me and Becky the truth when us ast'd you 'bout Naomi."

"Silas, how come?" Mr. Willie asked, then paused, turned to me with a motion of his head, and asked Papa, "Ain't you gon' send yo' little boy back up in the field to walk 'long 'n' talk with my chillun while us talk?"

Papa turned and looked at me. I was about ten or fifteen feet away. "Oh, he jes' a little boy; he too little to understan whut us talkin' 'bout."

Returning to his question, Mr. Willie asked again, "Silas, how come you don' b'lieve I tol' you 'n' Becky the truth las' Sunday?"

"I don' 'zackly know, Willie, but I jes' got a feelin'—you know, jes' a feelin'."

"I see," Mr. Willie said and swung the back of his heel purposelessly into a growth of crabgrass and then pressed it back to the ground as if he were sorry he had disturbed it.

When Mr. Willie said no more, Papa added, "Willie, you know, I got a feelin' Naomi ain't on this plantation. I got a feelin' maybe her in Vicksburg or somewhere. 'N' since you 'bout the only one whut gits off the place reg'ly, I b'lieve you had somethin' to do with her gittin' 'way from here."

"How come her done run off?" Mr. Willie asked.

I think Papa felt trapped. Nobody had asked him that question before, and he hadn't thought out a good answer. And to him, I think, this wasn't really the question. He only wanted to know if Willie had helped his gal get away. Instead of answering, Willie was getting in his business.

"Well," Papa started off and paused a long time, "her, you see," then he stopped again. He had been looking down at the ground as if he were studying the tissue of the soil or the mud on his toes, which were pertruding from his wornout shoes. Then he looked straight at Mr. Willie and said, "Gawddamit, Willie, it ain't none o' yo' Gawddamn bizness how come her run off. I'm astin' you fer the las' time, Willie, did you help her git away, Gawddamit?"

Mr. Willie smiled and said, "Now, Silas, don' lose yo' head, don' lose yo' head." The smile never left his face.

"I ain't gon' lose my head, 'n' don't you worry 'bout that, but you gon' lose yo' ass ef you done helped my gal run off 'n' you don' tell me where you done took her. 'Cause ef I finds out 'n' you ain't done tol' me, yo' ass ain't gon' be wurth nothin'."

"Now, now, Silas, don' be like that."

"You Gawddamn yaller sonofabitch, is you gon' answer me or do I have to whup yo' Gawddamn ass right here in this field?" Papa said, advancing toward Mr. Willie with his fist doubled up.

Fearing Papa might kill Mr. Willie and get himself in a heap of trouble, I yelled out, "Mr. Win done got him to do it, Papa!"

Both turned toward me.

"Whut you talkin' 'bout, boy?" Papa asked, starting back to where I was.

"That chile don' know whut he talkin' 'bout, Silas," Mr. Willie said excitedly.

But Papa seemed not to have heard him. He continued walking toward me, not in a rush, but in a slow, studied movement, as if to give himself time to let what I had said soak in, or to give doubt a chance to race in from the back of his mind.

I wanted to run, but I froze in my tracks. Now that the words were out of my mouth, they seemed to take on a new and terrifying meaning. I realized they had saved Mr. Willie, but I was afraid they lost me my papa. As I stood there, I could hear Grandma as plain as day, saying, "No tellin' whut yo' ole crazy pa will do, ef he find out."

Papa was right upon me now, looking taller than ever as he stared down at me. "Whut that you say, boy?"

"Nothin', Papa, nothin'."

"Don't you lie to me, boy." He now had me by my shoulders, shaking me.

"Silas, that boy don' know whut he talkin' 'bout," Mr. Willie pleaded.

But Papa's ears were deaf to every voice but mine. "Boy, do you hear me?" he stormed.

"Yessuh, Papa, yessuh, Papa," I replied, trying hard not to repeat what I had said, yet I was so afraid after the shaking he had given me that I stood there, trembling.

"Boy, whut that you said 'bout Mr. Win?" Papa roared, grabbing my shoulders again and shaking me. "I say whut that you said 'bout Mr. Win?"

In tears, I slowly answered him. "Papa, Mr. Win he done tol' Grandma he done got Mr. Willie to take Naomi to Vicksburg." I purposely involved Grandma, hoping that she would be able to handle him the way she handled him about that note and the way she thought up black draught when Mrs. Susie came to the door.

But the way Papa turned on Mr. Willie after he had shaken the truth out of me made me afraid that not even Grandma would be able to talk any sense into him. "Gawddamit it, Willie, how come you ain't done tol' me?" he screamed. There were outrage and violence in his voice, but there was sadness, too, like the unconscious, sad overtones in the voice of almost every black man when he is singing—overtones that tell a tragic story of fear and shame and anger and dependence and lost dignity, lost respect, and lost love.

"I can 'splain, Silas; I can 'splain," Mr. Willie said hurridly as Papa approached him.

"Well, 'splain then, Gawddamit."

"Naomi was scared you was gon' beat her 'n' kill her baby," Mr. Willie said as fast as the words would come out of his mouth. "'N' her begged me to git her 'way from here." He was careful not to mention Mr. Win, and for just a flicker of a moment, the smile left his face.

But Papa hadn't forgotten that I had mentioned Mr. Win. A new tenseness came into his voice when he asked Mr. Willie, "Whut Mr. Win got to do with this?"

"Nothin', nothin', Silas," Mr. Willie said quickly. "He was jes' tryin' to help Naomi."

"Don' lie to me, Willie. White folks don' help no niggers, less'n they helpin' theyselves, too," Papa roared, shaking his finger in Mr. Willie's face. Then Papa's own face hardened, and his blackness seemed to turn blue black, his eyes bulged, and perspiration stood out on his forehead. "Willie, Gawddamit, whut is Mr. Win got to do with this? How come he helpin'?"

"B'lieve me, Silas, please b'lieve me, jes' 'cause he a good man," Mr. Willie said in a trembling, uncertain voice.

"Gawddamn yo' soul, Willie, is Mr. Win the one whut done spoilt my gal?"

But Papa didn't wait for a reply. In putting the question, he must have found the answer because he turned from Mr. Willie and took off again, running across the field just the way he had come, except that he seemed to be running faster and his feet took no care of the cotton. I was too scared to follow him. I watched as did Mr. Willie and his family until Papa disappeared behind Mr. Miller's tall corn.

Then I was swept up by Mr. Willie, who rushed for his car. "Us got to overtake yo' pa 'n' 'splain somethin' befo' he git to Mr. Win's," he said, opening the door of his car and pushing me in ahead of him.

It was the first time I had been in a car since he drove us to Vicksburg that previous fall. Even though the car was old, the seat felt soft, so much softer than the planks we used for seats in our wagon. My feet barely touched the floor, and I was too low to see out of the windshield, so I stood up with my chin resting on top of the dashboard, but Mr. Willie told me to sit down because I might fall. I sat back down, but I couldn't see where we were going, except out of the side window through which I could see we were taking a shortcut across the deadening and up through the far side of Mr. Jackson's farm over to the lane that ran in front of our house.

As we came up the lane toward our gate, Mr. Willie said, "Us gon' beat him; he still on Ben's place."

Within a few minutes, we were at our gate and I jumped out and opened it. Mr. Willie drove through and kept on going. I closed the gate and followed the car. Mama and Grandma were in our wagon driving out of the lot. After standing in the field a while watching us disappear nearly an hour ago, they had dropped their hoes, come to the house, and hitched ole Salt and Miss Lady to our wagon and come look for us.

"I'm sho' glad I got here befo' you left!" Mr. Willie yelled, jumping out of his car and running over to the wagon. "Silas been to my place 'n' he headed back here. He know Mr. Win done spoilt Naomi. But he don'." He got no further.

"Oh, naw, Willie, naw!" Mama screamed on hearing the news and began flailing her arms.

Grandma grabbed her and tried to comfort her. "Now, now, Becky, it ain't like you think, it ain't like you think."

"No'am, it sho' ain't, Miz Carrie; that's whut I was 'bout to tell Becky," Mr. Willie said, leaving his mouth hanging open without the smile.

"Naw, naw, Willie, don' tell me it was Mr. Win," Mama said and screamed a long wailing sound of fear and hopelessness.

"Now, Becky, baby," Grandma said, "you got to be calm at a time like this 'n' git a full understandin' o' whut done happen."

By now Mama had fallen onto the bed of the wagon and was wallowing and screaming. Both Grandma and Mr. Willie tried to calm her without any success. Papa, still running, was now nearing the house. As he came up to the wagon, Mr. Willie stepped back. "Whut done happen to Becky?" he asked in a wild sort of way.

"Nothin', her jes' excited," Grandma replied as calmly as she could.

"You done tol' her 'bout Mr. Win, ain't you?" he asked, turning to Mr. Willie.

"Silas, wait a minute, you don' understan'," Mr. Willie replied, moving back another step.

"I understan', Gawddamit, that white sonofaitch do spoilt my gal. 'N' you keep sayin' you don' understan'. Whut else is there to understan', Gawddamit?"

"Now, Silas, you listen to me," Grandma ordered, "it ain't like you 'n' Becky think."

"Ole woman, don't you come orderin' me 'round; I know you done laid 'round with white mens in yo' day, Gawddam yo' soul to hell, but Naomi ain't gon' do it, Gawddamit." All of Papa's pent-up hatred of Grandma over the long years came pouring out of his mouth like vomit.

"You crazy black sonofabitch, you!" Grandma came back with equal hatred. "Ef I hadn't had a white man, 'n' Gawd be my judge, I ain't had but one, how would Becky got her bright skin 'n' long straight hair you love so much, you black bastard, you?"

Again, like when Mr. Willie had asked him how come Naomi had run off, Papa had no real answer. Now Grandma had tied Mama's color and good hair to her laying around with a white man. Papa hadn't thought this through; he hadn't seen the connection before. But something inside him wouldn't let him back down; his hatred of Grandma and the shame she caused him was too deep for that.

Unable to mount a second attack against the main issue, he brought in a side issue with all the venom he could he had.

"Gawddamit, ole woman, don't you call me no black bastard," he stormed. "My pa 'n' ma was marr'ed when I was born. They ain't had no bastards like you."

"You can call Becky a bastard ef you want to, you black sonofabitch, but you would eat a bale o' her shit jes' to lay yo' black ass in the bed side o' her."

Before Papa could answer, if he had an answer, Mama opened her eyes and said, "Ma, you 'n' Silas stop all this bad talk. Then she got to her knees and crawled out of the back of the wagon. I think Papa was too ashamed or too afraid to help her. Instead, he ran into the house and reappeared with his new shotgun.

I ran to him, screaming, "Don't you shoot my Grandma, Papa!"

"I ain't stud'n that ole black bitch; I'm gon' settle things with Mr. Win. He ain't gon' lay 'round with Naomi 'n' git 'way with it, Gawdammit," he said, jumping off the porch and running across the field toward the store, where he thought Mr. Win would be.

"Naw, naw, Silas!" Mama screamed and took out after him.

I was right behind her.

She caught up with him and grabbed his free arm. "Please, Silas, please don' do nothin rash; stop 'n' think 'bout whut you is doin'," she pleaded.

Papa kept on going with Mama hanging on his arm, but I think he slowed a little. I don't know whether it was the burden of Mama's weight on his arm or a weakening of his resolve.

I had caught up with them. Mama continued her plea.

"Wait, Silas, please wait, don' do nothin' you gon' regret. Silas, wait 'tel you seen Naomi 'n' heard whut got to say 'bout this."

"Naw, I ain't gon' wait; I done waited too long already. Look at the preacher, he done waited while Mr. Win done had his gal in the cornfields 'n' evvywhere else on the plantation. 'N' his waitin' ain't got him nothin' but mo' shame."

I think Papa's will was bolstered by many pressures. He, too, was living in shame because Naomi was going to have a baby. Mr. Willie had revealed this by asking him how come his gal done run off; there were Mama and Grandma, with whom I think he thought things could never quite be the same again, and then there was Mr. Win, who he thought had caused all this—a white man who could do as he pleased with the folks on his place, while they had no rights at all. I think Papa thought he had come to the end of his row and there were no choices open to him but to stand up and be the man he had pretended to be.

Back down the lane, Mr. Willie and Grandma were coming in the car; along the way folks were standing in their fields, looking and wondering what the trouble was, but nobody said anything or tried to unterfer. Papa rushed on with Mama dragging back on his arm and me trotting at his side. We were still some distance from the store when Papa stopped to get through the barbed-wire fence and into the lane, where he could make better time.

As he pushed his gun under the fence and tried to shake Mama off so that he could grab a strand of the wire with both hands and step through the wire sideways, I yelled as loudly as I could, "Papa, don' hurt Mr. Win, it wasn't his fault; he didn't know it was Naomi in the dark!"

Mama let Papa go and turned to me, and Papa caught the wire and pressed it down and put one leg through the fence before he seemed to have heard what I had said. "Whut you say, boy?" he asked, half bent to keep the wire above him from tearing into his back.

"Yes," Mama added, "whut is this you say 'bout Mr. Win not knowing Naomi in the dark? Whut is you talkin' 'bout, boy?"

I explained to them what Willie Fisher and Naomi had told me. And Mr. Willie and Grandma, who had got out of the car and come over to the fence, told them what Mr. Win had said.

Papa, who had pulled his leg back through the fence and picked up his gun, was standing there looking wide-eyed first at me and Mama, then at Mr. Willie and Grandma, and then toward the store, seemed somewhat convinced by what we had said, until Grandma spoke up again. "'N' here you go running like a fool across the fields toward the sto' with yo' gun 'fo' anybody can tell you anything. "Runnin' 'n' you don' know whut you runin' fer."

"Old woman, don't you call me no foll; I knows whut I'm runnin' fer 'n' I know a lie when I hear one, 'specially when it come outa yo' ole black mouth."

"But us ain't lyin', Silas; why would us lie to you?" Mr. Willie asked, looking Papa in the eye.

"You lied to me 'n' Becky Sunday, didn't you, when you acted like you near 'bout didn't eben know Naomi, let 'lone where her was?"

"Well, that's different, Silas; I was tryin' to stall 'tel you cooled off 'n' got a real understandin' o' whut done happen," Mr. Willie explained.

"'N' 'nother thing, you keep sayin' I don' understan'; well, I sho' don' understan' how come Naomi gon' wait in the dark 'n' then jump in Mr. Win's car with him like he the onliest man in the worl'."

"Silas, don't you see," Mama said, "it wasn't jes' a man Naomi was after, it was a white man or someone very bright like Roscoe Jackson her was runnin' after."

"How come her want a white man or someone bright so bad?" Papa asked.

"'Cause her not only the spittin' image o' you, but her jes' like you," Grandma spoke up for the first time since she had called Papa a fool. "How come you'da died ef you hadn't got you black hands on Becky?"

Papa just stood staring off into space with his hands resting on the muzzle of his gun as Mama tried to explain further.

"'N', Silas, you know how bad Naomi want to be bright, so you know her would want bright chillun with good hair."

"But how come her gotta pick Mr. Win?"

"'Cause it was easy," Grandma said. "Like evvybody else on the plantation, her knowed Mr. Win was goin' with the preacher's gal next do', 'n' her knowed Mr. Win he drink. So her figgered out a way to take Lilly Mae's place one night, so her could have a bright baby."

Papa didn't say a word. He shifted his gun to his right hand, where he held it balanced with the barrel tilted toward the ground.

"Come on, y'all, 'n' git in my car 'n' let me take you back home," Mr. Willie said.

We all got through the fence and into his car, and he drove us home.

X

Silas's Family Visiting Pregnant Daughter in Vicksberg

Early the next morning, Mr. Willie was back. He picked up Mama and Grandma and took them to Vicksburg with him when he went to carry the mail. He said he was going to take them by where Naomi was staying and leave them until he came back from the post office with the Bend's mail. Papa had agreed not to go this time for fear of frightening my sister. So he and I went as far as the gate and opened it for Mr. Willie's car. We waved as the car moved down the lane, then we closed the gate and went back to the house to get our hoes and go to the field. We had to walk over part of the land where the weed killers had been spread before we got to the other part where it had not.

For sure the weed killers were working. Few if any weeds or grass were to be seen.

"It's jes as clean as my hand," Papa said as we walked along looking for weeds.

"Ef they put this stuff over the whole plantation, there ain't gon' be no choppin' much to do, is it, Papa?" I asked.

"Sho' ain't, boy, sho' ain't," he replied as we turned off from the grassless cotton and headed to where we had been chopping the day before when he dropped his hoe and ran to Mr. Willie's. Of course, Papa had picked up all the hoes later and had brought them home and shoved them under the house out of the dew.

Dead weeds and grass in the middle of the rows told us where we had chopped. After placing the bucket of water he was carrying under a bush to keep it out of the sun, Papa took the two rows he had had, and I took one of Mama's with my short-handled hoe to be next to him. The sun came up hot; there wasn't a cloud in the sky, but we chopped harder than ever, trying to finish as much as we could by the time Mama and Grandma returned from visiting Naomi. They had agreed not to ask her to come back home right now, unless she wanted to. She was to stay on in Vicksburg and have her baby there because, they said, "it wouldn't give the niggers on the place so much to talk 'bout."

And they were going to take the money they were saving to buy a farm and use it to pay her expenses as far as it would go, and pay the rest in the fall when our cotton was ginned. Mr. Willie had said the welfare might help. He said Mr. Win had sent a letter to them by him when he took Naomi to town, and he had given him twenty dollars to pay her board and room for a week or two. After that the welfare was supposed to help.

"Mr. Win done give you twenty dollars fer Naomi?" Mama had asked when Mr. Willie first told us the night before.

"Yes 'n' I got her a place fer three dollars a week, 'n' her can do her own cookin'. So I give the lady six dollars fer two weeks 'n' give Naomi the rest—fo'teen dollars.

"Bless yo' heart, Willie," Mama had said.

"Thank the Lawd," Grandma had added.

When Papa had heard what Mr. Willie said, he had gone into the house and returned with four crumpled five-dollar bills. "You give this to Mr. Win, Willie, 'n' you tell him ef us owe any mo' fer Naomi, fer him to let us know 'n' us'll pay him when us gin."

"Silas, I don' think Mr. Win want his money back," Mr. Willie had said.

But Papa had insisted that he take it. "Either Mr. Win guilty or he innocent," he had said. "Ef I was sho' he spoilt my gal intenshonally, I'd kill him, Gawd knows I'd kill him. But ef it like you say, 'n' he didn't know in the dark, then he sho' ain't guilty, 'n' he don' owe Naomi nothin'. 'N' long as I'm 'sponsible fer her, I'm gon' pay her honest debts."

By noon, Papa and I were down to about a dozen rows, and they were in a corner of our field, where they were getting shorter and shorter. I liked short rows; they made it appear that you were working faster and accomplishing more. With the help of Mama and Grandma when they got back, we would finish that afternoon and layby. This would give me two weeks to fish with Mama and Grandma and go to the association meetings before the split session of school started for six weeks of learning before cotton-picking time.

Papa was an artist with a hoe. He could bring the weapon down to with half an inch of a tender cotton plant and end the life of a dewberry sprout, a dandelion shoot, or a sprig of Johnson grass without touching the cotton stem or disturbing its roots. He hated Bermuda grass and cockleburs, which grew so close to cotton. And he used the corner of his hoe like a spear to root out these enemies. I don't think he ever got over the Williamsons actually planting Bermuda grass, Korean lespedeza, and fescue the next year for their expanding herd of white-faced cattle.

Mama and Grandma returned from Vicksburg in the early afternoon. Mr. Willie didn't stop to talk. They said he told them he had to hurry home and help with the chopping because they were still behind from Mrs Birdie being sick two weeks ago. In the field that afternoon, we chopped leisurely, knowing we could finish by night. Mama and Grandma reported on their trip. Naomi was fine. She was living with a widow lady, Mrs. Addie Jones, at 304 Second North Street up one of them hills in that hilly town. The welfare had already sent her to a doctor, who said her baby was due in the middle of October, about three months from then.

"'N' the lady her live with is wonderful, Silas," Mama said. "Her cook fer some white folks 'n' they 'low her to bring heapin' pans o' food home. Naomi eat most all it, 'n' her lookin' jes' fine, 'n' her seem happy."

"That's good," Papa said. "I'm so glad her doin' all right. I'm goin' with y'all next time."

"Her ast 'bout you 'n' her said her want to see you."

"Her do?" Papa asked, smiling. To know that Naomi still loved him made him gentler as he chopped.

"'N' Silas," Grandma said with some sweetness and some "I told you so" in her voice, "Naomi done backed up whut Mr. Win say 'bout her jumpin' in his car in the dark."

"Miz Carrie," Papa replied with indifference, "I jes' 'bout done fergot 'bout that. All I wants to know is that Naomi is all right."

"I'm sho' glad, Silas," Mama said softly as if Papa's words were the answer to long hours of prayer. "'Cause her a good girl."

"Yes, her a good girl; I knows that now down in here," Papa said, patting the space over his heart. "Don' nobody have to tell me now, I knows fer myself."

I think he meant he had come to this conclusion after long meditation over what all of us had tried to tel him. He must have lay awake last night thinking about it, and this morning, when he went to the privy first thing, and all during the day as we chopped up and down the cotton field.

"'N' after the baby done come, Silas, the lady in Vicksburg gon' git Naomi a job with the lady next do' to where her is cookin' at," Mama explained. "Her say her can git somebody to keep Naomi's baby fer her while her work."

"Us could keep her here at us house," Papa said with a big grin on his face.

"Maybe after 'while," Mama agreed, "but us better let this thing blow over firs'."

"Yes," Grandma added, "'cause there ain't no tellin' how Mr. Win's wife, that ole Miz Susie, would take it ef her found out."

"'N' some o' these niggers on the place would be sho' to tell her," Mama said.

"I guess y'all right, but us can go to see her once in a while, maybe evvy month or two," Papa suggested, looking up toward the sun and measuring the time against the amount of chopping still to be done.

"Yes, Silas, us can do that," Mama replied.

The talk then drifted to the fishing we were going to do during layby time, about getting my clothes ready for school—patching my pants, making me some shirts, and making me a new asafetida bag to keep around my neck to ward off the diseases some of the other children might have. And they talked about the revival and the church associations and the basket meetings and the picnics.

Papa wondered about the crop, how much cotton we were going to make, and how we were going to come out at settlement time. And he counted up the debts, mostly the cost of the tractor work, the fertilizer, the poison, and the weed-killer stuff. "Us ain't took up much rations at the sto', 'cause us growed most o' them—us salt meat 'n' vegetables 'n' us chickens plus the fish us done catched 'n' the dewberry us done picked," Papa said, shaking his head in self-satisfaction.

I am sure he thought of the money we were going to owe the lady for keeping Naomi, but he did not mention it. I think he thought it was too delicate a matter. Mama or Grandma might take it to mean that he thought it was a burden or something we ought not have to pay.

"This cotton look good," Mama said as we neared the end of the last three rows. "It look better 'n' better evvy time us chop; us gon' come out all right."

"Us sho' is," Grandma agreed, "'cause I jes' got a feelin' the Lawd is with us."

Papa didn't say anything, but there was a broad smile on his face.

When school started, I soon found out that just about everybody knew Naomi was in Vicksburg and was going to have a baby for Mr. Win. I wasn't surprised that Willie knew because he lived next door and he and Lilly Mae were in and out of our house all the time, getting milk regularly and a little sugar or meal or lard when they ran short, and they were always short. But General Lee and Silvester also knew, as did almost everybody else at school, except Mrs. Taylor. If she knew, she didn't let on.

But among the children, and I am sure, among their parents, too, there was more envy than malice. Having a baby for one of the plantation owners carried a certain amount of status on the place, except with Mama and Papa and few others, like Mrs. Nettie Woodson. The family was bound to benefit a little: Maybe get a larger cotton allotment, less add-on interest and other charges on the bill at the store to be taken out at settlement time, and somewhat easier credit.

The easier credit Lilly Mae used to get at the store, however, was gradually being shut off, Willie said. And they thought it was because of Naomi, while it probably was because Mr. Win had found another girl on the plantation or in Vicksburg and had lost interest in Lilly Mae. "Done started astin' her to take a bath sometime 'n' brush her teeth," Willie told me. "so her'll smell clean like yo' sister smelt that time he had her las' winter."

"Is Lilly Mae gon' bathe evvy week like Naomi 'n' brush her teeth with charcoal 'n' bakin' soda?" I asked as we walked home from school.

"Naw, her say whut he want her to brush her teeth fer, since he don' never kiss her in the mouth. Her say all Mr. Win wanna do is kiss her on the neck 'n' git her to put her tongue in his ears."

"Put her tongue in his ears? That would sho' tickle me," I said.

"Lilly Mae say it don' tickle him; her say it make him hot. 'N' her say when he hot 'n' drunk, he don' think nothin' 'bout her bathin' and brushin' her teeth like yo' ole black black sister do."

"My sister ain't black," I protested.

"Her is, too. Black 'n' shiny as Miz Susie's new car."

"Her ain't," I insisted. It was one thing for me to call Naomi black, but it was something else for Willie or other people to do so.

"Evvybody on the place know yo' sister is black 'n' yo papa is black, 'n' yo' grandma is black," Willie said, pushing the word "black" out of his mouth like it was something nasty.

"Willie, I'm tellin' you, don't you call my papa 'n' them black," I said forcefully, doubling up my fist.

"Whut you gon' do 'bout it?" he asked.

"You call 'em black again," I replied, "'n' I'm gon' pop you up side yo' head, that's whut I'm gon do."

"You hit me, River, 'n' I'm sho' gon' tell my sister 'N' her gon' tell Miz Susie Mr. Win done sent Naomi to Vicksburg 'n' is keepin' her there 'n' payin' all her 'spenses," Willie threatened.

"He ain't payin' all my sister's 'spenses; Papa is 'n' the welfare," I argued.

"You don' have to lie 'bout it, River. Evvybody know Mr. Win done sent Naomi to Vicksburg 'n' is payin' to keep her there so Miz Susie won't fine out. But her sho' gon' find out ef you hit me, 'cause Lilly already say her gon' tell her ef Mr. Win keep messin' with her 'bout credit at the sto'."

"Let her tell her, I don' care, but her bet not tell no stories, 'cause ef her do, my papa gon' come over to yo' house 'n' whup her ass," I said boastfully.

"Whup whose ass?" Willie asked.

"Yo' sister's ass, that's whose, ef her tell any stories on Naomi."

"You let 'm try it 'n you'll see whut my papa will do," Willie challenged.

"Yo' papa ain't nothin but a jackleg preacher," I said, but immediately I was sorry I had said it. Because I knew Papa would whip me ef he ever heard I had said such a thing about Reverend Fisher, although he himself said it all the time. I was sorry, too, because I thought Reverend Fisher had some special arrangements with the Lord, and he might tell Him on me.

Willie's reply increased my sorrow and my fear. "I'm gon' sho' tell Papa whut you done said, 'n' he gon' put you outa the church," he said with finality as he turned off at his house.

Put me outa the church after all my praying, I thought.

"'N' after all yo' lying, too," the ole devil seemed to be saying. "Pretendin' you done seen a sign when you ain't seen nothin', jes' tol' the preacher whut Willie done tol' you."

Tears gathered in my eyes, and I ran home crying.

"Whut you cryin' 'bout, River?" Grandma asked as I came up on the porch, where she was sitting.

I buried my face in her lap and said in a muffled voice, "Willie Fisher gon' git his papa to put me outa church."

"Fer whut?"

"'Cause I tol' him my papa would whup his sister ef her tol' Miz Susie stories on Naomi 'bout Mr. Win payin' her 'spenses in Vicksburg," I said, postponing the part about him calling her and Papa and Naomi black and about me calling his papa a jackleg preacher.

I barely got the words out of my mouth before Grandma stopped patting my head and raised her arms high in the air with a scream. "Naw, Jesus! You know us way hard 'nuff 'thout that." She said something else, but her words were smothered by my own crying, which was increased by her alarm.

"Can his papa put me outa church, Grandma?"

"Naw, 'cause he ain't the pastor; he jes' helpin' out Reverend Whitten, the pastor, but that ain't whut I'm worried 'bout right now, boy. I'm worried 'bout that gal tellin' Miz Susie 'bout Naomi. Ef that fool gal tell that, us sho' gon' be put off the place, 'cause Miz Susie is mean, do you hear me?

Mean. I sho' hopes yo' ma 'n' pa hurry up 'n' come home from fishin', 'cause they got to do some-thin' right away."

I felt better knowing that Grandma wasn't worried about the preacher putting me out of church. I began dryin' my eyes while Grandma kept calling on the Lord. Soon I saw Mama and Papa coming up the lane, and I ran to meet them.

"Look whut us done catched," Mama said, coming through the gate ahead of Papa, who held up a long string of perch, carp, and cats. Papa and Mama looked so happy with their catch that the thought of the bad news Grandma and I had for them brought tears into my eyes.

"Whut you cryin' 'bout, River?" Papa asked as we walked toward the house.

"Nothin'," I said, not wanting to be the one to tell them; Grandma could do that better.

"Nothin', you cryin' 'bout nothin' River?" Mama asked.

"No'am, I ain't cryin' 'bout nothin'."

"Well, whut is you cryin' 'bout, then?" Papa insisted as we walked into the yard.

Grandma was standing on the porch. "I'm sho' glad y'all done come."

"What River cryin' 'bout, Ma? You been cryin', too. Whut's wrong?"

"You ain't heard nothin' from Naomi, is you?" Papa asked.

"Naw, us ain't heard nothin' from Naomi," Grandma said, dabbing at her eyes.

"Well, whut is it, Ma?" Mama asked in irritation.

"It's 'bout the preacher's gal, Lilly Mae," Grandma replied slowly.

"Whut 'bout her?" Mama questioned.

"Her know 'bout Naomi being in Vicksburg."

"Well, jes' 'bout evvybody know her in Vicksburg, Miz Carrie," Papa put in.

"But the white folks don' know, 'cep'n Mr. Win," Grandma said mournfully.

"'Course, they don' know, Miz Carrie," Papa said impatiently, putting the fish down on a corner of the porch.

"Well, this chile say Willie Fisher done tol' him Lilly Mae gon' tell 'em; gon' tell Miz Susie," Grandma said.

"Naw, naw, Ma," Mama cried out, "that gal ain't gon' do that."

"I wouldn't put it pas' her; when Willie tell you this?" Papa asked.

"This edenin' comin' from school," I replied uncertainly, fearing I was going to have to tell him what I had called the preacher.

"How come he say that?"

"'Cause I doubled up my fist at him when he said you 'n' Naomi 'n' Grandma was black."

"He called us black?"

"Yessuh, he sho' did 'n' he say ef I hit him he was sho' gon' tell Lilly Mae 'n' her was gon' tell Miz Susie 'bout Naomi."

"Silas, you don' reckon that gal would sho'nuff tell Miz Susie, after all the food 'n' clothes us been givin' 'em 'n' milk evvy time us churn?" Mama asked.

"It jes' jealousy, that's all it is, Becky," Papa replied. "I 'speck I oughta go over there after supper 'n' talk with Reverend Fisher. He'll put a stop to that."

"But you don' know that gal, Silas," Mama said. "Since her mama died year fo' las', her ain't min'in' her papa 'n' nobody else. You let me go 'n' talk with that gal. Hurry up 'n' clean the fish 'n' I'll take some o' them 'long."

As soon as Mama had finished milking, she grabbed about half of the fish they had caught and put them in an empty lard bucket and took them over to Reverend Fisher's. Then she came back for meal and lard and took along some white potatoes and two heads of cabbage out of our garden. It was dark when Mama returned; she had helped Lilly Mae cook the food and feed the children and Reverend Fisher. But with all her cooking and doing, there had been no time or opportunity to talk with Lilly Mae about not telling Mrs. Susie.

"I tol' her to come over here tomorrow 'n' I'd give her some mo' things," Mama said as she sat down to the fried fish Grandma had cooked. "You don' know how bad off they is," she added. "No clothes much fer anybody but Lilly Mae 'n' Willie 'n' the preacher, 'cep'n the few things us done give 'em las' winter. That's how come you don' never see the other chillum out in the yard. How Reverend Fisher can set 'n' read the Bible with all them naked, hongry chillun 'round him is beyond me."

"'N' let the weed 'n' grass take his cotton 'n' corn, 'cep'n this year when that weed-killer stuff is keepin' his field clean, is mo'n I can understan'," Papa added.

"I think he jes' done los' heart," Grandma said, "since Bessie Mae died. He loved her 'n' folks say they went through thick 'n' thin together. You know, folks say he had a big church in Valley Park years ago 'n' was doin' good when he had to marry her."

Grandma was about to repeat to Mama and Papa as if for the first time what she had heard the folks on the plantation say about Reverend Fisher and his wife. I had heard it so often, I almost knew the story as well as Grandma. At first she would whisper it to Mama and them when she thought I was anywhere nearby, later they talked about it openly same as they talked about crops or about church.

"After Reverend had to marry Bessie Mae, 'n' her was jes' a girl," Grandma said, "the folks in the church, they say, sort o' set down on him, 'specially some o' the sister who had their hats set fer him. 'N' year by year he would come up shorter 'n' shorter with his conference claims. Then the year before he come to the Bend, they say he had less 'n ha'f his dues at conference time 'n' when he made his report, the bishop pointed his finger at Reverend and said, 'Fisher, ef you looked after the Lawd's work 'stid o' livin' in 'dultry, you 'd have yo' claims.' Right there, they say he los' his church, 'cause he looked the bishop straight in the eyes 'n' said, 'That's a lie 'n' I don' care who said it.'

"'N' they say the bishop jumped up 'n' yelled, 'Fisher, you gon' regret this 'cause I'm gon put you on the shortest grass in the conference.'"

"It was a shame," Mama said, "fer the bishop to send Reverend here with Bessie Mae 'n' them chillun as assistant pastor o' us little church."

"They say the Williamsons was tryin' to help out when they give him a few acres o' cotton to work. But Reverend jes' ain't cut out to be no preacher," Papa said.

"He jes' a natchal-born preacher, Silas," Mama added.

"He is that, he is that," Grandma put in.

And he was a natural-born preacher. He could say, "You know, Jesus; You know how it is," with the right moan to start the congregation to stamping its feet and some members to shouting. And as he warmed to his sermon whenever Reverend Whitten would let him preach, he could sweep the congregation on to the canvas of his imagination with painted words that regaled the people in the Promised Land of their dreams with no boll weevils to fear, no cotton to chop or pick, and no more coming out in debt.

Reverend Fisher looked like a preacher, too. He always wore his black tattered coat whenever he left home no matter how hot it was, and around his neck, as if made there, was a white collar turned backwards and attached to his black vestment bib. Looking out from the sleeves of his shabby coat were soiled white cuffs that knew no shirt. And Reverend Fisher seldom took quick steps like Papa and the other men on the plantation rushing to the field or to the barn or to the wagon. His steps were slow and deliberate as if he was never in a hurry, and his tan face was calm and gentle and wore a smile that was cheerful and confident, not like Mr. Willie's, which seemed to be owned by somebody else who ordered his mouth open and dared him to shut it.

But like my father said, Reverend Fisher wasn't cut out to be a farmer. Grass took his cotton while he read his Bible and he came out in debt every year. But they said Mr. Win never balled him out the way he did other farmers when too much grass got in their crops, and even though he never cleared anything, the plantation owner always gave him a few dollars anyway. Maybe it was because of Lilly

Mae, or maybe it was because Mr. Win and Mr. Walter thought the preacher had some special connections with the Lord.

Papa, who had been mostly listening while Mama and Grandma talked about Reverend Fisher, cleared his throat and said, "Befo' y'all git carry 'way with the reverend's preachin', us better make sho' that gal don' go tellin' Miz Susie 'bout Naomi."

"I done tol' you I'm gon' talk with her tomorrow when her come to git the food 'n' things," Mama said.

"Whut ef her don' 'gree?" Papa asked.

"I think her gon' 'gree, Silas," Mama replied. "Her ain't no real bad girl; he jes' ain't had no chance much."

"But her jealous," Grandma said, "'n' ain't no tellin' whut jealous gal'll do."

"Yes, jealousy is a terrible driver," Papa said. "It drive some folks like they is mules."

"Well, talkin' to her 'bout the only thing us can do," Mama replied. "After that it up to the Lawd."

It was my bedtime then, and Mama didn't let me forget it. So I heard no more that night about what they were going to do to keep Lilly Mae from telling Mrs. Susie.

The next morning, Papa let me ride with him on ole Salt as far as Mt. Olive, where I went to school, and then he rode on to the store to get some cloth for Mama to make us some new cotton-picking sacks. This left Mama and Grandma at home alone to talk with Lilly Mae when she came. Before Papa let me down from the mule, he reminded me not to say anything to Willie Fisher or anybody about what were talking about at home the night before.

XI

Owner's Envious Suitor to Tell Owner's Spouse about the Affair

When I returned home from school that day, Mama and Grandma were sitting on the porch, rocking and smiling. I knew that meant that Lilly Mae must have agreed not to tell Mrs. Susie. As usual, I walked to Grandma's chair first and put my arms around her neck and kissed her while she wrapped her arms around me and patted my back softly.

"Was Grandma's boy a good boy at school today?"

"Yessum, I sho' was," I replied and turned to Mama and gave her a hug and a kiss.

She was piecing scraps of cloth together for a quilt. She put her needle down for a moment and hugged me with one arm and a grunt. "Mama's little man, ain't you?"

"Yessum, where is Papa?"

"He down to Ben's. Ain't River a big boy, Ma?"

"Yes," Grandma agreed, "he sho' is a big boy."

These compliments made me really feel like a big boy. I had already been asking Papa when I was going to be big enough for a plow and a mule of my own, and he had said, "It won't be long, man; maybe when you is nine or ten."

It seemed that would never come, except at times like that when Mama and Grandma were saying I was a big boy. I picked up my first reader and my drawing book and went inside to change my clothes, but I kept my ears open so as not to miss anything they might say about Lilly Mae. Most of the talk, however, was about the basket meeting set for the fourth Sunday at our church. At first Mama said she was going to fry about three chickens and maybe bake a ham and cook two jelly cakes, a peach cobbler, two or three blackberry pies, and a heap of biscuits. My mouth watered as she talked about the peach cobbler and jelly cake. I liked those tall jelly cakes made out of thin layers of cake and thick layers of Mama's wild grape jelly.

Then Mama changed her mind. "But you know, Ma," she said, "this is kinda foolish, us talkin' 'bout cookin' up a lot o' stuff to waste at church with Reverend Fisher 'n' his chillun hongry next do'."

"You right, Becky," Grandma agreed. "It'd be a shame to waste all that victuals showin' off at church, 'n' po' Reverend 'n' his chillun gon' be hongry the next day with nothin' t'eat."

"'N', Ma, did you see Lilly Mae this mornin' grabbin' up that flour 'n' meal 'n' lard 'n' piece o' bacon like her ain't never seen none befo'?"

"Yes, I seen her 'n' I felt sorry fer her; her pretty, too."

"Well, I ain't gon' take all that stuff I been talkin' 'bout," Mama said. "I'm gon' take somethin', of course, to the basket meetin', but I'm gon' hol' back mos' o' whut I said I was gon' take, 'n' I'm gon' give it to Lilly Mae for Reverend 'n' them chillun. Not all at once, but some at a time over a week or two."

My heart fell at the thought of Mama not taking a big basket of food to church, but I wasn't too worried because I knew Silvester's mama and General Lee's mama and Mrs. Mary Moses were going to have big baskets.

When I had changed my clothes, I went into the kitchen and dipped up a big cup of buttermilk out of a crock and cut a slice of cornbread from the hoecake that lay warm in the skillet on the back of the stove. I crumbled the bread into the milk, added a heaping tablespoon of sugar, stirred it up well, and spooned it down. Then I skipped out of the house, hollering back to Mama that I was going up the lane to get ole Beulah and bring her to the gate. I had given up on hearing any more about how Mama and Grandma had made out with Lilly Mae until supper, when I knew they would be telling my father about it. As I went for the cow, I threw at birds and fence posts with clods of dirt almost as hard as rocks.

At supper that night, Mama started telling Papa about Lilly Mae's visit while she was still placing the food on the table. "Lilly Mae 'greed with us," Mama said, "that there ain't no use stirrin' up these white folks fer nothin'. Said her was jes' talkin' when her tol' her brother, Willie, her was gon' tell Miz Susie."

"Well, that's good," Papa said. "I'm glad I don' have to go over there 'n' straighten that gal out."

"I'm glad, too, Silas," Mama agreed, "'cause that might be the sho' way to make her tell Miz Susie."

"Her wouldn't tell nobody when I got through tellin' her 'n' her pa whut I'd do ef her went tellin' stuff on Naomi to the white folks," Papa boasted.

"Silas, there some chillun like Naomi whut you can scare by talking 'bout beatin' 'em," Mama argued, "but Lilly Mae ain't one of 'em. That gal ain't scared o' nothin'. Her been hongry as a dog 'n' col' 'n' naked; whut her got to scared o'?"

"Becky, you tellin' the truth," Grandma said, "'n' that's whut keep me kinda worried. I'm scared o' folks whut ain't scared o' nothin', 'cause they ain't got no bounds; they do anything."

"You don' think her'd tell Miz Susie, do you, Ma, after her done tol' us whut her did, do you?" Mama asked.

"Come to think o' it, I ain't sho'. That gal might say one thing when her see victuals, 'n' 'nother thing when her hongry again, 'specially ef her hongry 'nuff."

"Or mad 'nuff," Papa said.

"Yes, mad at Naomi or Mr. Win."

"Her already mad at Mr. Win," I said, "'cause he want her to bathe like Naomi 'n' brush her teeth. 'N' he been cuttin' down on credit fer her at the sto'."

"I thought it mus' be somethin'," Mama said, "'cause they ain't had a speck o' food in that house yistiddy when I took that fish over there."

"Boy, how you know 'bout Mr. Win cuttin' down on credit fer 'em at the sto'?" Papa asked.

"Willie done tol' me."

"Whut else he done tol' you, boy?" Papa wanted to know.

"Nothin', cep'n Willie say his sister think Mr. Win tryin' to put her down," I replied.

"Becky, did her say anything 'bout this to you 'n' Miz Carrie?" Papa asked.

"Naw, her ain't breathed it to us."

"This here kinda serious," Papa said, "I think I better go over after I finish eatin' 'n' talk with Reverend 'bout it."

"Now, you jes' talk to him, Silas, 'n' don' go orderin' him 'round like you do sometime," Mama advised.

"Woman, I got sense, I ain't no fool," Papa roared.

"I know you got sense, Silas, but sometime you fergit," Mama said apologetically.

"Well, I ain't gon' fergit, Becky."

"Whut you gon' tell Reverend?" Mama asked.

"I don' know exactly, Becky. I'm jes' gon' talk with him, you know?"

"Well, you better plan whut you gon' say so you'll be sho' to say the right thing, Silas. Maybe I oughta go with you," Mama suggested.

"Naw, you don' need to go; I'm jes' gon' have a man-to-man talk with the preacher."

"But whut you gon' say, Silas?" Mama insisted.

"Oh, I'm jes' gon' 'splain the whole situation to him 'bout Naomi 'n' Lilly Mae 'n' Mr. Win. 'N' I'm gon' tell him it ain't gon' do nobody no good fer Lilly Mae to go tellin' Miz Susie 'bout this. 'N' I'm gon' tell him ef her do, it might end up with both them 'n' us bein' put off the place with nowhere to go."

"That sound good, Silas," Grandma said. "The preacher will listen to that."

"Yessum, thanky, Miz Carrie," Papa replied in a grateful voice that seemed glad she had backed him up and blocked any further criticism from Mama about what he was going to say to Reverend Fisher.

But it wasn't over yet.

"Now, don' go tellin' him with all them chillun listenin'," Mama warned. "Git him outa the yard 'n' off to hisself."

"Gawddamn, Becky, do you think I'm a sho'nuff fool?"

"Naw, Silas; I'm sorry. But I know you got so much on yo' min' with Naomi in Vicksburg 'n' all; I was jes' tryin' to help you make sho' you gon' git the preacher to keep Lilly Mae from tellin' Miz Susie," Mama explained.

"Well, I know whut you meant, Becky. I'm gon' be careful," Papa said, getting up from the table.

"Can I go with you, Papa?" I asked, following him to the door.

"Naw, you can't go," he said firmly. Then he paused and looked back at me and said, "Man, you stay here with yo' mama 'n' yo' grandma."

I followed as far as the porch. Papa walked carefully between the rows of cotton as he made his way over to Reverend Fisher's, not much farther from our house than it was out to the lane. There was no fence at the preacher's house because he didn't need one. He had neither chickens nor hogs nor even a dog. We had had two dogs, but they started eating our chickens and my father shot them. I don't know whether Reverend Fisher ever had a dog or whether he ever raised chicken and hogs, but he had none now. Whenever a member of the church gave him a hen or a tired old rooster, Willie usually tied it by the leg to a pillar of the house for a day or two until it was killed and cooked.

The preacher and Willie were sitting on the edge of the porch with their feet hanging down. Papa stood for a moment where the fence ought to be. Then he walked forward a step or two with both hands in the back pockets of his overalls. He was looking back more at the cotton and pointing to something rather than looking forward toward Reverend Fisher and Willie.

The preacher eased his feet down to the ground and walked toward Papa. They shook hands and stood for a moment talking, then they walked off down through the field looking at the cotton. Two small heads popped out of the door and seemed to be watching Papa and the preacher, who were some distance from the house now and had stopped and were looking into cotton squares. I knew they must have been talking about boll weevils and about how clean the weed killer kept the field.

After a few minutes, they were no longer looking at the cotton, but at each other, and the preacher was making the same motions with his arms that he made in church when he preached. Finally, they walked back toward Reverend Fisher's and stopped again and talked with the preacher, making the same vigorous gestures with his arms. The sun was now almost down and looked like a big red ball rolling down behind the levee. When Papa and Reverend Fisher had finished talking, Papa walked on home slowly, but the preacher did not go home immediately. Instead, he walked back across his field to the fartherest corner down by the lane. There he leaned on a post and looked off to where the sun had gone down and only the glow remained.

Mama and Grandma had joined me on the porch by the time Papa walked into the yard. He sat down beside me on the edge of the porch with one foot on the ground and the other propped up on the porch with his fingers laced around his knee. His back was braced against a post.

"The preacher," he began, "ain't knowed nothin' 'bout Lilly Mae 'n' Mr. Win. Thought his prayers 'n' the Lawd had opened the way fer him to keep on gittin' credit at the sto'. In fact, he was sho' the Lawd had answered his prayers. But he was puzzled 'bout the way the Lawd had used Lilly Mae in answerin' 'em. He kept on sayin', 'The Lawd sho' work in strange ways sometime.'"

"Silas, whut he say 'bout keepin' that gal from tellin' Miz Susie?" Mama asked.

"I'm comin' to that, Becky," Papa replied. "Firs' Reverend wanted to know how come us ain't tol' him 'bout Naomi 'n' had him pray fer her. He say the Lawd in all these things."

"He can't pray fer hisself," Mama said. "Ef he do it don' do no good; how he gon' pray fer Naomi?"

"But he git 'long somehow," Grandma said. "No matter how the weeds take his cotton, 'n' how po' the after-collection is on the second and fo'th Sundays, he 'n' them chillun eat some kinda way, 'n' they gits a few clothes, 'bout as much as the rest o' us gits with all us plowin' 'n' choppin' 'n' pickin'."

Mama had struck a sore point with Grandma, downgrading the preacher's prayers. She herself had counted on prayers too long, and they had done too much for her to question anybody's prayers now.

"Yes, Ma, I knows that, 'n' I didn't mean it the way you think," Mama said, "but prayers can't do evvything; us got to do some things fer usself."

"Prayers can do mo'n you think," Grandma argued, "'n' don't you never let doubt force you to close the do' to hope, Becky. The church 'n' hope 'n' prayers 'n' Gawd is all us po' nigger got. All."

"You is right, Miz Carrie," Papa said, repaying her for the support she had given him when he was preparing to go see Reverend Fisher.

"Well, I'll say again, y'all, I didn't mean it the way Ma is takin' it; I know whut prayer can do," Mama said, "but Reverend Fisher's prayers don' seem to git no results."

"Gawd's ways ain't us ways, Becky," Grandma insisted. "Us don' always understan' Him."

"Whut else did the preacher say, Silas?" Mama asked, ignoring Grandma's last remark.

"He say he gon' talk it over with the Lawd 'n' the Lawd gon' take care o' it."

"Ain't he gon' talk with Lilly Mae, Silas?"

"He didn't say, Becky," Papa replied. "All he said was that he was gon' talk it over with the Lawd."

"Well, all I can say," Mama said with a hint of disappointment in her voice, "all us better start prayin' 'n' hopin' the white folks, 'specially Miz Susie, don' find out 'bout Naomi."

"Course, I don' know much 'bout prayin' like Miz Carrie do, but I sho' felt better after talkin' with Reverend," Papa replied, getting up off the edge of the porch and walking out to the barn to see if the mules were all right for the night.

I ran after him.

XII

Sharecroppers Worry about the Cotton-Picking Machines

Two weeks passed, and it was the fourth Sunday: basket meeting day. Maybe somebody's prayers had worked, we thought, because as far as we knew, Lilly Mae had not told Mrs. Susie.

Mama and Papa had been to Vicksburg to see Naomi, and she was doing all right. The cotton was opening fast, and the stalks were loaded with bolls. Within a week or two, it would be time for picking and school would be out again. Ordinarily, people would be happy at basket meeting with the prospects for a big crop so good, but they weren't. Mr. Win and Mr. Walter had gone to Memphis to an agricultural fair, where all kinds of new farm implements were to be on display. And some folks were saying they had gone to look at mechanical cotton pickers. They said Mr. Fuller had already bought two for his plantation right up the levee beyond Fitlers, and he was going to us them this fall to harvest his crop. If they worked, folks were saying Mr. Fuller was going to get rid of just about all his half-hands. And although it was a bright and sunny day for the basket meeting, most folks minds didn't seem to be on eating. They were wondering if Mr. Win and Mr. Walter were going to come back from Memphis with a cotton-picking machine, if it would really pick cotton, and what was going to happen to them if it did.

The grown folks' minds may not have been on eating, but we children's certainly were. General Lee, Roosevelt, Silvester, and I darted from one part of the long tables to another, asking for cake, cobbler, fried chicken, biscuits, and pie until our hands were full. Then we took seats on the ground beneath a section of a table where the baskets sat. The tables were built by placing long boards on carpentry horses. The boards and horses were shoved under the church when not in use. But on almost every second and fourth Sunday, when Reverend Whitten, the pastor, came up from Vicksburg to preach, the boards' end horses were dragged out and made into tables, which were covered with tablecloths, starched and ironed sheets, and flour sacks just as they were for basket meetings. That was because Reverend Whitten held afternoon services in addition to morning services. In this way, he could get back to Vicksburg before night, but it made church last all day. So all the families brought their dinner to church and spread it out on the tables and fought the flies off with dishrags and leafy branches.

Under the tables was the favorite spot for most of us children because there were fewer flies there to fight. The sheets came almost to the ground, hiding the horses and shutting out the pests. Sitting there, we could hear the grownups talking as they stood by the tables eating when we weren't talking too loud or giggling our heads off. That day, above the sound of our giggles as we raced through the food, I heard my father and Mr. Ben and Mr. Willie talking about the mechanical cotton picker.

"Reckon that cotton pickin' machine gon' work?" Mr. Ben was asking.

"I don' know," Mr. Willie replied. "I seen one or two o' 'em in town, but I ain't seen one pick no cotton."

"I jes' don' see how they can make a machine whut can pick cotton with all them leaves and bolls evvywhichawhere," Mr Ben argued.

"But I heard a white man say in Vicksburg jes' a few weeks ago that them machine can pick," Mr. Willie said. "He said the thing straddles a row o' cotton with two things somethin like small barrels whut whirl 'round with some things like nails stickin' out o' 'em. 'N' he said the nail things gouge the cotton outa the bolls 'n' some kinda tubes sucks the cotton off the nails 'n' blows it up into a big basket on top o' the machine," Mr. Willie explained.

"You heard 'bout Mr. Fuller buyin' two o' 'em, ain't you?" Papa asked.

"Yes, I heard 'bout that," Mr. Willie replied. "'N' you know, Mr. Win 'n' Mr. Walter done gone to Memphis to look at 'em."

"You don' reckon Mr. Win 'n' Mr. Walter gon' buy one them things, do you, Willie?" my father asked with just a tiny note of fear in his voice.

"Silas, I can answer that," Mr. Ben said. "Mr. Walter might be in fer buyin' one, 'cause they say his wife, Miz Rhoda, don' think niggers oughta be kept on plantations like this, in old rundown houses, 'n' with no school much. Her a good lady, but her wanna help in the wrong way. Where us goin'? But now Mr. Win he ain't gon' never 'gree to that," Mr. Willie said. "He'd be los' without a heap o' niggers on the place."

His voice weakened, and he stumbled a little as the last few words came out of his mouth. I knew he wished he hadn't said them in front of Papa. But I think my father was too preoccupied to notice.

"Yes, Ben," Mr. Willie came back, "but Mr. Walter he the oldest 'n' he the boss; whut he say go."

"Well, ef that machine work," Papa said slowly as if he was trying to solve a riddle, "'n' the Williamsons git some like Mr. Fuller done done, then whut's gon' happen to the niggers here at the Bend?"

I didn't hear anybody's reply because both of my hands were empty by this time, and I rushed out to refill them. General was right behind me; Silvester and Roosevelt had already gone. Silvester had probably hidden some of his in his bosom or was off hiding it in his papa's wagon. That's the way he was, always hiding part of what he had to eat, and then pulling it out after everyone else has finished, and then eating it slowly before our envious eyes. This is what he did at school every day with the stick of candy he bought off Mr. Tobe's truck. He would hide it in his pocket and beg us for ours until recess was over and our candy was gone. Then he pulled his out and gnawed on it secretly in class. If you asked him for a piece of his candy, he pretended to be deaf.

General Lee and I returned to our places under the table with both hands full again. In Silvester's place sat Willie Fisher with both of his hands full also. His slender fingers tore into the chicken leg he had with a swiftness and a directness I had seldom seen before. He pushed most of the top joint into his mouth and followed it with a piece of pound cake, stuffing his mouth so full that his thin cheeks puffed out, making his eyes seem more deep set than ever. Folks said the only time the Fisher children ever got enough to eat was at a basket meeting.

General Lee and I slowed our gulping of food to watch Willie mostly because we were already full. "Isssssss that some o' Mizzzzzzzzzzz Viney Jackson's chhhhhhhhhhicken you got?" General asked Willie. "Herrrrrrrr sho' got some goooooooood chicken."

"Naw," Willie replied, "this piece o' chicken come outa Miz Nettie Woodson's basket. Her got some good chicken, too." With that the rest of the upper joint disappeared into his mouth to be followed by a big bite of dewberry pie.

"Yoooooooo mama got the bessssssss' jelly cake, River, but Mizzzzzzzzzzzz Mary Mosssssssssssses got the bes' dewberry pie," General commented as we watched Willie.

As Willie turned to one side to let his legs stretch out flat on the ground to give his stomach more room, the torn side pocket of his pants gapped open wide and something pink and silky-looking could be seen. Before I could catch myself, I said, "Oh, look, General! Willie got on his sister's drawers." In spite of all Mama and Grandma had told me about being nice to Willie so Lilly Mae wouldn't tell Mrs. Susie about Naomi, the words slipped out. "I'm jes' playin'," I said, trying to withdraw my charge before Willie became angry.

But he wasn't angry or ashamed; he was proud. "Yes, I got on some soft pink rubber drawers, all right, but they ain't my sister's," he bragged.

"Lemmmmmmmme see?" General asked.

"See," Willie said, pulling his torn pocket open wider so that General could get a good look.

"Youuuuuuuuu sho' is got on youoooooo' sister's drawers."

"They ain't my sister's drawers," Willie protested.

"Effffffff they ain't yooooooo' sister's, whose is they, then?"

"Annh hanh," Willie boasted, "wouldn't you like to know."

"Youuuuuuuuuuu know they is yoooo' sister," General insisted.

"They ain't neither," Willie said stoutly, unzipping his pants and trying to turn the waistband down far enough down to show us something. "They got a name sewed in 'em," he added.

"Whuttttt name? Lillllllllllly Mae?" General asked, laughing.

"Soon as us finish eatin', us can go out to the toilet 'n' I'll show y'all," Willie bragged.

We gulped down the rest of our food and followed Willie to the privy, but it was full and we had to wait. As soon as Mr. Gus and Mr. Stock came out, we ducked in. Willie pulled his pants down to his knees and rolled down the pink girdle an inch or two.

"See, I tol' you these ain't my sister drawers."

Sure enough there was a name embroidered in the waistband. It read "Millie."

General Lee, who was nearly as old as Willie but much larger, said, "Foooooool, whuttttttt you doin' with Miss Millllie's drawers on?" His eyes were stretched to nearly twice their size.

Willie only smiled. I was with him the first time I saw Miss Millie close up. It was early that summer right after she had come home from college. Willie and I were at play in his yard, trying to build a fire in what had been the hub wheel of a wagon wheel. We heard a horse walking toward us and looked around to see Miss Millie leading her horse with one hand and holding little Woodrow with the other. As usual he didn't have on any clothes and his teapot was showing. Willie was so afraid and ashamed for his little brother that he hid his face behind his hands and spoke in a whisper when he answered Miss Millie.

"This your little brother?" she asked gently, sweetly, with a wide smile on her face. She was just about the size and age of Naomi as she stood there holding little Woodrow. "He had wandered out to the lane," she said pleasantly. "You better keep an eye on him or I'm going to have a cute little boy."

"Yessum," Willie replied, looking toward the ground with his hands up in front of his face and making no move to take the boy off her hands.

Miss Millie, who was wearing yellow shorts and a long-sleeved blouse flowered with daffodils, said, "Come and get him," softly, patiently, as if she had all day. She looked a lot like her mama, Mrs. Susie, but her smile was broad like Mr. Win's and her eyes sky blue like his.

Lilly Mae and Daisy Lee appeared at the door. Lilly Mae looked straight at Miss Millie without a smile on her mouth or in her eyes and thanked her for bringing her little brother to the house. Then she went down the steps and picked up little Woodrow, gave him a gentle slap on his butt, and carried him into the house.

Miss Millie followed them with her eyes and then put one foot in the stirrup and sprang astride her horse almost effortlessly. "Bye," she said, waving her crop as she rode off smiling.

Willie and I ran after her to close the gate. We hopped on the bottom of the gate framing and rode it as the gate swung to the big post to which it fastened. But we did not fasten the gate. Instead, we ran out into the middle of the lane and watched Miss Millie riding down past Mr. Ben's. She looked back once, still smiling, and waved at us again. Willie jumped up and down for a while and then stood there, watching until Miss Millie was out of sight.

We were both charmed by her smile. It seemed as genuine as a bale of cotton, and Willie's mouth stood wide open in wonderment. As we turned to close the gate, he said, "Damn, ain't her pretty," licking his lips with his tongue as if he had just eaten. I remember the eager, hungry look on his thin face, much like the way he looked as he stood there in the toilet, showing us her pink girdle he was wearing.

General Lee asked again, and there was some fear and alarm as well as delight in his voice this time, "Foooooooooooool, I say, whhhhhhhhhhhhhhhhhut you doing with Misssssssssssss Millie's drawers on—woooooooooooooooowe!"

"'Cause I done took 'em, that's how come," Willie replied boldly.

"Youuuuuuuuu didn't take take 'em offffffffffffff 'n her, did you, fool?"

"Naw, I took 'em off the clothesline in her backyard yistiddy when I left a note fer Miz Susie," Willie explained.

"A note?" I asked in alarm. "Whut note?"

"A note Lillie Mae tol' me to leave in the do'."

"Whut fer?"

"'Cause Mr. Win done gone off to Memphis 'n' ain't give her no note to git some groceries at the sto'."

"But Mama done carr'ed y'all some food yistiddy edenin'," I said.

"That was yistiddy edenin'," Willie replied. "I took the note yistiddy mornin' when us ain't had nothin' much to eat since Thursday 'cep'n onion gravy 'n' hoecake 'n' the milk yo' Mama give us."

"Did Miz Susie give you a note to the sto'?" I asked.

"Naw, her didn't know I left it. I slipped it in the screen do' and run. As I run 'round the house, I saw these pretty pink drawers hangin' on the line 'n' I took 'em 'n' put 'em in my bosom. Ain't they pretty? I started to give 'em to Lilly Mae, but they too small fer her," Willie said.

As I was about to ask him what was in the note, Mr. Gus knocked on the door and told us to come on out of the privy. Outside, I stayed close to Willie, wanting to ask him and yet afraid to know what was in the note. Finally, it came out. "Whut the note said, Willie?" I asked.

"It said somethin' was goin' on in Vicksburg."

My heart jumped. "Whut goin' on in Vicksburg?"

"I don' know," he replied, "'cep'n Mr. Win done sent yo' sister there."

"Her done tol' Miz Susie," I said to myself as I left Willie and worked my way through the crowd to the table where Mama was.

Most of the chicken and cake and pie and biscuits she had spread on the table were gone, and she was standing a piece away, talking with Mrs. Mary Moses; Grandma was sitting by the table with her arm resting on it.

I walked up to the side of Grandma's chair and leaned against her and whispered, "Lilly Mae done sent a note to Miz Susie."

"Whut you say, River?"

I don't know whether she didn't hear me, or wanted to make certain what I had said, or wanted to delay her mind's reception of such bad news.

I whispered again, "Willie say Lilly Mae done sent a note to Miz Susie."

Grandma sprang up like a paper clown springs out of a toy box. "Lawd, Jesus," she said and sat back down, clutching at Mama's arm. "Becky, I ain't feelin' well; us better go."

"Whut's the matter, Ma?" Mama asked, turning away from Mrs. Mary and stooping down by Grandma.

"I got a sharp pain right here," Grandma said, placing her hand on her chest.

"Lemme git Silas," Mama said, "'n', us can go."

As she walked away to look for my father, Mrs. Mary stooped down by Grandma and said with a quite smile, "It jes' a little indigeshun; you done et too much."

"Yes, Mary," Grandma agreed. "I bet you is right."

Mama soon reappeared and started clearing off the table, putting what was left into our basket. "Silas be 'long in a minute, Ma."

"Her gon' be all right, Becky," Mrs. Mary said comfortingly, "jes' a little indigeshun; her done et too much."

"Thanks, Mary. I hopes you right."

After a round of goodbyes, we got into our wagon and started for home.

"I ain't really sick," Grandma said when we were a clod's throw from the church. "But this boy say Willie Fisher done tol' him Lilly Mae done sent a note to Miz Susie. 'bout Naomi."

"Naw, Ma, naw, her ain't," Mama said in a rising voice.

"That's whut Willie say, 'n' he got on a pair o' Miss Millie's drawers," I added.

"Pair o' Miss Millie's drawers? Pair o' Miss Millie's drawers, did you say, boy?" Papa asked excitedly.

"He sho' is," I said, "'cause I seen 'em. He done showed 'em to me 'n' General Lee."

"Oh, naw, naw," Mama said with tears of fear gathering in her eyes.

"Whut that fool boy want with Miss Millie's drawers?" Papa asked, not really seeking an answer, I think, but expressing the astonishment that had just penetrated his mind.

"Ef the white folks finds out that boy done stole Miss Millie drawers, there gon' be a heap o' trouble on this place. Whut can us do, Silas?" Grandma asked prayerfully.

"I don' know, 'cep'n talk to Reverend Fisher again 'n' that boy o' his 'n 'n' git this thing hushed up, but I don' know as it will do any good."

"Course, Silas, Reverend's gon' talk mostly 'bout prayin' but you might be able to talk some sense into that boy," Mama advised.

"'N' don' fergit to talk to that Lilly Mae 'n' find out what her done wrote Miz Susie," Grandma added.

"Lawd, I done clean forgot all 'bout the note that gal done sent up to Miz Susie's 'bout Naomi," Mama said helplessly.

"'N' that Miz Susie sho' gon' tell Mr. Win when he git back from Memphis," Papa added.

"Her gon' do mo'n that," Grandma put in, "her gon' threaten to leave him with her mean self 'n' go back to her folks over at Rollin' Fork. 'N' her sho' gon' make him put us off the place."

"Naw, Ma, don' say that," Mama pleaded.

"Naw, ef Mr. Win 'splain it right," Papa said, "'n' show there ain't nothin 'tween him 'n' Naomi, Miz Susie might not press him too hard."

Although Mama was crying, she chuckled at whut my father said. "Silas, how he gon' 'splain? Is he gon' tell Miz Susie he done mistook Naomi fer Lilly Mae?"

"Naw, I guess he can't say that."

"He sho' can't," Grandma added.

"Ef they do put us off, Silas, with us crop almos' made, where us goin'?" Mama asked.

"I don' know," Papa said quietly. "Maybe," and then he seemed to have second thoughts as he paused for a long time, apparently seeking an alternative but not finding one, and so he began again. "Maybe us could go somewhere 'n' pick cotton by the hund'ud 'tel us found a place."

"'Ef' us own crop almos' ready fer pickin', 'n' us got to start all over again pickin' by the hund'ud. Lawd, have mercy," Mama mourned.

"Things gon' be all right, Becky, honey," Papa said, whipping the mules lightly with the cotton ropes that were the reins.

"Yes," Grandma avowed, "the Lawd He gon' make a way; He always have 'n' He always will."

With that everyone was quiet as the wagon squeaked over the ruts, moving toward home behind Ole Salt and Miss Lady, who knew the way home as well as any of us. It was a hazy afternoon with clouds drifting in the sky. In the distance, the green levee was dotted with grazing cattle that increased in numbers every year as cows dropped calves. Some folks said it was a race between cotton and cattle, and the cattle were winning. But it didn't seem so as we drove along the road with cotton growing as far as we could see. The leaves were turning brown and the stalks were laden with fat half-opened bolls out of which puffed the snowy fiber.

Late that afternoon, shortly after Mr. Stock and Mrs. Viney and Silvester had driven Reverend Fisher and Lillie Mae and Willie home with two large bags of food for the other children who had no clothes to wear to the basket meeting, Papa and I went over to their house to find out what Lilly Mae had written in the note to Mrs. Susie and why Willie had stolen Miss Millie's underthings. Mr. Stock always drove Reverend Fisher to church because he was one of the hostlers on the place and he passed early en route to the plantation barn and lot to see about the workstock and then on to church. They had stopped at the gate and dropped the Fishers and driven on in their wagon.

Papa took me along, I think, either to confront Willie and prevent him from lying or to prove me a liar. As we walked into the yard, Reverend Fisher rose from his shuck-bottomed chair and came down the steps to meet us.

"Come on in, Brother Henry, you 'n' River," he said, extending his hand.

"Naw, Reverend, us won't come in 'n' bother the chillun," Papa said, shaking the preacher's hand stiffly. "I jes' wanna have a little talk with you again."

"Certainly, Brother Henry, certainly, that was certainly a good basket meetin' today, wasn't it?"

"It sho' was, Reverend, it sho' was," Papa replied.

"We can set right here," the preacher said. "Willie go in the house 'n' git the other chair."

"Willie went into the house and brought the other chair while Reverend reached up on the porch and lifted down the one he had been sittin in. "Why don't you 'n' Willie go play, River, while yo' father 'n' me talk."

"Yessuh," I said and went over to the corner of the porch where Willie was leaning.

The three smaller children—Addie Lou, Lucy, and Woodrow—were huddled on the other end of the porch. Lilly Mae and Daisy Lee were inside. Papa and Reverend were talking very low and we couldn't hear what they were saying as we swung on the pump handle, but soon Reverend called out, "Lilly Mae!"

There was no answer.

Then he looked over to where we were playing and said, "Willie, go tell yo' sister I say come here."

Willie ran into the house and came right back out, saying, "Her comin', Papa."

In a moment, Lilly Mae appeared in the doorway. "Whut you want, Papa?" she asked coldly.

"Come here a minute; Brother Henry want to ast you 'bout somethin'."

"I ain't got time," she replied and turned back into the house, closing the door behind her with a slight jar.

Reverend Fisher stood up and made a step as if he were going into the house and bring her out. But he stopped there, brought his foot back, and sat down.

Papa jumped up and mumbled something to the preacher and then said, "Come on, River, us goin' home."

"Wait, Brother Henry," Reverend with a kind of a plea in his voice.

"Wait fer whut?" Papa asked as we walked out of the yard. He was silent almost all the way home. But just before we reached our own yard, he said, "A preacher raisin' chillun like that. That gal oughta be mine; I'd whup her 'tel her couldn't set down."

I knew what he meant because he had burned my backside with a strap many times—and Naomi's, too.

"Whut Reverend Fisher gon' do 'bout Willie havin' Miss Millie's underthings?" I asked.

"Unh, I clean forgot 'bout that boy; that gal made me so mad. I guess it's the preacher 'n' the Lawd fer that now, 'cause I sho' ain't goin' over there nomo'," Papa said as we walked into our yard.

We scraped off the mud that had stuck to our feet as we walked on the damp bare ground between the cotton rows going over to Reverend Fisher's and coming back. Then we went inside to tell Mama and Grandma the bad news about the way Lilly Mae had acted.

"Her jes' went in the house 'n' slammed the do' when her papa tol' her I wanted to ast her somethin'," Papa explained. "Said her didn't have time."

"Said her didn't have time 'n' slammed the do'?" Mama asked in astonishment.

"That's 'zactly whut her did, didn't her, River?"

"Yessuh, that's whut ole Lilly Mae did, Mama," I said, feeling proud that Papa had called on me to witness his statement.

"That's whut I been sayin'," Grandma spoke up. "You can't trust that gal, 'cause her ain't 'fraid o' her papa 'n' nobody else."

"Ef her was mine fer a few minutes, her'd be so scared after that, her'd never slam another do' as long as her live," Papa vowed with increasing anger in his voice.

"Maybe you could scare her, Silas, 'n' maybe you couldn't, but us got to do somethin' befo' Miz Susie tell Mr. Win when he come back 'n' all the trouble start with us right in the middle o' it," Mama warned.

"But whut can us do?" Papa asked. "Ain't no use in tryin' to talk to that gal, 'n' you know the preacher ain't gon do nothin' but leave it in the hands o' the Lawd, where it already at."

"Maybe the hands o' the Lawd is where it b'long," Grandma said, "'cause ain't nothin' y'all did done no good."

"Ma, I know us have to have the Lawd with us, but us gotta help usselves, too," Mama replied with conviction.

"Maybe you could talk to Paralee 'n' git her to talk to Miz Susie fer us," Papa suggested.

"Whut, 'n' have the whole thing spread all over the plentation?" Mama asked. "You can't trus' nothin' to Paralee; her tell evvything her know 'n' a lot her don' know."

"Well, Becky, whut can us do, then?" Papa wanted to know.

"I don' know, Silas; I'm jes' tryin' to think," Mama said and paused a while. Then she added, "Maybe Miz Rhoda would talk to Miz Susie. Ef anybody can 'suade Miz Susie, it's Miz Rhoda, tho' they don' always set horses."

"You gon' ast Miz Rhoda to talk to Miz Susie?" Papa asked skeptically.

"Ain't nobody else us can ast, is there?" Mama replied.

"Naw, ain't nobody else much," Papa said, "but I jes' don' trus' white folks much as you."

"I know you don't, Silas, but white folks already knows. Miz Susie sho' know, ef her done read that note, 'n' her white," Mama said with a cock of her head as if to seal the argument and forestall any further comments Papa might have about white folks.

"I guess you right, Becky," Papa agreed slowly. "When you gon' talk to Miz Rhoda?"

"First thing in the mornin'," Mama said.

"All right, ef you think so, Becky," he replied.

The next morning, Mama put on a starched gingham dress and a clean apron and got into our wagon, which Papa had hitched up. I got in beside her to ride as far as the school. She drove back across the plantation and up the lane toward Wilmyra, where Mrs Rhoda lived. Folks said ole Captain

Williamson, Mr. Win and Mr. Walter's great-grandfather, named the house for himself and his wife, who was named Elmyra. Mama stopped the wagon when we reached Mt. Olive and I jumped down and ran into the church yard and joined the other children. Mama drove on; Wilmyra was up the road a piece where the lane bent.

In the yard on the shady side of the church near the door where the choir went in and out on Sunday, Willie and General Lee were in an argument.

"Jessssssssss' one mo' day," General was pleading. "Ittttttttttt ain't hurt for me tooooooooo keep 'me oneeeee mo' day."

"But I want 'm," Willie insisted. "You promised at church yistiddy when I let you wear 'em that you'd pull 'em off soon as you got to school 'n' give 'em back to me."

"Welllllllll, jes' let me wear 'em 'telllllllll recess then," General begged.

"Naw, I want 'em now," Willie said.

"Jesssssssss 'tel recess, 'n' IIIIIIIIII 'clare fo' Gawd, IIIIIIIIII give 'em to you."

"All right, jes' 'tel recess, 'member, but ef you don' give 'em to me then I'm gon' goose you I'm sho is," Willie threatened, snapping his fingers and fluting his lips with intake suction that sounded something like a loud kiss.

General jumped and warned, "Donnnnnnnnnn' you do that, Willie."

"Whut he got o' yo'n?" I asked.

"You know, Miss Millie's drawers," Willie replied.

"Papa say there gon' be trouble on the place of the white folks finds out you don' stole Miss Millie's underthings," I warned.

"How they gon' find out less'n yo' ole crazy black papa tell'em?" Willie asked.

"My papa ain't gon' tell 'em, 'n' he ain't black."

"Welllllllll, ain't nobody else gonnnnnnnnn' tell 'em, 'n' they sho'feels good," General said.

"Them drawers fit you, big as you is?"

"Theyyyyyyyyyy sho' do; they gottttttttttt rubber in 'em 'n' they feel tight 'nnnnnnnnnn' good, al-llllllllllmos' like rubbing my legggggggggggg 'gainst her'n."

"Whut you wanna rub yo' leg 'gainst Miss Millie's fer?" I wanted to know.

They both laughed and pointed their fingers at me. "'Cause it would feeeeeeeeeel good, boy," General replied.

"Eben jes' wearin' her drawers feel good," Willie added.

"Whut feel good?" I asked, pressing my hand against General's butt.

They laughed again and General said, "Shit, a littttttttle boy like you donnnnnnnnnnnnn' know nothin' bout it; ain't you never seen Miss Millie, boy? How old is you, anyhow?"

"Six 'n' a ha'f goin' on seben," I boasted.

"River jes' a baby," Willie said.

"I ain't no baby neither," I protested. "I'm bigger'n you is."

"Bigger'n I'm is," Willie mocked me, "'n' you don' know how come Miss Willie's drawers feels good."

"Letttttttt him 'lone," General ordered, "heeeeeeeeee'll find out bout gallllllllllls 'n' drawers when he git bigger."

The bell saved me. It rang out for the taking in of school. We rushed around to the front of the church and lined up with the other children and marched in. Miss Taylor stood at the door with the bell in her hand. We took our seats for classes, but I couldn't keep my mind off General Lee and Willie wearing Miss Millie's underthings and saying they felt good.

When I got home from school that day, I wanted to ask Papa why wearing Miss Millie's drawers made Willie and General Lee feel good, but I was afraid to. Anyhow, he and Mama and Grandma were still reviewing Mama's visit to get Mrs. Rhoda to talk with Mrs. Susie to keep her from pressing Mr. Win to put us off the place when he got back from Memphis. From the pieces of the conversation, I gathered that Mrs. Rhoda had agreed to talk with Mrs. Susie. And she had told Mama not to worry. Papa and Mama were happier than they had been for weeks. Most of the conversation dealt with the crops. In Mama's lap lay the heavy material Papa had bought for her to make new cotton-picking sacks.

"After you done et somethin', River," Mama said. "I want you to pump the machine; I'm gon' make some new sacks."

"Yessum," I replied, anxious to race the sewing machine as Mama made long runs sewing up the sides of the sacks and hemming them. I liked pumping the shaft, which propelled the machine, when Mama was making sheets or cotton-picking sacks. But I hated the job when she was gathering the sleeves of a blouse or the waist of a skirt and it was stop and go all the way.

All the time I was pumping the machine, I was wondering how I was going to ask Papa about General Lee and Willie feeling good because they were wearing Miss Millie's underthings. I decided that Papa wasn't the one to ask; he might get excited again about the white folks getting stirred, and I didn't dare ask Mama. Grandma was the one. If she knew, I was sure she would tell me without making a big to-do over it.

After Mama finished two sacks, it was time for her to milk the cow and cook supper, while Papa fed and watered the mules and piddled about the barn and lot. When I had brought ole Beulah to the lane gate and picked up enough chips around the woodpile to make a fire in the kitchen stove, I rushed out on the front porch where Grandma was rocking to ask her about this good feeling Willie and General were having.

I sat down on the floor beside her chair She slowed her rocking and said, "Watch yo' fingers, River, don' git 'em under the chair."

"No'am, I ain't," I said.

"You miss Naomi, don't you?"

"Yessum, I sho' do, Grandma. When is her coming back home from Vicksburg?"

"I don' know. Yo' ma 'n' yo' pa talk like her might stay there 'n' git a job," Grandma said.

"I sho' hope her come home."

"You gon' help look after the baby ef her come home?"

"Ef her 'n' Mama let me; they might not trus' me with it."

"Soon as the newness wear off, 'n' Becky 'n' Naomi gits tired o' holdin' it, they gon' be glad to trus' you."

The thought of Naomi coming back home with a baby excited me, and I forgot all about asking Grandma about Willie and General. When the thought of their good feeling came back to me, I was seated at the table where the conversation was on how many bales we were going to make and a trip to Vicksburg to see Naomi and pay the lady where she was staying. I decided to wait and ask Naomi.

XIII

Silas Arrested as Suspect of Owner's Murder

I guess Mr. Win and Mr. Walter got back from Memphis Tuesday because Wednesday morning before day, the sheriff and two deputies came and arrested Papa and put handcuffs on him. They said he had killed Mr. Win. When Papa tried to speak, the shorter of the two deputies slapped him across the mouth and said, "Shut up, nigger, we know you done it, Gawddamit."

"Silas ain't done nothin', Lawd know he ain't done nothin'!" Mama screamed.

"Ain't no need o' you lyin', nigger woman, 'cause we gon' beat the truth outa this black sonofabitch," the sheriff said.

I started toward the sheriff to bite him on the leg, but Grandma grabbed me as I attempted to bound past her. "Let me go, Grandma!" I yelled. "These ole mean mens ain't gon' take my papa nowhere!"

"He's a nervy little sonofabitch, ain't he?" the sheriff said. "Y'all better teach him some Gawddamn sense or he'll never live 'tel he grown."

"Whut he wanna live 'tel he grown fer? Why should he wanna live a'tall down here," Mama bawled, moving closer toward the sheriff.

"You yellow bitch!" the sheriff stormed. "Don't you know you talkin' to white men?"

"I don' give a damn who you is! You let my Silas go!" Mama screamed.

With that the sheriff slapped her as hard as he could and she stumbled back and fell. Papa, whose hands were held behind his back by the handcuffs, snatched away from the two deputies and started toward Mama, but the shorter deputy struck him full in the face with his fist and drew his gun.

"I don' wanna have to kill you, nigger," he said, "but ef you make another move like that, I'm gon' let you have it, you black bastard."

I broke away from Grandma and ran and knelt down by Mama, who was stretched out on her side. I pressed my face against hers and felt her warm tears. "Don' cry, Mama, please don' cry," I begged.

"I oughta 'rest all you niggers," the sheriff said.

"Please, suh," Papa pleaded, "please don' 'rest my wife 'n' child 'n' my mother-in-law; us ain't done nothin'."

"Shut up, nigger, Gawddamit!" the sheriff roared. Then he ordered the deputies to put Papa in the car and he followed them out of the house.

In a moment, I heard the car doors slam and the motor start up. Mama and I got up off the floor and walked to the door where Grandma was already standing. The car was out at the gate leading into the lane. The taller of the two deputies got out of the car and opened the gate. Papa was sitting in the back seat with the short deputy; the sheriff was driving. The car turned up the lane in the early-morning light, heading toward the store and the houses where the white folks lived. Mama kept repeating, "Po' Silas, po' Silas," until the car was out of sight. Then she turned away from the door with fresh tears in her eyes.

"Don' cry, Mama," I said, but she paid me no mind and went and fell across her bed and sobbed with her back heaving and settling and quivering like a hurt bird.

I crawled into the bed beside her and put my arm around her as far as it would go. Grandma stood by the bed, patting Mama's back just above my arm.

"Silas ain't done nothin' 'n' they done took him to jail!" Mama moaned. "Ain't no tellin' whut gon' happen now, 'specially ef Silas lose his head."

"Ain't no tellin' whut mighta happen right here, ef the sheriff 'n' them two deputies hadn't snapped them handcuffs on him befo' he knowed it with his hands behin' his back," Grandma said.

"Yessum, it all happen so quick," Mama recalled through her tears. "Silas went to the do' to see who was knockin' so hard; us was sound sleep. 'N' when he open the do' they grabbed him 'n' put them handcuffs on him. They musta heard 'bout Silas, 'cause they ain't give him no chance."

"Well, you 'n' me both know Silas is a mean nigger, but he ain't no fool," Grandma said. "He knowed he couldn't do nothin' with them three white mens with his arms handcuffed behin' him."

"You right, Ma, so he sorta took low, but there ain't no tellin' whut might happen when they git him to Vicksburg, or eben 'long the way," Mama sobbed.

"Becky, don't you worry 'n' fret yo'self, baby," Grandma said. "The Lawd gon' take care o' Silas."

In my own anger and helplessness, Grandma's words brought me comfort. They gave me a vision of God as a giant standing so tall that he could have one foot on the plantation at the Bend and the other one in Vicksburg, the boss of everyone, including the sheriff.

"The church 'n' prayer 'n' the Lawd is all us po' niggers got," Grandma often said. And until that morning, I had thought she was just saying something to be saying it, pretending there was somebody to help when she really knew there was no one. But as I lay by Mama's side, feeling her back rise and fall as she sobbed in anguish, and as I recalled my father standing there with his arms handcuffed behind him and the deputy's pistol in his stomach, Grandma's words no longer seemed empty, but full of strength and power that reached all the way to heaven, where God was, and brought Him down to the plantation to help us. And I knew her words were going to reach the Lord and draw Him to the jail where Papa was, although I never found Him in the cornfield when I prayed to get religion.

Mama finally stopped crying and sat up on the side of the bed with her arms around me. "My little man," she said. "Ma, River is our little man while Silas is gone, ain't he?"

"Indeed, he is," Grandma replied strongly, running her fingers through my hair.

"I don' know where to turn, Ma," Mama said, looking in the ceiling as if to find the answer there. "I turned to Miz Rhoda, 'n' it ain't done no good. Things eben worser now than they was. Now somebody done kilt Mr. Win."

"You jes' turn to the Lawd," Grandma suggested.

"I'm doin' that, Ma; I'm prayin' hard as I can."

"Well, He gon' work things out," Grandma said with certainty. "Us knows Silas ain't done nothin' 'n' the Lawd knows Silas ain't done nothin' 'n' the Lawd gon' git him out, but I sho' hopes they beats his ass good while he in there to bring him down a notch 'n' curb his hot temper."

"That's whut I'm scared o', Ma," Mama replied. "I'm scared they gon' try to beat him 'n' he gon' hurt somebody 'n' be in some sho'nuff trouble."

"All us can do is trus' in the Lawd," Grandma offered.

"I trus' in the Lawd, Ma, but I gotta do somethin' mo'; I gotta talk with somebody 'n' git help fer Silas." Mama paused and then said, "I'm gon' talk with Ben 'n' Mary, 'cause they oughta know 'bout this trouble us in anyhow, 'n' maybe they can tell us whut to do. Maybe they can tell us mo' 'bout whut done happen to Mr. Win."

Mama washed her face and combed her hair and rolled it up into a ball behind her neck as she always wore it, put on a fresh dress and apron, and walked out of the house toward Mr. Ben's. "You stay with Ma 'n' be a good boy, River!" she hollered back as she started down the turnrow, holding her dress up out of the early-morning dew.

"Yessum, Mama," I replied.

About an hour later, Mama returned and sat down at the table where Grandma was drinking her coffee and I was drinking milk and sopping biscuits and molasses. "Ben 'n' Mary say they saw a car here at us house at daybreak 'n' wondered ef there was some trouble," Mama reported. "When I tol' 'em the sheriff done 'rested Silas 'n' 'cused him o' killin' Mr. Win, they cried mo 'n' I did. They cried fer Silas 'n' they cried fer po' Mr. Win. They didn't know he was dead 'tel I tol' 'em."

"Lawd, Ben 'n' Mary is sho'nuff friends," Grandma said.

"They is that," Mama added, "'n' they say i oughta go back up 'n' see Miz Rhoda' 'n' 'splain to her that Silas ain't left this house las' night 'n' couldn'ta killed Mr. Win."

"That's a good idea, Becky; is you goin' to see Miz Rhoda?" Grandma asked.

"Yessum, I guess so, Ma; I don' know whut else to do."

"Can I go with you, Mama?" I asked.

"You can go as fer as school," she answered.

"School? Is I gotta go to school today, Mama?"

"You sho' is."

"Becky, do you reckon you oughta send him to school today?" Grandma asked. "It's gon' be all over the plantation 'bout Mr. Win bein' killed 'n' Silas 'rested 'n' the teacher 'n' the chillun gon' be lookin' at him 'n' ast'n' him all sorta questions. Reckon he oughta go to school 'n' face all this by his-self?"

"I reckon you right, Ma; I hadn't thought o' that."

Then Mama hitched up the wagon and drove across the plantation over to the other arm of the lane. I stood in the road leading behind our house and watched the wagon turn past Mr. Riley Jones and head toward Mr. Hamp's. Although I could see it no longer, I kept looking in that direction as if somehow my vision would follow the wagon. Finally, I began picking up clods and throwing at birds. When I was tired of this, I walked down to our cornfield and sat down on the ground. The sun was a quarter way up the skies and the dew had dried. The corn was turning brown and the leaves moved stiffly in the breeze.

Although repeated plowing and chopping had kept the weeds and grass down in the corn as well as in that part of our cotton where the weed killer had not been applied, there stood a fat jimson weed and two dandelions near my left foot. The yellow flowers of the dandelions had turned to snowy balls as light as feathers. I tried to pull one of the plants up, but it broke off at the ground, leaving only the stem and the crushed cotton-like ball and a few jagged leaves in my hand, while the root held firm in the ground. But I persisted, digging into the soft earth with my fingers until I was able to catch hold of the root and pull it up. The light brown root was long and tapered like the tail of a rat, but from it grew dozens of tiny shoots. When I laid the root beside the stem of the dandelion, it was just as long if not a little longer than the stem, indicating how well the plant was equipped to survive. And yet the weed killer that had been put down on part of our cotton killed these and other plants even before they could begin to grow.

I think I somehow realized then that only useful things would be permitted to grow on the plantation or perhaps any place else. And as Papa had often said, when weed killers and mechanical cotton pickers made sharecroppers like himself useless on the plantation, there would be no place for them there anymore, and they would have to move, perhaps finally to town when all the plantations had the stuff to kill weeds in their cotton and machines to pick the fiber.

Somehow this made me think of Naomi in Vicksburg, and I was less hopeful now that she would ever return. *Maybe,* I thought, *me 'n' Papa 'n' Mama 'n' Grandma will move there.* But my mind paused and started back over the list, stopping at "Papa." Then crowded in all the thoughts of his arrest, the mean sheriff and his deputies; how Mama was slapped and Papa struck in the face and held at gunpoint. My eyes filled with tears and I jumped up and ran back to the house where Grandma was.

When Mama returned from Mrs. Rhoda's, some of the grimness had gone out of her face. Once in a while as she related what had happened, a tiny smile wrinkled the corners of her mouth. She said that when she had explained to Mrs. Rhoda that Papa had been at home all night and hadn't seen Mr. Win since before he went to Memphis, Mrs. Rhoda's attitude changed.

"At firs' her treated me like dirt," Mama said. "Her voice was col' 'n' mean. Ast me, 'Whut you want now? Yo' husband done killed Mr. Win, ain't that 'nuff?' That's whut her said befo' I could hardly open my mouth," Mama explained.

"Her so nice, I didn't b'lieve her could ever be mean, but with somebody done killed Mr. Win, I guess her excited, 'specially when her think her talkin' to the wife o' the one whut done it," Grandma said.

"You right, Ma. I can't rightly fault her fer the way her talked to me at firs'," Mama agreed. "Then when I tol' her Silas ain't had no reason to kill Mr. Win, 'cause he ain't blame him fer Naomi, 'n' he done paid Mr. Win back the twenty dollars he spent on Naomi, gittin' her to Vicksburg 'n' all, Miz Rhoda said her 'membered I done tol' her that befo'," Mama added.

"Whut else her say?" Grandma asked.

"Her ast ef Silas didn't kill him, who did?"

"Whut you tell her?"

"I tol' her I don' no'am."

"Reckon who did kill him?" Grandma asked.

"I ain't got no idea, Ma."

"Well, one thing fer sho'," Grandma said, "he was kilt 'bout some woman."

"'N' the only gal he was goin' with is that gal next do'," Mama said, "'cause he didn't b'lieve in goin' with but one gal at a time; evvybody say that."

"But Lilly Mae couldn'ta killed him, 'cause they ain't got no kinda gun in that house; the preacher don' b'lieve in guns," Grandma said.

"You don' reckon the preacher borrowed a gun 'n' killed him, do you, Mama?" I asked.

"Hush yo' mouth, boy," Grandma ordered. "Reverend Fisher wouldn't hurt a fly."

"You know somethin', Ma," Mama said, "although Mr. Win didn't b'lieve in havin' but one gal at a time on the plantation, he may have been tryin' to put Lilly Mae down like River said Willie tol' him, 'n' maybe Mr. Win did have another gal."

"Like you say, he could, Becky," Grandma agreed, "but I can't think o' no gal on the place whut's mean 'nuff or crazy 'nuff to kill Mr. Win, 'cep'n that gal next do', 'n' I don' b'lieve her done it."

"I don' think so neither," Mama added. "'N' 'mongst the mens, Silas 'n' Hamp Davis 'bout the only ones hotheaded 'nuff to kill a white man, 'n' us knows Silas didn't do it, 'n' Hamp ain't had no reason to do it."

"Naw, Hamp ain't done it," Grandma agreed.

"You know, Ma," Mama said, "it coulda been a white man off'n one o' these other plantations 'round here whut did it. They coulda got in a fight 'bout some gal another."

"You right," Grandma said. "'Member that time 'bout ten years ago when a white man killed another one up in Humphreys County 'bout some nigger gal?"

"Yessum, I 'member," Mama replied. "That's how come I said whut I did."

"Did Miz Rhoda think a white man coulda done it?" Grandma wanted to know.

"Ef her did her ain't mentioned it," Mama replied. "You know how white folks is; they ain't gon' 'cuse one o' they own, long as a nigger's 'round."

"Do her still think Silas done it?"

"I don' no'am," Mama answered, "but her say her 'n' Mr. Walter gon' git to the bottom o' this, 'n' fer me not to worry, 'cause ef Silas didn't do it, he ain't gon' be kept in jail fer it."

"Well, us know Silas ain't done it 'cause he been right here in this house all night 'tel the sheriff come here 'n' got him," Grandma said firmly, patting her foot slowly and drawing on her pipe.

"Us sho' know he ain't done it, Ma."

"Where was Mr. Win kilt at anyhow? Did Miz Rhoda say?"

"Yessum, she say he was kilt over by the levee jes' below us house here. Her say he was found by Miz Susie 'n' her chillun, little Mr. Win 'n' Miss Millie. Miz Rhoda say after Mr. Win didn't come home 'round midnight, Miz Susie 'n' her chillun went to look fer him. They drove almos' to Vicksburg, hopin' to meet him on the road comin' back from seein' Naomi, like the note said."

"You mean that gal tol' Miz Susie in that note that Mr. Win was goin' to see Naomi in Vicksburg?" Grandma asked.

"Her sho' did; tol' a lie like that."

"Have mercy, Jesus," Grandma said, raising her hands high in the air and bringing them down against her knees with a loud sound. "Did they go all the way to Vicksburg 'n' look fer Naomi?"

"No'am, they didn't know where Naomi live at, so it wasn't no use goin' all the way in. They was hopin' to meet him on the road; that woulda been proof 'nuff fer 'em," Mama said.

"After they didn't meet him, they come back 'n' looked 'round the plantation, hanh?" Grandma asked.

"Yessum, that's whut Miz Rhoda say they done. Her say they found him layin' by his car over by the levee in that little clump o' trees over there."

"Was he dead, Becky?"

"Yessum, Miz Rhoda say they put him in they car 'n' drove him to the hospital in Vicksburg, but he was dead."

"Po' thing 'n' he was a good man," Grandma said in a mournful voice. "Ran 'round after nigger gals, but he was good to 'em; furnished 'em credit at the sto' 'n' all."

"Yessum, he was good-hearted. Look how he looked after Naomi; sent her to Vicksburg 'n' got her a place to stay after Silas acted a fool 'n' wanted to beat her," Mama recalled.

"He sho' did, po' thing," Grandma agreed.

"Was he shot, Mama?" I ventured to ask.

"Yes, River; Miz Rhoda say he was shot in the chest. Her say his car do' was open 'n' his cowhyde whip was laying by him on the ground."

"Musta been tryin' to whup somebody," I said.

"I guess so," Mama replied slowly, thoughtfully. "You know, Ma, that whup on the ground oughta prove Silas didn't do it, 'cause evvybody on the plantation, including the white folks know don' nobody whup Silas, less'n he handcuffed like he was when that little ole deputy hit him."

"Yes, ain't nobody gon' try to whup him with no whup; that ole crazy black fool will sho' stand' up fer hisself," Grandma said.

"Don' call Silas no crazy black fool, Ma, 'n' he down yonder in Vicksburg in jail," Mama ordered.

"I ain't meant no harm, Becky."

"When us goin' to see Papa, Mama?" I asked.

"Don' know, River. Miz Rhoda say can't nobody see him 'cep'n Mr. Walter 'n' his lawyer."

"Wonder ef Naomi know 'bout it," Grandma said in a whisper as if my sister was listening.

"I guess not," Mama replied, "less'n Willie tell her when he go to town to take the mail, but I sho' hope he don't, 'cause ain't no use bothering her with her baby due in 'bout a month."

"That gal sho' a heap o' trouble, jes' cause her want a white baby," Grandma remarked more to herself than to Mama or me as she sat back in her chair.

"'N' mostly 'cause o' you, Ma, with all yo' talk 'bout bein' black 'n' jes' the spittin' image o' ole black Silas," Mama said heatedly, fighting back tears as she rose and walked toward the kitchen.

"Well, I was so disapp'inted when Naomi come here so black, but I didn't mean no harm talkin' 'bout it," Grandma said sorrowfully.

"You may nota meant no harm, Ma, but you see whut done happen," Mama hollered back from the kitchen. Unable to hold back her tears any longer, she sat down at the kitchen table and sobbed. Between sobs, she cried out accusingly, "You 'n' yo' talk 'bout black day after day, 'n' buyin' bleach cream with evvy nickle you could lay yo' hands on, 'n' rubbin' that chile like you could rub the black off."

I stood by the table and tried to help Mama dry her eyes on a corner of her apron.

"Mama's big man," she said, reaching out with one hand and folding me in her arm.

Grandma joined us in the kitchen. "I'm sorry, Becky," she said, patting Mama's shoulders, "but I couldn't he'p it; I always been shame o' bein' black; that's how come I fought it so hard. I'm is sorry, Becky, baby."

"That's all right, Ma, I know how it is, Ma," Mama said, still sobbing.

"You can't never know how it is, Becky, 'cause you ain't never been black with short kinky hair," Grandma said, taking the chair by Mama's side and placing a tired old hand on Mama's soft long hair as if by touching it she could transform her own into silky locks. Then she, too, began to cry, not quietly like Mama, but in a loud, deep wail, as if her sorrow came up from a well inside her a mile deep. "Lawd, Lawd, have mercy, Jesus," she said over and over, and I found myself crying again.

XIV

Deceased Owner's Envious Suitor's Note to Owner's Spouse

When we had had our cry, Mama got up and began cookin' supper. I brought in the chips to start the fire and then I went for the cow and put a few ears of corn on the ground for her. In the barn, I put corn in the trough for the mules and pumped water for them outside. Grandma watched the pots and churned while Mama milked.

Mama got back to her visit with Mrs. Rhoda while I was holding the cloth strainer for her to pour the milk from the bucket through it into a crock.

"Miz Rhoda ast me again ef I knowed who sent that note to Miz Susie," Mama began calmly, but with a question, it seemed, in the back of her mind, as if she was puzzled about what the white woman was thinking.

"Whut you tell her?" Grandma asked.

"I tol' her like I tol' her befo'," Mama replied. "I tol' her I jes' heard that somebody had left a note in Miz Susie's do' tellin' her 'bout Mr. Win done sent Naomi to Vicksburg to have a baby fer him."

"Whut her say then, Becky?"

"Her ast me who I heard it from, 'n' I tried to think o' somebody else to say, but I couldn't think o' nobody, 'cause I hadn't 'spected her to wanta know 'zackly who tol' me. So I had to tell her River done heard it from some chillun at church," Mama said, having delayed telling us all this time because she hated to admit she had involved me.

"You tol' her River done tol' you, Becky?"

"Yessum, 'n' now her wanna talk with him; tol' me to bring him up there firs' thing in the mornin'," Mama replied shyly, apologetically.

"I'm goin' to the white folks' house, Mama?" I asked excitedly because I had never been there. I had passed the two large white houses with their red chimneys and their large posts on the front porch many times, but I had never been inside one of them, not even the yard. And I had wondered how they looked inside, if they had Bible pictures pasted on the walls like those at our house, including the torn one I had won at Sunday school. And if they had any, I wondered where they got them because they didn't have a church on the plantation, and I had never heard of them going to church. Then as I thought of facing the white lady and talking with her, I became afraid. "Do I have to go, Mama?"

"Yes, River, in the mornin' I'm gon' take you up to talk to Miz Rhoda."

"I'm scared, Mama," I said, letting the cloth slip a little and some of the unstrained milk get in with the other.

"Oh, River, look whut you did," Mama complained.

"I'm sorry, Mama. I didn't go to do it."

"I know," she said as we strained the milk again into another crock.

"Mama, I don' have to go up to Miz Rhoda's, do I?"

"Course, you gotta go."

"Don' be scared, boy," Grandma spoke up. "White folks ain't nothin' but folks."

"Miz Rhoda is a nice lady," Mama added.

"Yessum, but I'm scared."

"Miz Rhoda ain't gon' bite you, boy," Grandma assured me.

"Yessum. Whut her wanna see me fer?" I asked.

"Her wanna ast you who tol' you somebody done sent a note 'bout yo' sister, Naomi, to Miz Susie," Mama explained.

"Willie done tol' me Lilly Mae done sent him with a note to put in Miz Susie's do'," I said confidently. "Didn't you know that, Mama? I done tol' you 'n' Papa 'n' Grandma Sunday right after the basket meetin'."

"Yes, I knowed," Mama replied, "but I didn't wanna tell Miz Rhoda that."

"How come, Mama?"

"'Cause niggers don' tattle to white folks on one 'nother."

"I ain't gon' tattle, Mama. I'm jes' gon' tell Miz Rhoda whut Willie done tol' me."

"Well, that's tattlin'," Mama said. "Tell her you don' 'member."

"But I 'member, Mama."

"I knows that, but you jes' tell her you don' 'member."

"Or, Becky," Grandma spoke up, "he can tell her three fo' diff'ent boys, jes' don' say 'zackly."

"That's right, Ma; he can tell her it was General Lee 'n' Silvester 'n' Willie 'n' Roosevelt. You can say you heard 'em talkin'. That way you won't be tattlin'."

"River, jes' tell her you heard 'em talkin'," Grandma said, reinforcing Mama's words. "'N' 'member," she added, "niggers don' go tattling to white folks on other niggers, you hear?"

The next morning, when the mules and hogs and chickens had been fed and watered and ole Beulah milked while nibbling on ears of corn, I sopped molasses with four or five hot biscuits. Then Mama bathed me in the washtub, greased my hair with some of her hair grease, wiped my face with the dishrag so it wouldn't be dry, and put out my Sunday suit and shoes for me to wear up to Mrs. Rhoda's with a lie in my mouth.

All the way in the wagon, Mama kept reminding me to say I heard about the note at church last Sunday from Roosevelt Harris, General Lee, Silvester Robinson, and Willie Fisher. She shifted Willie's name in the order several times, but it never came first. Finally, she settled on making it last, and she repeated the list over and over. "Now this all you know," she said. "You don' know nothin' 'bout who sent the note or nothin'. Jes' say you heard the boys say that somebody done sent a note to Miz Susie's, do you hear?"

Mama took the back road again so we wouldn't have to pass the store where some meddling white men might be sitting. Along the way everybody waved, and Mr. and Mrs. Riley Jones came out to the wagon to say how sorry they were that Silas was in jail, but they said everything would turn out all right. Mr. Hamp Davis, the Sunday school superintendent, also stopped our wagon and expressed his sympathy. He said Mrs. Davis didn't come out with him because she was ailing. Mama said she would come by to see her soon. As we passed the church where school was held, Lucy Lee and Viola Jones were running to the privy.

Up the road from the school stood Mrs. Rhoda's house. Mama pulled ole Salt and Miss Lady into the lane that led back of the barn and tool shed, where a few red and a lot of green tractors were parked. Then we came to the pecan grove that hid the barn and tool shed from Wilmyra. Mama drove into the grove and hitched the mules to a post. As we walked through the backyard, I noticed the chickens had a special yard all their own that held them in so that they couldn't roam all over the whole yard as they did ours, messing everywhere, even on our porch.

Mr. Tobe David's son, Frank, was mowing the large green lawn with a tractor-drawn mower. He seemed to enjoy mowing around the trees and shrubs, swinging his mower around them in tight circles. I think he was pretending not to see us because he didn't wave back when Mama and I waved at him, although he was only a short distance away. And his mother, Mrs. Ida, was slow about answering Mama's knock. Finally she came to the door of the back screened porch and unhooked the door after Mama had knocked several times. Maybe she didn't hear the knocks because Mama knocked gently, timidly as if she wasn't suppose to knock on white folks' doors, even the back doors, and was a little afraid. But from the way the cook acted, I think she heard the knocking all the time.

"Whut you want now? Done come to 'fess up that you stole Miss Millie's girdle that was hangin' on the line?" Mrs. Ida asked, holding the hook of the screen and standing in the middle of the doorway as if to block our entrance with her body. I wondered how a woman could be so mean whose husband made such good ice cream and smiled so friendly from his truck.

"Us ain't stole no girdle," Mama said, but her voice lacked the force of innocence because she did know who had taken the garment.

"You can deny it all you wanna, but Mr. Walter gon' find out," Mrs. Ida warned, 'cause he on the lookout for the thief to nail him down fer sho' 'n' find out who done killed his brother, po' Mr. Win. Course, you might as well know, I think they got the one."

"I don' car whut you say, Ida; I knows 'n' Gawd knows Silas ain't kilt nobody," Mama said strongly.

"Well, one thing fer sho', Mr. Win is dead 'n' he ain't kilt hisself," Mrs. Ida came back.

"I didn't come here to argue with you, Ida; I come to see Miz Rhoda."

"Us ain't got no time to see you 'cause us all is busy. You know po' Mr. Win's fune'al is tomorr'," Miz Ida insisted.

"I ain't come to see no us," Mama said impatiently. "I come to see Miz Rhoda; her done ast me to come 'n' bring River, 'cause her wanna talk to him."

"I sho' don' know whut Miz Rhoda done that fer, 'cause her busy 'n' I'm is busy," Mrs. Ida replied, still blocking the door.

"Well, her sho' done tol' me to come."

"I think y'all better come back 'nother time after Mr. Win's fune'al," Mrs. Ida concluded, closing the screen door and rehooking it.

Then a calm and gentle voice from inside the kitchen asked, "Who is that, Ida?"

"It's these folks whut done kilt po' Mr. Win, Miz Rhoda," Mrs. Ida replied.

"Oh?" Mrs. Rhoda said, and then there was a long pause while she walked toward the door, where the cook was standing.

She moved a few inches aside as Mrs. Rhoda approached. "It's that Silas Henry's folks, Miz Rhoda," she said coldly.

"Open the door, Ida, and let them in," Mrs. Rhoda said. "I asked Becky to come back this morning and bring her little boy along; I want to talk with him. Come right in," she added as the door swung open.

"Thanky, ma'am," Mama said with a cramped smile of appreciation on her face.

"Let's go out on the side porch, where it's cooler," Mrs. Rhoda said, leading the way through her kitchen with a gleaming white stove, a large white refrigerator, and rows and rows of cabinets everywhere.

While I was still looking back, admiring the shiny white kitchen, my feet sank into carpet so soft I came near falling. I was in the dining room, where there were a large oval table, cushioned chairs with high backs, a broad buffet, and a china closet in which stood sparkling dishes with angels painted on them.

Through a door off the dining room, I saw shelves of books that reached from the floor to the ceiling. I never knew there were so many books before. In our house, there were only the Bible, my first reader, Naomi's arithmetic, and two or three other books. These were all. In Mrs. Rhoda's house, there must have been several thousand books. Mrs. Rhoda led us across her wide hallway, the carpet never stopping. There were a table and more soft chairs. On the walls were Bible pictures with angels like some of those on our walls, but ours were pasted on like wallpaper. These were in beautiful frames.

From the hallway, we went through the living room with two long red sofas and four or five over-stuffed chairs that looked as soft as ginned cotton. At one end of the room sat a huge television set, and before the fireplace was a brass screen out of which projected polished and irons that looked too pretty to place firewood on. Over the mantlepiece hung a tall picture of a soldier with a sword in his hand. I froze in my tracks on the soft carpet, gazing at the handsome soldier with mustache and side-burns and eyes so blue and real under the visor of his gray hat that for a moment I thought he was looking at me and wondering what I was doing in this house.

"Come on, River," I seem to have heard Mama saying, but I did not move.

Then I felt soft hands gently resting on my shoulders.

"That's Mr. Walter's great-grandfather, Captain Winfield Scott Williamson, who fought at Shiloh and Vicksburg and Chickamauga," Mrs. Rhoda said, not with bursting pride, but in a kind of neutral voice that was merely conveying information.

I wondered what he was fighting about and where these strange places were. Of course, I knew where Vicksburg was, but I had never heard of Shiloh and Chickamauga. I did not ask Mrs. Rhoda, however, as she led me out of the room and onto the porch, where Mama and I sat together on a pretty couch that moved back and forth like a swing.

Mrs. Rhoda stood by me for a moment with her hand on my head. "Becky, you have a cute little boy," she said. "You call him River?"

"Yessum," Mama replied. "That's his name."

"It's an unusual name," Mrs. Rhoda said. "How did you come to name him that?"

"Us named him River 'cause he was born one night as us was crossin' the Sunflower River," Mama said. "Us thought it might be a sign o' good luck fer the baby to come while us was on the bridge."

"It's an unusual name, but it's a pretty name," Mrs. Rhoda said, patting me on my head and then taking a seat in a large soft chair right in front of us. "Becky, have you told him why I want to talk with him?" she asked.

"Yessum, Miz Rhoda. I done tol' him you wanna talk to him 'bout who said somebody done sent a note to Miz Susie's," Mama replied, putting an arm around my waist and letting her hand rest on my leg. I was glad she did because it made me feel safer, although somehow I was not really afraid of Mrs. Rhoda even though she was the first white person I had ever seen close up, except Mr. Win when he was in our cornfield with Lilly Mae and that time in the store when I gave him the note from Naomi.

"Your mother said someone told you that a note about your sister had been sent to Mrs. Susie," Mr. Rhoda said, leaning forward and looking me straight in the eye with eyes as blue as the sky, "and I want to know," she continued, "who told you this?"

"Some boys, some boys at church," I said in a high scared voice that grew its newfound fear, I think, from the sharp contrast between the house we lived in and this beautiful home that made me think I had died and gone to heaven.

"Some boys?" Mrs. Rhoda repeated. "What boys? What are their names?"

"Willie," I started off, although Mama had trained me to put his name last, and I felt her arm around my waist jump a little, or maybe it was more of a quiver or a tremble like a trapped rabbit you are holding. "'N' General Lee 'n' Silvester 'n' Roosevelt," I added slowly with my eyes on my hands, which were locked in my lap. I felt scared now in a desperate kind of way because I was lying. I wanted to look up to see what Mrs. Rhoda's eyes were saying—whether they still smiled in kindness or were dim and doubtful—but I was afraid to, afraid that my own eyes would give me away. Yet I felt that I owed Mrs. Rhoda something more, something honest, and I was about to tell her that Willie was wearing Miss Millie's underthings when she cut me off.

"What were the boys saying, River?" Mrs. Rhoda asked. "Try to remember exactly what they were saying about the note. Did they mention who sent it?"

My head felt hot and my tongue was dry, and all my fear settled in my eyes, pumping out tears that ran down my face. "I don' no'am," I said almost in a whisper. I had been reinforced by a vision of Grandma standing by our wagon before we drove off, saying over and over, "River, now 'member, niggers don' tattle to white folks on one 'nother." But I was torn between this unwritten code and a desire to be honest with Mrs. Rhoda, who didn't seem to me exactly like white folks, especially the white folks Mama and Papa talked about.

"Now, River, don't be afraid; I'm trying to help your papa," Mrs. Rhoda said. "Try hard to remember more of whut the boys said at church."

My mouth was open, my eyes had become unglued from my hands, and I was looking at Mrs. Rhoda again. I was ready to tell her the truth, not only because it was the truth, but because I wanted to please her, to see the smile in her eyes again, to renew her kindness, to feel her hand on my head. I might have been anxious to tell her the truth, too, to help Papa, but I don't think so. To us, Papa was only temporarily in jail and would soon be out because we knew he had not killed Mr. Win. Of course, we knew nothing about the intricacies of the law and circumstantial evidence.

But before I could blert out all I knew, I heard a door slam and a heavy voice calling, "Rhoda!"

"We are out on the side porch, Walter!" Mrs. Rhoda said, rising and walking toward the living room door.

Mr. Walter, big and tall with graying hair, appeared. Before he said a word, he caught Mrs. Rhoda's face in both his hands, as if one hand could not hold her mouth in place, and kissed her.

Then looking toward us, he said, "I see, Becky 'n' her boy come up to see you. Howdy, Becky; howdy, boy."

"Mornin', Mr. Walter," Mama and I said almost in unison as we stood up in the presence of the plantation owner. But I am sure my quiet words were nearly drowned out by Mama's voice, loud and clear and thankful that I had been interrupted by Mr. Walter's appearance.

"I don't know if the boy has told you," he said, "but I think we've solved at least part of this thing."

"You have, Walter?" Mrs. Rhoda replied. "I'm glad."

"Yes, we just caught a boy in the store wearing one of Millie's girdles." Mama gripped my hand tightly as if the words had pulled on a muscle in her arm.

"A boy wearing one of Millie's girdles, did you say, Walter?" Mrs. Rhoda asked. "Whatever would he want to do that for?"

"I don't know," Mr. Walter replied. "It's the damnedest thing I ever heard of."

"I, too," she said. "I heard of college kids conducting their spring panty raids, but I don't recall having read anywhere that they took girdles or that they went so far as to wear them."

"Well, this boy, General Lee, they call him, was certainly wearing Millie's. You know, he's one of Tom 'n' Luiza's children."

"Yes, the name always struck me," Mrs. Rhoda said, "and he has a bad speech impediment."

"He's the boy, 'n' he's goosy, too. That's how Lige discovered he was wearing Millie's girdle," Mr. Walter explained.

"Well," said Mrs. Rhoda, rising again and moving closer to Mr. Walter.

"This boy," Mr. Walter continued, "came to the store a while ago with a note from Tom for a sack o' flour 'n' a plug o' tobacco. I approved it 'n' when Lige was placing the flour on the boy's shoulder, he fluttered his fingers under the boy's arm and made a couple of *spooo-spooo* sounds. The boy jumped 'n' screamed 'n' fell on the floor, wriggling like a worm. During his agitation, his shirt came up 'n' his pants slipped down some, 'n' there he lay in a pink girdle that was almost black with dirt. If we hadn't been lookin' for Millie's girdle, which Paralee said someone stole off the line, we'd never have noticed it," Mr. Walter explained with a look between puzzlement and disgust on his face.

"I thought a girl had taken it," Mrs. Rhoda said, "and I was planning to drive around a bit and observe the wash folks have on their lines. I don't imagine many of the women on the place wear girdles."

"No'am, they don't," Mama added. "I'd say almos' none o' 'em."

"Well, you won't have to do that now," Mr. Walter said, moving back to the door as if ready to leave.

"Walter, you don't think the boy killed Win, do you?" Mrs. Rhoda asked.

"I don' know," Mr. Walter replied. "When Lige kicked the boy 'n' asked him where he got Millie's girdle, he stammered out something about Willie Fisher, the preacher's boy. So I called Jack Warrenton, the sheriff, 'n' he's on his way; he's gon' track it down."

"River, here, said Willie and General Lee and some other boys were talking about someone having sent that note to Susie," Mrs. Rhoda pointed out to Mr. Walter.

"Well, River was sure right," Mr. Walter replied, walking toward me. "Yo' name River?" he asked, bending down a little.

"Yessuh," I said.

"I think I recall Silas tellin' me his boy was named River. It's a good name, especially for a boy on our place right here by the ole Mississippi." Then he ran his fingers through my hair and patted my shoulder. I felt proud and I wasn't afraid anymore.

Turning to Mrs. Rhoda, Mr. Walter said, "I gotta get back to the store to be there when the sheriff comes. I don't want any rough stuff; I just want the sheriff to find the guilty person 'n' 'rest him. I'll be back soon as he comes to take you 'n' Susie to Vicksburg to finish the arrangements for Win's funeral."

"All right, Walter. I'll be ready," Mrs. Rhoda replied, walking with him as he left the porch.

Mama and I sat there quietly. I was thinking about the ole sheriff and what he was going to do to General Lee and Willie and others as he and his ole mean deputies swept over the plantation looking for the one who killed Mr. Win, no matter what Mr. Walter told them not to do. But slowly it was occurring to me that the sheriff was going to find the guilty one and let Papa out of jail. This brought me a good feeling.

When Mrs. Rhoda came back out on the porch, she said, "Becky, you and River can go now; I don't think we'll need you anymore, and I hope your husband will soon be freed. Thank you for coming."

"Thanky, ma'am," Mama replied, taking me by the hand and leading me behind Mrs. Rhoda, who preceded us.

I followed reluctantly, wanting to stand and look at the pictures and the beautiful furniture and walk and rewalk over the soft carpet.

In the kitchen, Mrs. Ida was a changed woman. With a broad smile, she handed me a chocolate-covered cookie. "This is fer you, River," she said, adding, "Ain't he cute? Got good hair, too."

I was so surprised and frightened that I did not say anything.

"Ain't you gon' thank Miz Ida after her done give you a cookie?"

"Thanky, ma'am," I said quickly, wondering why Mrs. Ida had changed so suddenly.

"Ida, isn't he a nice little boy?" Mrs. Rhoda asked.

"Yessum, he sho' is, he sho' is," Mrs. Ida said, "'n' Becky 'n' Silas is nice, too, Miz Rhoda."

"Becky, thank you again for coming, and thank you, too, River," Mrs. Rhoda said.

"Thanky, ma'am!" Mama and I hollered back as we walked down the steps and out toward our wagon.

Frank, who had stopped his tractor and was doing something to the mower, waved and yelled, "How y'all?"

Mama did not wave back; she merely said, "Good mornin'," in a cold kind of way, barely looking in his direction. And as if anticipating my own wave and greeting to Frank, she gave my hand a quick jerk. "Two-faced niggers," she said almost under her breath. "Frank 'n' his mama so friendly all of a sudden. Mr. Walter musta tol' 'em 'bout Gene'al Lee 'n' Willie. Niggers make me sick."

As we drove toward home, Mama said she felt sorry for Tom and Luiza and that boy, General Lee, because she felt sure the ole sheriff and his deputies were going to manhandle them. "No tellin' whut they'll do to that boy fer wearin' Miss Millie's girdle. I guess us shoulda got word to'em 'bout that boy bein' mixed up with Willie Fisher, but us had 'nuff troubles o' us own."

"Is they gon' let Papa outa jail, Mama?" I asked.

"Yes, soon as they finds out who kilt Mr. Win. Course, all the sheriff's gon' find out from them boys is that Lilly Mae done sent that note to Miz Susie, 'n' us know that already, but don' nobody know who done kilt him. I still say it was some white man fightin' with Mr. Win over some o' these gals."

We returned by the same route we took to Mrs. Rhoda's, waving again as we drove along, but this time there was life in our wave and a smile on our faces. Papa was going to be free.

After we passed Mr. Riley Jones' cornfield and before we got to ours, we could see Reverend Fisher's house. There was a car there.

"Lawd, I b'lieve that's the sheriff's car," Mama said with a groan and whipped the mules with the lines to hurry them along.

As we rounded our house and headed toward the lot, the ole sheriff and his deputies were dragging Lilly Mae out of her house. She was screaming and kicking and pulling back, but they put her in the car, where we found out later Willie and General Lee were already seated. Then they slammed the door and drove off.

Reverend Fisher and his four remaining children stood on their porch crying. Mama drove into the lot and left the mules still hitched to the wagon while we rushed over to find out why the sheriff had arrested Lilly Mae. We rushed, but not too fast, because Mama said she wanted to give the sheriff plenty time to be well up the lane before we got there.

As we walked into the yard, Reverend Fisher came down the steps to meet us. Tears were in his eyes and blood was running down one side of his face. "Oh, Sister Henry," he said, "the sheriff done 'rested Lilly Mae 'n' Willie 'n' one of the deputies struck me with his gun when I tol' him to take his hands off Daisy Lee."

"I'm so sorry," Mama said. "Was he gon' 'rest her, too?"

"No'am, he wasn't gon' 'rest her. You know, Daisy lee gittin' to be a big girl; she almos' leben, 'n' that ole deputy wanted to feel all over her. 'N' when I tol' him to take his hands off my chile, he called me the dirties names you ever heard 'n' struck me with his pistol."

"It's a shame the way some o' these white folks treats us," Mama moaned. Then walking closer to Reverend Fisher, she told him, "This a bad place on yo' head, Reverend. River, run home 'n' tell Ma to send a piece o' old sheet or a couple o' pillowcases 'n' the jug o' turpentine so I can fix Reverend's head."

I ran swiftly through the cotton patch and returned with the things Mama sent me for. Grandma was following on her stick. She took part of the torn piece of sheet and dried Reverend Fisher's face and head after she had washed his head under the pump. Then she dabbed the cut place with turpentine and bandaged it while he sat on the steps.

"Thank you kindly, Sister Henry," the preacher said as Mama helped him up off the steps and into the house. There the cotton from the tick was strewn everywhere. "The sheriff 'n' those deputies did this," he said. "They was lookin' fer the gun."

"Thssst, thssst, thssst," Grandma lamented. "Now you set down, Reverend, while me 'n' Becky git things straight."

The other children and I helped pick up the cotton and refill the tick so that Reverend Fisher would have some place to lie.

"They searched evvywhere 'tel they found it," he said, "after the sheriff had called Lilly Mae a jealous wench who had kilt Mr. Win in a fit of jealousy, 'n' she hollered, 'Naw, it was a accident.'"

"It was a accident?" Mama probed gently.

"Yessum, Sister Henry. Lilly Mae said she accidently shot Mr. Win while they was tusslin' over the pistol after he done tried to whup her," Reverend said, stretching out with a slight groan on a quilt Mama and Grandma had spread over the tick.

"Mr. Win done tried to whup Lilly Mae fer writin' that note to Miz Susie, ain't he?" Mama asked straightforwardly, indicating it was all becoming clear to her now.

"Yessum, that's whut Lilly Mae tol' the sheriff," Reverend replied. "She say Mr. Win come down the lane that night 'n' parked in front o' our house 'n' blinked his lights as usual, and she run out 'n' got in the car with him. Us musta been sleep. Anyhow, she say he was real drunk 'n' come near runnin' in a ditch on the way over there by the levee, where he stopped the car 'n' tried to whup her fer writin' that note to his wife. 'N' when she grabbed the whup 'n' snatched it outa his hand, he turned to his car 'n' got his pistol outa the glove 'partment. She say while they was tusslin' over it, it went off 'n' kilt Mr. Win. Lawd, Gawd, 'Our children shall bring damnation upon our heads,'" he quoted from the Bible.

"Po' Lilly Mae," Mama moaned.

"Yes, that po' chile," Grandma added.

"I'm sho' glad it was a accident," Mama said.

"Yes, Sister Henry, I know it was a accident, 'cause I b'lieve whut Lilly Mae said."

"I do, too, Reverend," Mama said softly, "'n' a accident is diff'ent from murder, a whole lot diff'ent."

"It sho' is," Grandma agreed.

"'N' you don' have a heap to worry 'bout, Reverend," Mama added.

"No'am, 'cause my daughter sho' ain't no murderer 'n' Gawd know that 'n' evvything is in His hands, 'n' he ain't gon' permit his own to suffer."

"That's right, Reverend," Grandma said. "That's right."

"But it hurt my heart," Reverend Fisher said, "to know that my own daughter, my own flesh 'n' blood been havin' relations with Mr. Win or any other man outa wedlock."

"But us can't be 'pletely 'sponsible fer us chillun nomo'," Mama said. "They headstrong 'n' can't nobody do nothin' with 'em sometimes."

"Yessum, sister, but they still our 'sponsibility. The Lawd placed the 'sponsibility in our hands," he replied with fresh tears settling in his eyes.

I had been looking around the room while we picked up the cotton and while Mama and the preacher were talking. It was the first time I had ever been inside Willie's house. The walls were bare. Not even newspapers or Bible pictures were pasted there. And there was no dresser or wardrobe or washstand. In the kitchen stood a bare table and a small stove standing on two legs and two stacks of bricks. The wretchedness of the house might not have struck me so forcibly, had I not just returned from Wilmyra, where Mrs. Rhoda and Mr. Walter lived. The soft carpet and beautiful furniture and framed pictures and painted dishes were still in my mind.

When I got back to our house a little later to pick up chips and make a fire for Mama to cook something for the preacher and his children, I was glad I had gone inside Willie's house after my visit to the white folks' house. This reduced somewhat my full awareness of the drabness of our home.

XV

Silas's Jail Release and the Helplessness of Black Sharecroppers

The next day, Papa came home with Mr. Willie and so did Willie Fisher and General Lee. The sheriff had whipped the boys with his belt and kept them in jail overnight. Dried tears were still on their faces and fear seemed to have been driven into them like one drives a stake into the ground to mark the boundary of his land.

Mr. Willie, who still left his mouth hanging open when he talked, said he had wanted to go to Mr. Win's funeral at the funeral home there in Vicksburg but had decided not to because he was afraid that the presence of a colored person might upset Mrs. Susie. So he went directly to the jail and picked up Papa and the boys, but he was going to the graveside services here on the plantation.

"Willie offered to take me by to see Naomi," Papa said, "but I didn't want her to see me looking like this."

"Silas, you did right," Mama said.

"Yes, 'specially in her condishon," Grandma agreed.

"Well, I'm gon' go on up here 'n' take Tom his boy 'n' 'liver the mail," Mr. Willie said, "'n' then git ready fer the burial. Y'all goin', ain't you?"

"Yes, us goin'," Papa replied. "Ain't gon' be 'tel fo' o'clock, is it?"

"That's right, fo' o'clock," Mr. Willie said, walking down the steps.

"I'm sho' muchoblige to you again, Willie, fer bringin' me home," Papa said.

"Yes, thanky, Willie," Mama added.

"Don' mention it, Silas, you 'n' Becky; it wasn't nothin'!" Mr. Willie hollered back as he got into his car.

Papa had a funny odor, and his eyes seemed dimmer and more fixed. They moved somewhat slower, too, as if to focus better on what they saw or as if they saw more now than before he went to jail. Also, he seemed to speak slower as if some unexpressed thought stood behind every word.

"I know you hongry, Silas," Mama said, "'n' I done already cooked; 'n' I got a big pan o' hot water on the stove so you can take a bath."

When Papa had shaved and bathed and put on his Sunday clothes for Mr. Win's burial, we sat down to eat. Papa said the blessing in a quiet voice that broke into a muffled groan as he finished and tears rolled down his face. I had never seen him cry before.

"Us is sho' helpless," he said in a broken voice while Mama patted his back and tried to calm him. "The sheriff," he continued, "can come 'n' 'rest you fer nothin' 'n' hit you 'n' threaten to kill you, 'n' slap yo' wife, 'n' there ain't nothin' you can do 'cep'n waylay him 'n' kill him."

"Naw, naw, Silas," Mama pleaded, "that ain't the way. Ef you do that, you gon' be in a whole mess o' trouble sho'nuff."

"Naw, Silas, don' do that," Grandma warned.

"I know, Miz Carrie," Papa said, "but up to yistiddy edenin', I couldn't think o' nothin' while I was in jail, but gittin' eben with that ole sheriff 'n' 'specially that little sawed-off deputy sonofabitch o' his'n they call Roy Bates whut done hit me 'n' jabbed in the stomach with his pistol."

"Jes' don' think 'bout it, Silas," Mama advised. "It's all over now; you is outa jail 'n' back home with us, 'n' us can still farm here. Mr. Walter 'n' Miz Rhoda don' seem to be hol'in' nothin' 'gainst us, do they, River? Us was up there yistiddy fer River to 'splain whut he knowed 'bout the note Lilly Mae sent to Miz Susie's, 'n' they was jes' as nice, 'specially after Mr. Walter done found out Gene'al Lee had on Miss Millie's girdle."

"Boy, you didn't go tattlin' to white folks, did you?" Papa asked in a fighting voice, looking me straight in the eye.

"Nawsuh, Papa, nawsuh," I answered quickly, "I didn't tattle to the white folks, did I, Mama?"

"Naw, Silas," Mama said, "River didn't tattle a'tall; Mr. Walter 'n' Mr. Lige found out at the sto' when Gene'al come up there to git some 'bacca 'n' a sack o' flour fer Tom 'n' Luiza. 'N' that fool boy was wearin' Miss Millie's girdle; 'n' like Mr. Lige always do, he goosed him 'n' he fell out on the flo' 'n' his pants come down 'n' they seen the girdle. That's how they found out; River didn't tell 'em, but I was scared tho' 'cause Miz Rhoda was questionin' him mighty close jes' befo' Mr. Walter come."

"Well, jes' so he didn't tattle," Papa said firmly. "Ef there anything I can't stan' it's a nigger whut go tattlin' to these damn white folks."

"Nawsuh, Papa, I sho' ain't tattled," I repeated.

"Silas, how come you is actin' the way you is?" Mama asked. "I done tol' you Mr. Walter 'n' Miz Rhoda ain't hol'n' nothin' 'gainst us, 'n' they ain't gon' put us off the place."

"Us is jes' so Gawddamn helpless," Papa said, wiping away the tears that still rolled down his cheeks. "These damn white folks 'cide evvything fer us."

"It's the Lawd whut 'cides, Silas," Grandma said. "I been tellin' y'all us po' niggers ain't got nothin' but the Lawd 'n' us church 'n' us prayers."

"Yessum, I know, Miz Carrie," Papa replied. "I b'lieves you, too. But I done learnt a heap in jail in them two days. White folks is givin' niggers the short end o' the stick evvywhere."

"They is?" Mama asked.

"They sho' is; you oughta hear them niggers talk. There's niggers in that jail from evvywhere all round here, eben from Sharkey, Yazoo 'n' Issaquena Counties. Sheriffs done took 'em there fer safe keepin' 'cause Vicksburg's got the biggest jail."

While we finished eating, Papa told us about several men he met in the jail. He said in the cell next to his was a man from Deer Creek who was sentenced to die for killing his landlord because he wouldn't settle with him. Said the landlord had started using weed killers and then had bought two cotton-picking machines. At the end of the first year, he had the machines, he put about half the folks off his place, sowed more land to pastures, and added more cows. During the second year, Papa said, the man refused to furnish his folks, and that fall he put them all off, except five young fellows and their families. He kept the men to drive the tractors and combines and cotton pickers and their wives to catch the few weeds the weed killers somehow missed.

Papa said the man said those who were put off had nothing. The man refused to settle with them, claiming they owed everything they made off their cotton for fertilizer and poison and weed killer and tractor work and picking, although the folks had picked some of their cotton themselves, especially in the low, wet patches where the picker couldn't go. And they had done some of the plowing and a lot of the chopping on part of their farms.

Papa said the man told him when he stopped to think that he and his family had done all that plowing and chopping and picking for nothing, not even food, because they hadn't eaten anything all year but greens and potatoes out of their garden and a chicken or a rabbit now and then, he got so mad he could hardly see. So he got his shotgun one day and waited in the bushes near a bend in the road and let the landlord have both barrels when he slowed his car down to make the turn.

The man swore, Papa said, and others agreed that the picker really works, except when it rains a lot and the heavy machine bogs down in the field. Said one of the pickers on a good day can pick a bale every couple of hours, or six or seven bales a day—as much as forty people.

"As much as forty people?" Mama asked in wonderment.

"That's whut he said," Papa replied. "Said the thing move down a row of cotton almos' as fast as a man can walk, jabbing cotton outa the bolls with dozens o' steel finger 'n' suckin' it up through tubes into a basket on top o' the machine."

"Lawd, Gawd, Almighty!" Grandma cried out. "The white folks done made a thing like that?"

"Yessum, they sho' is," Papa replied. "'N' fo' or five in jail say all the plantations 'round Rollin' Fork 'n' Anguilla, Mayersville, 'n' Panther Burn got 'em. 'N' jes' as soon as they git 'em they put the folks off, no matter whut kinda promises they done made 'bout 'You can stay here long as you live.' 'N' all the land they can't plant to cotton 'cause o' them 'lotments, they plant in grass fer mo' cattle."

"Lawd, Silas, where is the folks goin'?" Mama asked.

"They say they goin' to Vicksburg, 'n' Jackson 'n' Greenville 'n' Memphis 'n' on up North, wherever they got kinfolks or friends. But the white folks don' care where they go, jes' so they git off'n they place."

"You say the folks eben goin' up North, Silas?" Grandma inquired to make certain she had heard him right.

"Yessum, Miz Carrie, they sho' is."

"Ain't it mighty col' up there?"

"Yessum, they say it git real col' up there," Papa replied.

"Silas, you reckon Mr. Walter gon' git some o' them machines, now that Mr. Win's dead? They say Mr. Win was the one whut been hol'n' back," Mama said with fear crowding out the calm that had been in her voice.

"I wouldn't be surprised ef he got some," Papa said, "'cause ef whut them fellows in jail say is so, evvy plantation gon' git 'em sooner or later. Whut us gotta do is git us a place o' us own."

"How us gon' do that," Mama asked, "when us ain't got but thirty dollars, 'n' us owes some o' that fer Naomi?"

"I knows us ain't got no money much," Papa replied, "but one them fellows in jail say the gover'ment 'low credit to po' folks like us to buy farms o' they own."

"A fellow in jail tol' you that sho'nuff, Silas?" Mama asked with cautious hope.

"Yes, he sho' did, Becky. It was a fellow who used to live on the edge o' the hills over near Lexington," Papa explained. "He say the gover'ment done loan hund'erds o' folks money over there to buy farms."

"Colored folks?" Grandma asked in doubt.

"Yessum. He tol' me some colored 'n' some white," Papa said. "'N' that's whut stopped me from thinkin' 'bout killin' that damn sheriff. I'm gon' see 'bout gittin' some credit from the gover'ment next time I go to Vicksburg."

"Tint's good, Silas," Mama said, "that sho' sound good. I hope that nigger was tellin' the truth."

"I think he was tellin' the truth, Becky, 'cause some o' the other fellows said they had heard somethin' 'bout the gover'ment helpin' folks to buy farms. Anyhow, I'm sho'gon' see 'bout it," Papa said, pushing his chair back from the table. "I'm gon' put on my jumper 'n' hitch up the mules; it's near'bout fo' o'clock."

"You right, us better git started, ef us goin' to the burial," Mama said, getting up from the table, too. "Us be ready by time you git the wagon hitched up."

At the white folks' little cemetery right across the road from where Mr. Walter and Mrs. Rhoda lived, the family and some white folks I had never seen before sat close to the opening in the ground, while the colored folks stood back a ways behind them. The hearse backed up to the little gate that led off the lane into the cemetery. There, six white men, including Mr. Lige and Dr. Boyd, took hold of the casket as it came out of the hearse and carried it over to the grave and placed it on some straps stretched across the opening, where it sat while the white preacher conducted the rites. I didn't know there were white preachers before; I had never seen any. And I hadn't even thought about white churches because there wasn't one on the plantation. Once in a while I had seen the white folks at our church when an old person died who had been a good hand on the place. I had come to think that churches were only for colored folks.

The preacher opened his Bible and read a long time from several different pages, then he prayed a short prayer and made a talk. He addressed the family and the white folks and then he said to the colored folks, "I'm glad to see you here, too, because you also are Mr. Win's friends."

Then of Mr. Win, he said, "Winfield Williamson, a good and kind man, has been cut down before his time. He was relatively a young man with many useful years before him. His dear widow and his two fine children and his older brother and his sister-in-law, however, will carry on the work he might have performed."

As the preacher called off the family by relationship, I noticed for the first time that Mrs. Susie was not in mourning. Instead, she was wearing a bright green dress as she sat between Miss Millie and a man they said was her father, Mr. Jim Tate of Rolling Fork. There was nothing sad or grave about her face. She sat with one foot well forward as if to help push in the dirt that would bury her husband.

Miss Millie wore black and dabbed at her eyes continuously. I thought about her pink girdle Willie had stolen and I wondered again why it made him and General Lee feel good when they wore it.

Looking again at the preacher, I picked up more of his words. He wasn't saying anything about heaven or hell, or about Mr. Win's devotion to the church, or about crossing the Jordan, or golden slippers or white robes or pearly gates. He was talking about the Williamson plantation and how much cotton it grew, the number of families it took care of, and its top rank among the plantations of the area.

"And unlike some other plantations in this section," he said, "the Williamsons have not rushed to replace their colored folks with white faced cattle, or brought in machines to reduce the need for them and turn them out to pasture like old horses and mules. To pasture, I might say, in the towns and cities where the grazing is short and nubby. There is a kind of humanitarianism on this plantation that puts people ahead of profits." I had never heard that big word before, and I wondered what it meant.

"I know, however," the white preacher continued, "that sooner or later the Williamsons must catch up with the times or they will not survive. But both Mr. Win and Mr. Walter have told me many times that they hope to develop a training program that will prepare you folks," he said, looking around at the colored audience, "for employment in town. Mrs. Rhoda has spoken of it to me many, many times."

There were some quiet "Amens" and then a hush among us like the silent ripple of of waves in a pond following the leap of a fish.

The preacher said a few more words I do not recall, then he prayed another short prayer and said, "Amen." As a mechanical device lowed Mr. Win's body into the ground, the preacher picked up a rose that lay on the casket and dropped it back gently, petal by petal, saying, "Ashes to ashes and dust to dust...."

As the casket disappeared, the family was silent, but among the plantation folks there were sobs and a few outcries of "Have mercy, Jesus!" and "Lawd, Lawd!"

Then all the people made their way to the wagons or cars. Most of them came in our direction, saying, "Sho' glad you out, Silas," or "Us knowed you ain't done nothin'." It was said quietly, both in keeping with the mood of the occasion and in some small fear that overjoy over Papa might not reflect, I think they thought, a proper awareness of our family's part in the white folks' tragedy.

XVI

Reverend Fisher and Family Thrown Off the Plantation

The next morning, after the funeral first thing, I was helping Papa in the lot before going for the cow in the lane when we saw Mr. Walter and Mrs. Rhoda drive up to Reverend Fisher's house. The preacher went out to the car where the plantation owner and his wife were sitting. They were too far away for us to hear what they were saying as he talked through the window to them for a long time. Finally, both Mr. Walter and Mrs. Rhoda got out of their car and walked slowly into the yard with Reverend Fisher.

We could see the heads of the children sticking out of the front door and the window as they watched their father talk with the white couple. Mrs. Rhoda, with her arms folded, looked more toward the ramshackle house from which the children were peeping then at the preacher. And her husband stood with both hands in the back pockets of his trousers. His feet seemed to be kicking at a patch of grass toward which he looked intently as if this was what he had come to Reverend Fisher's house to do. It was as if neither wanted to look the preacher in the eye as they talked to him. At the end of their conference, Mr. Walter brought out of one of his back pockets what looked like a billfold. He took something out of it and handed it to the preacher, and Mrs. Rhoda, who had gone back to car and got her handbag, also handed Reverend Fisher something. Then they got into their car and drove away.

Papa kept currying the mules as if he would rub the hide off them while we watched. I pretended to be pumping water, but the pump handle was still more than it was in motion. As soon as the Williamsons' car was back in the lane, Reverend Fisher came running toward our house through the dewey cotton.

"Brother Henry," he said, almost out of breath, "I gotta move; Mr. Walter 'n' Miz Rhoda say Miz Susie want me off the place befo' night."

"Her do? Befo' night?" Papa asked in a desperate voice that revealed his fear that we might be next.

"Yessuh, that's whut Mr. Walter say she said," the preacher replied. "Where is I'm goin', Brother Henry?"

"I don' know, 'cep'n to Vicksburg."

"They give me twenty-five dollars; Mr. Walter give me twenty, 'n' Miz Rhoda give me five."

"That's 'nuff to git you 'n' the chillun a place in town far a while," Papa said.

"But where we gon' stay?"

"Whut 'bout us pastor, Reverend Whitten? Maybe he could help you find a place fer you 'n' the chillun to stay 'tel you could look around."

"Yes, Brother Henry, I thought o' Reverend Whitten," the preacher said, "but he ain't doin' well hisself with two little churches that can't half pay. I hate to ast him to help me find a place, 'cause he might feel duty bound to put us up in his small house. So I'd rather not ast him."

"I understan', Reverend," Papa said, scratching his head. "Letme see. Becky done said somethin' 'bout the welfare in Vicksburg that help folks. It's helpin' Naomi."

"Yes, Brother Henry, I think I heard somethin' 'bout the welfare years ago when I pastored in Valley Park, but that's been a long time."

"I don' know nothin' 'bout it myself, Reverend, but I think Becky know. Us can go ast her," Papa said.

In the house, Mama and Grandma expressed great regret that Mr. Walter and Mrs. Rhoda would let Mrs. Susie make them put the preacher off the plantation.

"Is that all he done said," Mama asked, "that Miz Susie say her want y'all off the place befo' night?"

"Mr. Walter say her said her didn't want none o' Lilly Mae's kin on no land she got ownership in," and then the preacher paused a long time, looking from Papa to Mama as if to see if they clearly understood. "Course," he added, "Mr. Walter 'n' Miz Rhoda say they didn't want me 'n' my family pushed off like this. Said ef it was left to them, I could stay at least 'tel Lilly Mae's trial is over 'n' she is proved innocent or guilty."

"They nice; both Mr. Walter 'n' Miz Rhoda is nice," Mama said.

"Ain't no two ways 'bout it," Reverend Fisher said, "they sho' been born again."

"Amen," Grandma said. "Amen."

"Course Miz Susie, evvybody say, been crossways the world evvy since her come to the Bend," the preacher recalled.

"Folks say her ain't never been satisfied with Mr. Win since her marr'ed him 'n' come over here from Rollin' Fork, 'n' they say he ain't been much satisfied with her. They say her col'," Mama said, "'n' got back trouble 'n' that whut make Mr. Win run 'round so much with these gals on the plantation."

"Well, her sho' tryin' to git eben now," Grandma pointed out.

"Her sho' is," the preacher agreed, "'n' I wouldn't be a bit surprised ef her sol' her part o' the plantation to somebody else jes' fer spite."

"You don' reckon sho'nuff her would do that, do you, Reverend?" Papa asked, "'cause that might put Mr. Walter in a bind."

"I wouldn't put it pas' her," Grandma spoke up.

"I wouldn't put it pas' her neither, Sister Johnson," Reverend Fisher agreed. "Course, I don' blame her too much fer hatin' Lilly Mae, 'cause Lilly Mae was wrong. The Bible say, 'Thou shall not commit 'dultry,' 'n' that's whut Lilly Mae was doin'."

"Reverend, it ain't gon' do no good to talk 'bout Miz Susie 'n' Lilly Mae now," Papa said. "Us gotta help you find a place to stay in Vicksburg. Becky, whut 'bout that welfare place whut helpin' Naomi?"

"I don' know nothin' much 'bout it," Mama answered, "but Willie Woods, he know."

"That's right, he sho' do," Papa said. "I'll drive you down to Willie's in my wagon while Becky milk 'n' cook breakfast fer us 'n' you 'n' yo' chillun."

"Can I go, Papa?" I asked, pulling on his sleeve as he moved toward the door.

"Naw, man, you stay here 'n' help yo' mama," Papa replied. He knew when he called me "man" he could deny me anything.

So I said, "Yessuh," and released his sleeve.

While he hitched up the mules to the wagon, I carried stove wood into the kitchen and went for the cow.

When Papa and Reverend Fisher came back from Mr. Willie's, Mama was all ready with breakfast—bacon and molasses and grits and eggs and hot biscuits. The preacher ate as if he hadn't eaten in a week. As usual, I limited myself mostly to hot biscuits and butter and molasses. I stirred butter and hot bacon grease into the syrup until it was almost white, then I sopped it up with four or five biscuits.

While we were eating, Papa reported that they had caught Mr. Willie before he left to go to the store to pick up the mail. Papa said Mr. Willie wasn't going to leave the Bend until around 10 o'clock, and he was going to come by Reverend Fisher's house and pick him up and take him to Vicksburg so he could be looking for a place while he returned and picked up the children.

"He say he gon' take Reverend by where Naomi stay," Papa said, "'n' see ef the lady her stay with can help 'em find a place."

"Ef that lady can't help," Reverend Fisher spoke up, "then I'm goin' by Reverend Whitten's 'n' see ef he know of a place."

"'N' ef he don' find a place in Vicksburg, Willie say he know a place near Red Wood where he 'n' the chillun can stay a few days," Papa added. "'N' then next week Willie gon' help him git in touch with the welfare."

"That's good," Mama said. "Willie don' grin at the white folks fer nothin'; he can help you when nobody else can."

"Cep'n the Lawd," Grandma said. "Don' fergit the Lawd."

"Amen, Sister Jones, you certainly right," Reverend Fisher said. "We musn't fergit the Lawd, 'cause He's evvything."

"Well, you 'n' the Lawd better hurry, Reverend, so you can git yo' things together 'n' be ready when Willie come," Mama said in a voice that meant, "Shit, I am tired o' Grandma 'n' the preacher draggin' the Lawd into evvything."

"Thanky, Sister Henry. I'm gon' hurry," Reverend Fisher replied, shoveling more grits out of the dish and smearing them with butter. "I still got mo'n a hour 'n' that's plenty time fer me to git my few things together. You gon' help the chillun git ready, ain't you, Sister?" he asked helplessly.

"Yessuh, Reverend Fisher," Mama replied softly, trying to gain forgiveness, I think, for the way she had used the Lord's name. "Us gon' help the chillun pack 'n' be ready when Willie come fer 'em." Now there were tears in Mama's eyes, which she tried to wipe away with her hands. I think the full meaning of what was happening to Reverend Fisher and his family was just finding its way into her mind.

"Don' cry, Sister Henry. The Lawd will provide," the preacher said, patting her on the shoulder as he rose from the table. "I'm gon' have a place fer me 'n' the chillun by the time Brother Woods gits back to Vicksburg." For all his pretense of confidence, there were doubt and fear in his voice he could not hide.

I think Papa sensed the preacher's fear because he quickly added, "Oh, sho', Reverend, you 'n' Willie gon' find a place."

"The Lawd is gon' help him," Grandma added.

"I sho' hope so, Reverend," Mama said. "'N' tomorrer, me 'n' Silas goin' to both the churches 'n' ast.'em to take up a collection fer you, 'n' us gon' send it to you Monday by Willie." All the time Mama was putting into a large pan all that was left from breakfast plus some grits and biscuits that she never brought to the table. "Take this to the chillun," she said. "It's good 'n' hot."

The preacher took the pan, tears welling up in his eyes, and for a moment, just a moment, his eyes and face seemed to indicate that all the faith and hope he had generated in others on the plantation had abandoned him in his own hour of need. Before turning to go, he shook our hands and then rested his hand on my head.

"Gawd bless you all," he said and walked down the steps and through the gate without looking back. He didn't look back, I think, because the tears that were in his eyes were probably running down his face.

In a little while, we heard Mr. Willie's horn blow, and all of us went out on the front porch to wave goodbye to Reverend Fisher. He came out in his Sunday clothes, carrying a box. His children accompanied him, even little Woodrow, who didn't have on a stitch of clothes. The preacher waved to us and hollered, "Goodbye, y'all!" At the car he stooped and hugged each of his children. As the car pulled off, he waved back to them and they kept waving at him until he and Mr. Willie were out of sight.

They were still standing in the yard when we went over to help them pack and get ready to join their father that afternoon in Vicksburg. The ragged clothes the children had on, an extra dress of Daisy Lee's, a slip and two dresses of Lilly Mae's were all the clothing they had. Mama sent me and Papa back to our house to get our tubs, washboard, and a bar of soap so that she could wash up everything.

After we brought the tubs, Papa went into the preacher's house and brought out the two shuck-bottomed chairs and placed them on the ground backside up to form a bench by the side of the house for the tubs. Then he made a fire in the stove and heated the water he and I and Willie had brought from the pump. When Mama was ready to wash, the children threw clothing out of the window to her. She held them up and shook her head. Only two blouses and Daisy Lee's dresses were worth washing. Willie had on his patched suit and a hopeless shirt.

When the wash was finished and on the line, Mama said to Papa, "Silas, these chillun gotta have some mo' clothes. I want you to go to the sto' with me so I can take up on credit a few yards of gingham 'n' make 'em some things. 'N' I think River got some shirts he can give Willie."

"No'am, no'am!" I screamed. "I don' wanna give my shirts to Willie, no'am."

"Now, River," Mama, said, "you not actin' like Mama's little man."

"No'am, no'am!" I screamed again, shaking my head vigorously. "I want my shirts, Mama, I want my shirts!"

"Silas, go git all River's things 'n' give 'em to Willie," Mama ordered. "They too big fer us little baby."

"Naw, Papa, please, Papa!" I screamed louder than ever and fell on the ground, kicking in protest.

"Git up from there, boy; whut's the matter with you?" Papa said in gruff voice, coming over to where I was lying.

"Please, Papa, don' give my things to Willie," I begged, getting part way up off the ground.

Papa snatched me the rest of the way. "This ain't no way fer a big boy to act, is it, man?" He knew he had me.

As I dried my eyes, knowing I had lost, I turned my head to see Willie standing near me. His hands were held together in front of him, and tears were running down his face, which he made no effort to wipe away. The picture my mind snapped of him has been with me ever since.

When I had finished drying my eyes, I went and caught Willie by the hand. "I'm a big boy, ain't I, Papa?" I asked, looking at him and Mama trying to hide their smiles.

"Yes, man, you sho' is a big boy," Papa replied.

I led Willie over to my house and gave him a pair of my good pants and two shirts. Mama had made the shirts for me for Easter. I now had three Sunday shirts left and two pairs of pants.

"You giving Willie some o' yo' things?" Grandma asked when she saw me handing him the shirts and pants.

"Yessum, Grandma," I said.

"That's nice; you a big boy, River."

When Mama and Papa returned from the store, Willie and I pumped the machine while she made the clothes for the other children. She made two garments apiece for them, bathed the children in our tubs with Daisy Lee's help, gave them their new clothes to put on, and brought them over to our house to eat. After we had eaten, we sat on the porch until Mr. Willie came. We couldn't play because they had on their new clothes.

In a little while Mr. Willie came. He announced that Reverend Whitten was helping the preacher find a place. We hugged each of the children as they piled into the car. Their extra clothes were in one box and two fried chickens were another. They waved as Mr. Willie pulled off.

Before Papa took up the collection at each of the two churches that Sunday, he asked Mr. Willie to tell the congregations about Reverend Fisher's situation in Vicksburg. Neither Papa nor Mr. Willie explained why the preacher left the plantation so suddenly, but no one needed an explanation. They knew Lilly Mae had admitted killing Mr. Win and was in jail, and on top of that they knew the preacher's boy, Willie, had stolen Miss Millie's girdle. It was to be expected that the white folks would make the preacher move. And some said that if he had been living on some of the other plantations around, he would have been driven out with shotguns or maybe shot.

"Reverend Fisher 'n' his chillun is now livin' in Vicksburg, as you know," Mr. Willie began. "I drove him down yistiddy mornin' when I made my regular trip to take the mail so he could be findin' a place befo' I got back with the chillun in the edenin'. Well, Reverend Whitten done helped him find a place right away where they can stay fer a week or two 'tel he have a chance to look 'round. But he can't git on welfare fer thirty days, 'n' he ain't got but leben dollars to his name after he done paid his rent fer a week 'n' bought a few groceries. Course, they ain't gon' have to buy no clothes right away, 'cause Becky Henry done made the chillun some nice things befo' they left. But Reverend sho' need mo' money, 'cause things is so 'spensive in Vicksburg."

At each church, the folks marched up to the table and put down nickels and dimes because it was just before cotton-picking time and they didn't have much money. The total added up to four dollars and thirty cents.

What Mr. Willie did not tell the folks at church but practically whispered to Papa and us in our wagon was that Reverend Whitten had said the Vicksburg Branch of the National Association for the Advancement of Colored People might hold a big mass meeting the next week and raise some money for Reverend Fisher, and they might make a big protest about the way they were put off the plantation with their crop still in the field.

"Now, don't you tell nobody I tol' you this," Mr. Willie whispered, "'cause ef the white folks hear 'bout it, there could be mo' trouble." When he finished his mouth did not hang open, and there wasn't a sign of a smile on his face.

The four dollars and thirty cents Papa collected and sent to Reverend Fisher by Mr. Willie wasn't a drop in the bucket compared to what the NAACP raised at the mass meeting the next Sunday at one of the large Vicksburg churches. Mr. Willie came to our house that Monday evening and told us about the meeting. We sat on the porch, where it was cool. Papa had made a fire in the yard and covered it with dirt and wet weeds and grass to smoke the mosquitoes away.

Mr. Willie said the church was packed to hear Reverend Fisher tell about how he and his five children were put off the plantation after his oldest daughter was arrested for accidentally killing a white man while they tussled over his pistol he had pulled on her when she wouldn't let him whip her with a cowhyde whip. He said Reverend Fisher told him he told the folks how he had been order last Saturday morning to get off the place before night with nothing but what he and his children had on their backs. When he had finished, he said Reverend told him the folks came up and put one hundred eighteen dollars and forty-five cents on the table.

"A hund'ered 'n' eighteen dollars!" Papa exclaimed. "Thats almos' a bale o' cotton."

"Course, the pastor o' that church took out twenty-five dollars fer the use o' his church," Mr. Willie said.

"Ain't Reverend done tol' 'em Mr. Walter 'n' Miz Rhoda done give 'em twenty-five dollars?" Mama asked.

"'N' that's mo'n he ever cleared outa his cotton," Papa added, "with him 'n' them chillun eatin' up they cotton money at the sto' faster'n the boll weevils was eatin' up they cotton."

"'N' ain't he tol' 'em whut they had on they backs was all they had anyhow?" Mama wanted to know.

"You know he ain't tol' 'em that, Beck," Mr. Willie replied, "'cause ef he had, them folks wouldn't a give no hund'ered 'n' eighteen dollars."

"'N' I bet he ain't tol' 'em Mr. Win been takin' care o' 'em neither," Mama said self-righteously.

"Naw, course, he ain't tol' 'em 'bout his gal 'n' Mr. Win; you know he ain't tol' 'em that," Mr. Willie said. "He tol' me the NAACP man done tol' him the Williamson plantation jes' like all the rest 'round here, 'n' don' come tellin' him it ain't. So he made the Bend sound as bad as he could."

"Well, all these plantations is bad 'nuff," Papa said, "but the Williamsons 'bout the bes' I ever seen."

"It is that, Silas," Grandma agreed, "'n' it wasn't right for Reverend Fisher to go lyin' 'bout the place."

"He ain't 'zackly lied, Miz Carrie, he jes' left out some o' the truth," Mr. Willie explained. "But, you know, folks in town jes' ain't open 'n' honest like us country folks. Out here evvything is open like us farms, 'n' evvybody can see evvybody else's bizness 'cause it's growing right there in the field. Ain't no need o' tryin' to lie 'bout yo' cotton, 'cause evvybody can see it fer theyselves, 'n' they knows ef you got a good crop, or ef you ain't. Now in town it's diff'ent. Eben yo' next do' neighbor ain't gon' know where you works or how much you makes less'n you tell him, 'n' you can tell him anything you want to."

"But that don' mean you gotta lie," Grandma said firmly.

"Miz Carrie, you gotta put yo'self in the preacher's place in town with only leben dollars plus the fo' dollars 'n' thirty cents us done sent from the Bend, 'n' that little money runnin' out with the welfare three weeks off 'n' you don' know how you gon' feed yo'self 'n' yo' five chillun, 'n' yo' oldest chile in jail fer killing a white man."

"That do make a diff'ence, Willie, but he always 'pended on the Lawd," Grandma replied.

"I'm sho'," Mr. Willie argued, "he still 'pendin' on the Lawd, but ef you was in his shoes 'n' you seen a chance to help yo'self by leavin' out a little o' the truth, ain't you gon' do it?"

"Not ef it's lyin'." Grandma stood firm.

"Well, anyhow," Mr. Willie continued, "the folks done put a hund'ered 'n' eighteen dollars on the table, 'n' Reverend say he gon' rent a house 'n' git some furniture on credit. 'N' he say the N Double-A CP gon' defen' Lilly Mae when her trial come up. Now don't y'all breathe a word 'bout the N Double-A CP, do you hear?" And again his mouth did not hang open and there wasn't a sign of a smile on his face in the twilight.

"Don't you worry none, Willie," Mama promised. "Us ain't gon' say a thing 'bout that Double-A CP."

"The N Double-A CP is a good 'sosation, but the white folks don' understan' it," Mr. Willie explained. "That's how come I'm warnin' you not to mention it. There already trouble 'nuff on the place. I guess you know Paralee 'n' George is movin'?"

"Naw, where they movin' to?" Papa asked.

"To Rollin' Fork with Miz Susie," Mr. Willie replied.

"Us heard something 'bout Miz Susie might move," Mama said, "but us wasn't sho'."

"Well, Becky, her sho' gon' move. They say her gon' move this week," Mr. Willie replied. "'N' they say her astin' fer ha'f the plantation fer herself 'n' her chillun, 'n' Mr. Walter gon' have to buy it from her, ef he don' want her to sell it to somebody else."

"Lawd, Gawd, A'mighty," Grandma exclaimed. "That woman gon' do that with her mean self?"

"Her sho' is, 'leas' that's whut they sayin'," Mr. Willie answered. "Mr. Lige hisself tol' me."

"Reckon Mr. Walter got the money to buy her out?" Papa inquired.

"I don' know," Mr. Willie replied, "but Mr. Lige don' talk like he got 'nuff; said Mr. Walter is tryin' to borrow the money from the bank in Vicksburg. You know, 'cep'n fer las' year, crops ain't been good fer the las' three fo' years."

"They sho' ain't," Papa agreed, slapping at a mosquito that was singing near him, "but las' year was sho' a good un."

"It sho' was, Silas," Mama said, then turning to me, she ordered, "Poke in the fire a little, River, 'n' throw some too' dirt on it. Mosquitoes gittin' bad ag'in."

"You know us made a little money las' year, Willie, 'cause you took us to town where us bought some things," Papa said. "Then I bought 'nother mule 'n' put 'side some to buy a farm o' us own when us git 'nuff."

I missed some of the conversation while I poked in the fire and threw more dirt and weeds on it to get the smoke going again. When I came back up on the porch and sat on the floor beside Grandma's chair, Mama was saying how much we wanted a place of our own.

"That's fine, Becky 'n' Silas, that's jes' fine," Mr. Willie said. "All us gon' have to buy farms o' us own, ef Mr. Walter lose this place, 'cause there ain't go' be no mo' plantations us can move to. I been savin' a little from carr'in' the mail 'n' haulin' folks to town, 'n' I got my eye on thirty acres out 'round Valley Park, ef the man'll sell to me."

"You don' think Mr. Walter gon' lose the place sho'nuff, do you, Willie?" Papa asked.

"I jes' don' know," Mr. Willie answered, "but Mr. Lige got me scared, talkin' the way he do. Course, there gon' be a heap o' changes, eben ef he don' lose the place."

"You mean he gon' git cotton pickers 'n' mo' cattle?" Papa said.

"That's right, Mr. Walter gon' git cotton pickers like a lotta other plantations 'round here, 'n' mo' cattle. He got 'bout fifty or sixty head now grazin' on the levee. It wouldn't surprise me none ef he put mo' land in pastures 'n' got mo' 'n' mo' cows."

"You don' think he gon' put nobody off the place, do you, Willie?" Grandma asked.

"Whut he gon' do with all the folks ef he raisin' cattle 'stid o' cotton, Miz Carrie?" Mr. Willie said, replying to her question with a question.

"Lawd, Jesus," Grandma moaned, "look like the colored folks don' never win." In the years since then, I have wondered if everybody doesn't need a victory sometimes. And like Grandma said, it seems we don't ever win.

Papa slapped again at a mosquito as he spoke. "You know, Willie, ever since Mr. Win tol' us they was gon' try out that weed-killer stuff, I knowed ef it worked, 'n' it sho' worked, they was gon' try cotton picker next 'n' find out ef they works," he said. "Them fellers in jail say they sho' works."

"Ain't no doubt about it, them machines sho' works," Mr. Willie agreed. "They say some o' the plantations up in the sho'nuff delta picks evvy lock o' them cotton with machines. Mr. Lige say Mr. Walter ain't got no choice but to git some o' them picker, ef he gon' save the place."

"Whut 'bout the folks?" Grandma asked. "When us firs' come here in fifty, folks said the Williamsons don' never put nobody off they place. They say they said evvybody could stay here jes' as long as they live."

"Yessum, they say that's been the rule on the place since ole Cap'n Winfield Williamson's day. He was Mr. Walter 'n' Mr. Win's great-granddaddy," Mr. Willie replied, "but I don' know 'bout now; evvything done changed so."

"Well, no matter whut happen," Grandma said, spitting off the porch, "jes' so us don' have to move to town. 'Cause I don' wanna be cramped up in no town starvin' to death. I lived in Clarksdale two weeks once when Becky was a baby, 'n' that's 'nuff fer me"

"Now some o' the folks in Vicksburg do have it pretty tough, Miz Carrie," Mr. Willie said, "'n' I knows 'cause I go there evvy day 'n' I sees how they lives. But some o' the folks there lives pretty good. Folks say Miz Rhoda all fer lettin' the niggers go to town, less'n Mr. Walter 'n' all these other planta-tion owners sell us some o' they land so us can make a better livin'. Now you know they ain't gon' do that. They say Miz Rhoda say folks be better off in town, less'n they got some land o' they own, 'cause they chillun have better schools in town, 'n' they say her say that's the onliest way colored folks gon' git anywheres—education."

"I don' care whut Miz Rhoda say," Grandma argued. "I don' want nobody stickin' me up in no town where I can't raise no hogs 'n' chickens 'n' a patch o' collard greens."

"That's how I feels, too, Ma," Mama said, "but River might learn mo' goin' to school in town."

"I don' wanna go to no school in town," I protested. "I wanna stay out here on the farm with Papa 'n' help him plow 'n' drive a tractor when us gits one."

Papa reached over and patted me on the shoulder, and that made me feel good all over. "I'm jes' hopin'," he said, "us'll have a farm fer him to stay on, 'n' plow out in the fresh air 'n' drive us tractor ef us ever gits one."

"Us gon' sho' have a farm o' us own, ain't us, Papa?" I asked, sliding closer to his chair and catching his arm.

"I sho' hope so, River," Papa replied.

"Ef something do happen 'n' you have to move off the place, I'm sho' you gon' find a place," Mr. Willie said hopefully.

"You know, Willie, when I was in jail, I talked with a feller in there who said the gover'ment lend money to po' farmers like us to buy farms o' they own," Papa explained. "You heard any thing 'bout this?"

"Naw, I ain't, Silas," Mr, Willie replied. "The gover'ment sho' ain't help nobody 'round here buy no farm, 'specially no po' folks. It might be helpin' the rich white folks buy mo' land like it helpin' 'em plant mo' pastures fer they cattle to graze—land where niggers used to live 'n' grow cotton."

"This man in jail was from out 'round Lexington, he say. 'N' he say that's out pas' Yazoo City," Papa explained. "He say the gover'ment done helped a heap o' folks out there buy farms o' they own."

"Maybe so," Mr. Willie said thoughtfully, "but I ain't heard nothin' 'bout it. Course, there Mr. Bob Flagg, the county agent, in town there. You know, he come out here sometime 'n' talk with Mr. Walter 'n' Mr. Win. I could ast him ef he know antthing 'bout the gover'ment helpin' po' folks buy farms, but it sho' gon' git back to Mr. Walter 'n' he gon' wonder whut I'm astin' Mr. Flagg 'bout that fer."

"Naw," Mama spoke up, "don' do that, 'cause us don' want Mr. Walter to think us tryin' to leave; he might put us off befo' he woulda."

"Naw, that's right," Papa agreed.

"Let me see now," Mr. Willie said, searching his memory for something. "I heard 'bout a colored man 'tween here 'n' Vicksburg whut own a farm somewhere near Red Wood. He might know 'bout the gover'ment helpin' po' farmers. I'm gon' find out where he live 'n' ast him next time I gits a chance."

"Yes, you ast him, Willie, 'n' let us know whut he say," Papa suggested.

"I'm gon' do that, Silas, firs' chance I gits," Mr. Willie agreed. "Guess I better be goin', me 'n' Birdie gotta git us sacks ready; us gon' start pickin' next week."

"Yo' cotton open that good?" Mama asked.

"Yes, I'd say 'bout three fo' bales ready fer pickin'," Mr. Willie replied, getting up to go. "Course, jes' me 'n' Birdie be pickin', 'cause school ain't out yet."

"I don' think us can start 'tel week after next," Papa said. "Us cotton is late. I kinda think that weed-killer stuff had something to do with it."

"Don' seemed to make no diff'ence on my place," Mr. Willie said. "They put it down on six acres o' mine, but it sho' made choppin' easier on them six acres," he boasted, walking down the steps.

"How much you think you gon' make, Willie?" Papa asked.

"Oh, I don' know," Mr. Willie answered, walking back from our gate, scratching his head. "I'm hopin' fer leben bales on my ten acres."

"That's good," Papa said. "Us got eight acres; they cut us 'lotment back, but us hopin' fer a bale to the acre or mo'."

"That's 'bout whut you did las' year, ain't it?"

"That's right, a bale to the acre on leben acres," Papa said.

"I got thirteen bales las' year off thirteen acres," Mr. Willie said. "They done cut me down to ten this year, but thank the Lawd fer that."

"That's right, Willie," Grandma agreed. "Don' fergit the Lawd."

"No'am, you right. Well, goodnight, y'all."

"Goodnight," we all said as Mr. Willie got into his car and drove away.

XVII

Settlements of the Crops Diminished by New Farm Implementations

The day before school closed for cotton-picking time, two big vans passed the church. We could see them from the windows. Riding ahead were Little Mr. Win and his sister, Miss Millie, in their open car. She waved toward the school; must have been at someone going or coming from the privy. I couldn't see who it was from where I was seated. And I couldn't see Miss Millie too well because Little Mr. Win's head was in the way. But I could see her golden hair blowing in the breeze, and I caught just a glimpse of that friendly smile on her pretty face. It was a smile everyone on the plantation had seen as she rode up and down the lanes and across the turnrows every summer on her hay-colored mare. I saw it best that time at Willie's when she led his little brother out of the road and up to the house.

It wasn't a false smile like Mr. Tobe's when he was selling you an ice cream cone from his truck, or the fawning smile of his wife, Mrs. Ida, up in Mrs. Rhoda's face, or the scared, nervous smile of a farmer giving Mr. Win an excuse for the grass in his cotton, or the self-satisfied smile of one who has come out better at settlement time than he ever expected. No, it wasn't a smile to pay a debt or earn a reward. It was a smile given without cost because it wanted to be given.

The vans returned just as school let out that day. Mrs. Paralee and Mr. George were riding in the back of the first van and Miss Millie and her mother, Mrs. Susie, followed the second van in their big black car. Little Mr. Win trailed them in his racer. Miss Millie, who was driving her mother's car, waved quickly, more with her fingers than with her arm. Her smile was quick, too, as if to hide it from her mother. Neither Mrs. Susie nor Little Mr. Win looked either to the right or to the left but kept their faces pointed straight ahead like mules wearing blinders.

It was the last time I ever saw Mrs. Susie and her two children, but we never saw the end of the effects of their leaving. Mr. Walter had to mortgage the already over-mortgaged plantation to pay them out. And with the price of cotton depressed by bulging government warehouses of surplus cotton, things didn't look any too good.

That fall we picked out eight bales as Papa had expected, but when he came back from settling with Mr. Walter, there was no smile on his face. The weed-killer stuff, the fertilizer, the poison, and the tractor work plus what we had taken up at the store left us only $202. It was mostly in one-dollar bills with twelve dollars of it in silver dollars and fifty-cent pieces. As always, Papa and Mama spread it out on the bed and counted it several times. Then Papa handed Grandma twenty one-dollar bills. "Us had hope to give you mo', Miz Carrie," he said, "'cause you did a heap mo' pickin' this year with Naomi gone 'n' all, but us jes' didn't make it."

"This plenty fer me, Silas," Grandma replied, raising her skirt on the side and putting the money in her sack.

Papa gave Mama fifty dollars for herself and fifty more to put aside with the thirty they had managed to save from last year for a farm of our own. Then he gave me a silver dollar and two fifty-cent pieces, and kept the remaining eighty dollars to buy food and clothes and pay whatever Naomi owed in town. Two dollars was the most money I had ever had. I rubbed the three coins together for a while and then put them in my pocket and ran around, shaking my pocket to hear them clank against one another.

Mama had had her heart set on a washing machine, as much to sit on the front porch where everybody could see it, like Mrs. Viney Robinson's, as to be used for washing, "I think I'm gon' hold on to my money 'tel next year to buy a washing machine, Silas," Mama said, "'cep'n fer ernuff to buy a little cloth to make dresses fer Ma 'n' Naomi 'n' me, n of course to make a few things fer the baby. But 'cep'n fer that I ain't gon' buy nothin' else."

"That's good, Becky. Us gon' make ernuff next year to buy that washer fer you; I jes' feels us is somehow," Papa promised.

"Ef Mr. Walter don' lose the place," Mama added.

"Oh, he ain't gon' lose the place befo' next year," Papa assured her.

"I hopes you right, Silas."

"Sho' I'm right."

"I ain't 'zackly scared he'll lose the place befo' us picks us cotton next year, Silas, but I'm scared he gon' be in such a tight fix, he gon' figure us outa most o' us cotton like he did this year; only he gon' have to take mo'," Mama said.

"Yes, I know us oughta cleared mo' this year outa eight bales, but I didn't say nothin'," Papa explained. "I figure he up 'gainst it, 'n' Naomi 'n' us is partly to blame."

"You right, Silas, us is partly to blame, 'n' I'm glad you didn't say nothin' when he run us debt up," Mama said, "but I think he gon' be mo' up 'gainst it next year, less'n us makes a lot mo' cotton, 'n' with the 'lotments gittin' tighter 'n' tighter, I don' think us is."

"I guess you right, Becky. Ain't no way fer us to ever git ahead, less'n us gits us a place o' us own," Papa replied.

"I sho' hopes y'all gits one," Grandma said wishfully. "Willie ever talk to that man whut he say own a little farm out 'round Red Wood?"

"Ef he is, he ain't tol' me nothin' 'bout it," Papa said.

"He sho' ain't," Mama added. "When us go to town with him Sadday to see 'bout Naomi, us can ask him, 'n' maybe us can stop by with Willie 'n' talk to the man usselves."

"That's a good idee, Becky, 'cause you know how scary Willie is. He ain't gon' do nothin' whut might put him in bad with the white folks," Papa said with a kind of chuckle.

"Reckon he gon' wanna stop there, Silas?" Mama asked. "Mr. Walter or some o' the white folks might pass 'n' see his car 'n' wonder whut he doin' there."

"Ef it's a farm a nigger own," Grandma put in, "you can bet yo' life it ain't near no highway. White folks jes' don' 'low that."

"You right, Miz Carrie," Papa agreed. "I don' know but two three colored mens whut own they farms 'n' they is, like you say, way on the back side o' the communities where they lives."

"How come they farms so fer back, Papa?" I asked.

"I don' know, River, 'cep'n like yo' grandma say, white folks fix it that way. 'Cause white folks have all the say 'bout where the highway go," Papa replied.

"Well, fer one thing," Grandma added, "white folks don' sell no niggers no land up by good roads, 'n' fer another, ef by some accident they happens to own a piece o' land on a good road, white folks find some way to git it 'way from 'em. Seem they jes' don' want other niggers or white folks neither to know some niggers own land 'n' live in good houses. So they keep they tenant shacks up on the good roads."

"It sho' seem like that, Miz Carrie."

"Course, it's like that," Grandma said in a voice of certainty. "There was a nigger up on the highway near Clarksdale once whut owned two three hund'ered acres 'n' a nice big house left him by his ha'f-white pa who 'herited it from his white daddy. Long as the ha'f-white nigger lived there, wasn't no trouble, but soon as he died 'n' his black son took over, there was trouble all the time. Finally, the white folks burnt his house down 'n' drove him 'way from there. Said he was too biggity 'n' thought he was good as white folks."

"Sonofabitch," Papa said. "Ef I ever own a piece o' land 'n' some Gawddamn sonofabitch come tryin' to run me off it, that gon' be his las' day on earth, 'cause I'm gon' kill the sonofabitch, so help me Gawd!"

"Now, don' go gittin' all worked up, Silas," Mama said. "Us don' have to have no farm by no highway. It can be so fer back, us can hardly see the sun, jes' so it's us own land."

"I ain't gon' look fer no trouble, you know that, Becky," Papa said, "but ef trouble come lookin' fer me, the Lawd knows I ain't gon' run, not off my own land."

"Ef ever us gits a farm," Mama said, getting up to put her money away, "I hopes that'll be the end o' trouble, 'n' us can settle down 'n' fix up us own house, 'n' grow us own crops, 'n' put down roots like the trees. There would be no mo' movin' year after year, 'n' runnin' from plantations in the middle o' the night."

"Ain't gon' be much o' that nomo' nohow, Becky. It gon' be mostly niggers tryin' to find a place that ain't been took over by cotton-pickin' machines. White folks ain't gon' be tryin' to hol' niggers on they plantations no mo' they gon' be tryin' to git rid o' 'em."

"They done used the niggers up now, wore 'em out," Grandma said, "now they through with 'em. Got stuff to kill the weeds 'n' grass, machines to pick they cotton, so white folks don' need niggers no mo' to chop 'n' pick cotton. They ready to send 'em all to town to starve to death. Have Mercy, Jesus."

"Us ain't gon' have to go to town, Ma," Mama promised.

"No'am, Miz Carrie, us gon' find a place in the country where us gon' have a farm o' us own," Papa added.

"A farm anywhere, Silas, jes' so us don' have to move to town," Grandma moaned.

We were up early that Saturday morning to go to town with Mr. Willie. When he came around nine o' clock to pick us up, we were tired from waiting. The cow was milked and the chickens, hogs, and stock fed long before breakfast. Then we bathed and ate and put on our Sunday clothes, Mama had put on her shoes and taken them off many times, and Papa had been out to the lane three or four times to see if Mr. Willie was coming. Grandma put on her things and sat by the kitchen stove, drinking black coffee. I walked out to the lane with Papa every time he went. We walked hurriedly as if somehow that would cause Mr. Willie to rush. As anxious as we were about Mr. Willie's coming, there wasn't the excitement that there was the year before, when we had more money to spend in town. We were going to town mainly to see Naomi and find out what she needed and when the baby was coming.

Naomi had been gone since late spring, and I no longer missed her the way I did the first few weeks. But now that we were going to Vicksburg, it seemed that I couldn't wait to get there and see her.

Papa stood in the door, holding the framing; I stood by a post, alternately hugging it and swinging around it as we waited for Mr. Willie.

"Here he come!" Papa yelled and I ran out to open the gate.

We got into the car quickly and Mr. Willie headed down past Mr. Ben's and across the lower end of the plantation past Mr. Stock's and Mr. Miller Jackson's and Mr. Gus Hawkins' and Mr. Henry Woodson and Mrs. Nettie's and out to the lane on the other side of the place just below Mr. Willie's. He waved toward his house as we passed, but I didn't see anybody. And it had been that way almost all across the plantation. It was a cool, frosty morning, and smoke came from most of the chimneys. I think most of us, especially Mama, preferred not to see anybody much as we headed for town. The fewer folks Mama saw, the fewer she would have to explain that she hadn't gone to Vicksburg to get the washing machine she had been talking about but to see Naomi. And the fewer she had to explain that to, the fewer would be asking about Naomi, and fewer who asked about Naomi, the better we liked it.

We knew the folks were still whispering about Naomi leaving the plantation so suddenly, but they didn't say anything to us about it. Our going to Vicksburg would give them an excuse.

"Niggers gon' be jes' waitin' to ast us whut all us bought in Vicksburg," Grandma said, "'n' the next thing they gon' wanna know is ef us went by the jail to see Lilly Mae. 'N' then they gon' ast 'bout Naomi. Deceitful niggers."

"Let 'em ast all they wanna, us sho' ain't got to tell 'em," Mama said with an edge in her voice.

"Us ain't got no time to worry 'bout that; us gotta worry 'bout findin' us a place, like the other folks better be doin' 'stid o' talkin' 'bout Naomi," Papa said. "'N', Willie, ef you got the time, us would like to stop by 'n' talk with that colored man you say own a little farm out near Red Wood."

"I was jes' thinkin' 'bout that, Silas; found out where he live jes' the other day. It's off Sixty-One back over there a piece back o' Red Wood," Mr. Willie replied.

"Ef us stop by there goin', us might could go by the gover'ment place while us in town," Papa suggested.

"That's whut I think. They say it ain't fer off the highway," Mr Willie said. "Man at the service station say it's jes' 'bout two miles back in there jes' after us cross the bridge."

"That's good, Willie," Papa said with what started out to be a smile but which dried up before his teeth showed, as if doubt or fear that nothing would come of the visit caught his lips and held them together. "Then us can have that outa the way without makin' 'nother trip to town." His voice was flat and empty as if he had turned over a big watermelon and found it rotten underneath.

"Right, Silas," Mr. Willie approved. "Course, I gotta come to town evvy day anyhow, but you don't."

"Naw, the way us come out this year, us can't 'ford to come to town, 'cep'n when us gotta see 'bout Naomi," Papa explained. "Willie, us ain't cleared by little over two hund'ered dollars."

"I was disap'inted myself, Silas," Mr. Willie said. "Figgered my leben bales was gon' brine us leas' fo' hund'ered 'n' fifty dollars in the clear, 'cause us ain't took up much at the sto', with me gittin' paid fer carr'in' the mail, 'n' makin' a little somethin' haulin' folks to town, but us didn't clear but two hund'ered 'n' forty-fo' dollars. Time I buy shoes fer me 'n' Birdie 'n' us six chillun, 'n' two ti'es fer this old car, us ain't gon' have nothin' left much."

"Us didn't clear but two hund'ered 'n' two dollars, 'n' us had eight good bales," Papa said. "'N' us don' take up nothin' much at the sto' neither, 'cause us raise most all us food, 'cep'n coffee 'n' sugar 'n' flour."

"Look like ain't nobody on the place cleared nothin' much," Mr. Willie pointed out. "I hear Stock Robinson ain't cleared but two hund'ered 'n' twenty-three dollars off his twelve bales, 'n' Miller Jackson ain't carr'ed home but fifty-two dollars fer his ten bales. Course, he had a heap o' sickness. Emma was down fer two months 'n' two o' his boys was sick all spring with chills 'n' fever, 'n' you know, he los' his baby girl."

"'N' he ain't cleared but fifty-two dollars?" Mama asked.

"That's whut I hear, Becky."

"Whut did Henry 'n' Nettie clear, Willie?" Mama inquired with a little sly grin.

"You know they didn't come out with but six bales, don't you?" Mr. Willie said. "Well, I hear they ain't cleared but a hund'ered 'n' thirty-one dollars."

"Is that all, a hund'ered 'n' thirty-one dollars?" Mama said in pleased surprise.

"Ben 'n' me settled 'bout the same time," Papa said, "'n' he say he ain't cleared but a hund'ered 'n' sixty-fo' dollars."

"Well, po' Tom 'n' Luiza come out with jest forty-six dollars fer they five bales, 'n' some folks ain't cleared nothin'," Mr. Willie reported. Then he lowered his voice to a whisper as if Mr. Walter might be able to hear him from way out where we were. "Jes' 'tween us, Silas, I figger I cleared mo'n Mr. Walter give me credit fer."

"Us figger the same thing, Willie," Papa replied. "Course, I didn't say nothin, 'cause I reckon he up 'gainst it. There been so much trouble on the place this year."

"I think he sho'nuff up 'gainst it," Mr. Willie agreed, "'cause he done had to borrow money to pay Miz Susie out 'n' all."

"Willie, do you reckon he 'n' Miz Rhoda gon' be able to pull through?" Mama asked.

"Ef us can make good crops on the place next year, they might make it," Mr. Willie replied.

"I sho' hopes so," Mama said, "'cause they good white folks."

"Jes' as good as they come," Grandma added.

"Y'all is sho' right," Mr. Willie agreed, "'cause there one thing you can count on, the Williamsons gon' settle with you evvy year. I mean evvy year."

"They sho' do, Willie," Papa said. "You might come up a little short, but they gon' settle with you, 'n' that's mo'n you can say fer most o' these plantations."

Mr. Willie pressed harder on the gas as if to make up for lost time. We came around a clump of trees and up a little hill straight into the morning sun. Mr. Willie pulled down both sun visors, but the sun still struck me in the face. I put one hand over my eyes and leaned closer to Papa. In no time we had rounded a curve and come up behind more trees that shielded us from the sun again.

We crossed a narrow bridge that Mr. Willie said was over a neck of the Yazoo River. Then he pointed up ahead. "That's Highway 61. Soon as us cross the Yazoo River Bridge, us gon' turn off 'n' go by the colored man's farm. He Name Amos Ammons."

Mr. Willie may have explained things to us along the way the year before when he took us to Vicksburg, but I didn't remember. All my thoughts must have been on the things we were going to buy in town.

We came to a full stop at the highway and waited for several cars and trucks to pass before we got on it and headed south. We were barely on the highway when the long, tall Yazoo River Bridge came into view. We crossed it, turned left, and wound our way up through the hills. After about a mile on the narrow road, Mr. Willie stopped at a house and asked the man where Mr. Ammons lived.

"He live in the fourth house up the road," the man said, "'bout three-quarters of a mile from here."

"This is in the hills," Papa said as Mr. Willie drove on.

"It sho' is," Mr. Willie agreed.

"Ef a nigger own it, you oughta knowed it was in the hills," Grandma said, "'cause they can't git none o' that right delta land."

"I thought o' that, Miz Carrie," Papa replied, "but I thought there might be one nigger whut happen somehow to come by a piece o' delta land 'round here, like one or two did in Sunflower County."

"Up in these po' hills, I bet they don' git ha'f a bale to the acre," Mama said, "ef they grow cotton a'tall."

"I ain't seen no cotton yet," Papa said.

"Maybe they don' grow no cotton up here," Mr. Willie guessed, but just as he got the words out of his mouth, we rounded a hill and come up on a cotton patch. The stalks were no more than a foot high, and the bolls were far apart.

"Ef you can call that cotton, they grows it," Grandma said with a chuckle.

"This the fourth house," Mr. Willie said after rounding another hill. "Mus' be where Amos Ammons live."

He slowed down and pulled off the road a little. In the field near the house, a man was driving a mule-crawn stalk cutter. Papa and Mr. Willie got out of the car and walked toward him. I attempted to follow them, but Mama reached over the seat and caught the collar of my coat.

"Wait, River, might be a bad dog," she said.

The man stopped his cutter and got down off the machine and came to see what they wanted.

"Is you Mr. Amos Ammons?" Mr. Willie asked.

"Yes, I'm him," the tall brown farmer replied.

"I'm Willie Woods, the mail carr'er from Williamson Bend, 'n' this here is Silas Henry. He from the Bend, too."

"Pleased to meet you," the man said.

"'N' that's his family," Mr. Willie explained, pointing to us in the car.

Mr. Ammons came over to the car. "Won't y'all git out 'n' come in? My wife's in the house," he said in a friendly voice.

"Nawsuh, us don' have much time," Mama replied. "My husband, Silas, he come up here to ast you 'bout gover'ment credit to buy little piece o' land."

"Yes, I see," Mr. Ammons said, turning to Papa and Mr. Willie.

"Us heard the gover'ment is makin' loans to po' folks like us to buy little farms o' they own," Papa said, "'n' us thought you might know somethin 'bout it."

"Yes," Mr. Ammons answered, "the gover'ment do make loans to po' farmers, but it's mostly to help tide 'em over a year or two. They help 'em buy a mule or a cow or some chickens 'n' groceries 'n' feed fer livestock. Ain't no farmers through here got no loans to buy no land, but I heard o' farmers in other places whut got loans to buy land. They was mostly white, very few colored, but I hear there is some."

By now, Mrs. Ammons had come to the door. Seeing us in the car and the men engaged in conversation, she walked down the steps and out to the gate. "These folks from Williamson Bend, honey. Come on out 'n' meet 'em," her husband said.

She came to the car and invited us in, but Mama explained again that we didn't have much time. So Mrs. Ammons stood by the car with her hands rolled up in her apron and talked quietly with Mama and Grandma, while Mr. Ammons continued discussing government loans with Papa and Mr. Willie.

"You ever git any credit from 'em?" Papa asked.

"Yes, I got a loan to buy a couple o' mules three years ago, 'n' befo' that we bought a cow 'n' some baby chicks on credit. 'N' evvy year I borrow money from 'em to make my crop."

"Where the office at?" Mr. Willie wanted to know.

"In the post office building in Vicksburg."

"In the post office building? I go there evvy day 'n' I ain't seen no sign 'bout no gover'ment loans to farmers."

"It don' say that; it jes' say 'The Farmers Home Administration' on the little boa'd on the wall right 'long with the Extension Service 'n' the Soil Conservation Service 'n' the Commodity Stabilization Service," Mr. Ammons explained.

"I ain't hear o' none o' them," Mr. Willie said.

"You know 'bout the county agents, don't you? Mr. Flagg 'n' Mr. Burton Mackey?"

"I heard o' Mr. Flagg; he come to the Bend sometime 'n' talk with Mr. Walter 'n' Mr. Win. Course, Mr. Win he dead now, but I ain't never heard o' Mr. Mackey," Mr. Willie replied.

"Mr. Mackey is the colored county agent," Mr. Ammons said. "Him 'n' Mr. Flagg 'n' two women, Miss Williams 'n' Miss Dishmon, is the Extension Service."

"I see," Mr. Willie said thoughtfully.

"All these gover'ment agencies help farmers, mostly them whut owns land. They don' do much fer you ef you don' own no land," Mr. Ammons pointed out.

"But the one whut 'low credit do, don't it?" Papa asked.

"Yes, it help farmers whut don' own no land," Mr. Ammons said.

"Whut you say the name o' it is?" Papa inquired with a frown of puzzlement on his face.

"It's the Farmers Home Administration."

"Muchoblige, Mr. Ammons. That's the one us wanna see," Papa said.

"Jes' go right on up there 'n' see 'em. You never can tell; they might make you a loan to buy a piece o' land. You never can tell," Mr. Ammons repeated. "The man he name Mr. Warrenton, Mr. Ken Warrenton. He right there on the second flo'."

"Mr. Warrenton?" Papa asked with a new frown on his face. "Ain't he the sheriff?"

"Naw, the sheriff name Jack. He the sheriff's brother," Mr. Ammons explained.

"Oh, that's diff'ent; I don' never wanna see that damn sheriff no mo'," Papa said.

"Naw, he ain't the sheriff; you go on up there 'n' see him, 'cause you never can tell," Mr. Ammons said.

"Well, muchoblige ag'in, Mr. Ammons," Papa said with new confidence in his voice. "Us sho' muchoblige."

Papa and Mr. Willie got back into the car and we drove away, leaving Mr. and Mrs. Ammons standing in front of the white picket fence, which enclosed their pretty white house with blue trimming. I had never seen colored folks living in a painted house before. I thought our houses weren't supposed to be painted. When we first drove up, I thought we were at a white man's house and I kept waiting for him to come out. Then Mrs. Ammons walked out of the front door without a broom in her hands. And I was still puzzled about colored folks coming out of the front door of white folks' houses unless they worked there, until Mrs. Ammons invited us to come in.

Mr. Ammons was different, too. He had walked leisurely from his stalk cutter over to talk with Papa and Mr. Willie. He wasn't hurried as if someone was watching him and counting the time. And he gave direct answers without fumbling about and scratching his head, and he knew the exact names of government agencies, where they were located, and what services they provided. Mr. Willie had been going to the post office every day for years and years and he had never heard of these agencies. The difference, it seemed to me, was that Mr. Ammons owned his own farm and was his own man and not a landless tenant like Papa and Mr. Willie, staying or moving at the will of the plantation owner, clearing money for a year's work or coming out in debt by another man's figures, waiting sometimes indefinitely for settlement time while his children stayed home from school because they had no shoes.

XVIII

Sharecroppers Request Government Loans to Buy Own Farms

Visiting Mr. Ammons made me more anxious than ever for my father to own a farm. And it seemed that we would never get to Vicksburg and the post office, where Papa and Mr. Willie were going to talk with the government man about credit to buy farms of their own.

Finally, we were in town, driving up a street that ran up a high hill. There were the railroad tracks and the smell of coal tar.

"That used to be the river right over there," Mr. Willie said, pointing across the tracks. "Now it ain't nothin' but a lake. The river over yonder hehin' them trees."

"I bet there some good fishin' in there," Mama said.

"Used to be," Mr. Willie replied, "but not no mo'; too many folks fishin' in it, 'n' too many o' them little boats racin' 'round makin' noise."

"Look, Mama," I said. "That' s the sto' you bought yo' stove at."

"It sho' is," Mama said. "River, you sho' got a good memory, ain't he, Ma?"

"He sho' is; got a min' like a steel trap; don' let nothin' go," Grandma said.

Papa's hand, which hung down from the back of the seat, came down and rested on my shoulder. "His memory better'n mine," he said, glancing back at Mama and Grandma.

"Like my chillun," Mr. Willie added, "they can 'member evvything."

"There's the Valley," Mama said in admiration. "That's where I was gon' git my stove 'tel that ole man back there stopped us. How fer is this from the post office where you goin', Willie?"

"It ain't nowhere, right 'round the corner 'bout a block 'n' a ha'f."

"Well, me 'n' Ma 'n' River gon' come back here 'n' git the cloth fer the dresses 'n' a few things, Silas, while you 'n' Willie go to the gover'ment place," Mama said.

"Mama, I wanna go with Papa," I said, moving closer to my father and catching his coat.

"Don't you wanna go in the pretty sto' 'n' see all the pretty things?" Mama asked.

"No'am, I wanna go with Papa. Can't I go with you, Papa?" I begged.

"Can he go with you 'n' Willie, Silas?"

"I reckon so, Becky. It'll be all right, won't it, Willie?" Papa inquired.

"Sho'; might eben help, them seein' you with a little boy, 'n' they might make you a loan," Mr. Willie said as he pulled in back of the post office.

We got out of the car; Mama and Grandma tried to brush the wrinkles out of their coats and dresses with their hands; Papa and I stood stiffly by the side of the car while Mr. Willie opened the trunk and took out the mail bag.

"Us'll meet you right back here at twelve o'clock," Mama said. "It's ten-thirty now, is that all right?"

"That's fine, Becky," Mr. Willie replied, and Mama and Grandma walked back down the hill toward the Valley.

"Willie, how long it gon' take you with the mail?" Papa asked.

"Oh, I don' know; I tell you whut, why don't you 'n' River go on up there, 'n' I'll come up soon as I gits through with the mail?" Mr. Willie suggested.

"All right," Papa said, taking me by the hand and walking around to the front of the building, but he didn't walk with his usual stride. His steps were shorter and less direct, as if he was uncertain where he was going and not fully decided if he should go.

In front of the post office, a crowd of people were on the street like at the Bend when church let out. We walked up the steps and entered the post office. Papa looked all around, then we went to one of the windows, where he asked the man where the Farmers Home Administration was.

"Right up those stairs over there, the third door on your right."

"Muchoblige, suh," Papa said, and we mounted the stairs.

I counted the doors, only I was counting on the left. "This is it, Papa," I said, trying to pull him over to the left side of the hallway.

"Naw, River, the man said on the right."

Papa opened the next door and we walked in, taking off our hats as we entered. We walked up to the counter, which was much taller than the one at the store at the Bend. I couldn't see over it, but I could hear ladies talking and laughing.

It seems that we had been standing there an hour, when one of the ladies finally hollered across the room, "You want something, boy?"

I looked to try to see where the voice was coming from because I thought the lady was speaking to me. "Ma'am," I said, letting Papa's hand go and moving beyond the counter to a wooden fence and a gate. "Ma'am," I said again.

"I'm not talkin' to you; I'm talkin' to him," she said, looking Papa straight in the eye from where she sat.

The other ladies stopped laughing and looked at me and Papa.

"Yessum," Papa said, "is this the place where the gover'ment give credit to po' farmers to buy farms o' they own, ma'am?"

"It was when I came in here this mornin'," the lady said in a voice like Mama's whenever she was angry with Papa for being late for a meal and he asked if it was ready. She would reply coldly, "It was at six o'clock this edenin'."

"Well, ma'am, I come to find out 'bout gittin' one o' them loans," Papa said slowly as if trying not to let himself get out of hand.

"Whut's yo' name, boy?"

"River," I said. "It's River, ma'am."

The lady's face flushed, and she looked at me from where she was standing, a good six feet away, like we had some kind of disease, and she said, "Little nigger boy, will you keep yo' mouth shut?"

"He ain't meant no harm, ma'am," Papa said.

"Well, you better teach him to keep his big mouth shut befo' somebody shut it fer him."

"I'm sorry, ma'am; he jes' a little boy 'n' he thought you was talkin' to him when you said 'boy.'"

"Well, I'll let it go this time," she said, moving to a place at the counter five or six feet away. "What's yo' name?"

"Silas Henry, ma'am."

"Where you from, Silas?"

"Williamson Bend, ma'am."

"That place belongs to Mr. Walter Williamson, don't it?"

"Yessum."

"Does he know you down here tryin' to git a loan to buy a farm?"

"No'am, I don' reckon he do, I ain't tol' him yet."

"Well, Mr. Williamson could git awful mad at you 'n' us, too, fer helpin' you to sneak off his place."

"I ain't gon' sneak off, ma'am. I come here to see ef I could git credit to buy a piece o' land. Ef I git the credit, I'm gon' tell him I'm gon' move."

"I bet you gon' tell him; all the niggers say that. I bet you knee-deep in debt to Mr. Williamson, 'n' comin' down here tryin' to git us to help you sneak off."

"Ma'am, I don' owe Mr. Williamson a cent. I cleared two hund'ered 'n' two dollars this year, 'n' I save thirty dollars from las' year to pay down on a farm o' my own."

"Well, anyhow, our funds fer makin' ownership loans are exhausted, Silas, but we do have a little money for production loans. We might be able to lend you money fer fertilizer and poison fer yo' cotton, or to buy a mule," the lady said, "but you'll have to take an application form to Mr. Williamson 'n' git him to sign it, 'n' you'll have to have a written lease fer three to five years on the farm you rentin' from Mr. Williamson."

"Yessum, I got mules 'n' Mr. Walter got fertilizer 'n' poison. Whut 'bout a loan to buy a little piece o' ground?" Papa asked.

"I jes' tol' you our ownership funds are exhausted."

"Exhausted? Whut that mean, ma'am?" Papa asked, and the room came down in laughter.

Papa looked around the room at the ladies lying on their desk laughing their heads off. I think he was a little afraid at first, and then the lady to whom he was speaking smiled for the first time and said, "Silas, that means we are out of money for such loans."

"The gover'ment outa money, ma'am?" Papa asked with a puzzled look on his face. "How can the gover'ment be outa money?"

There was more laughter, enough to bring the supervisor out of his office.

"Whut's the trouble, Miss Harkness?"

"Oh, it's nothin', Mr. Warrenton; I was jes' tryin' to explain to this boy here that we are outa money fer makin' ownership loans."

"I see, but whut's so funny?"

"He can't understan' the gover'ment bein' outa money."

"Oh, huh huh huh," he grinned. "Sometimes I can't understan' it myself. Where you from, boy?"

"Williamson Bend, suh."

"That's Mr. Walter Williamson's place, ain't it?"

"Yessuh."

"His brother, Mr. Win, got killed up there this year, didn't he?"

"Yessuh."

"Well, boy, I might as well tell you right now, we don' make no loans to none o' the niggers on the plantations, less'n the landlords consent. You see, if we did, we could take away some o' they bes' niggers. 'N' I'm certainly not gon' do that to Mr. Williamson now while he in the fix he's in."

"Yessuh."

"He git any them cotton-pickers yet?"

"Nawsuh."

"I thought he hadn't. Now how he gon' git his cotton picked next year, ef we make you 'n' some o' these other niggers loans to go runnin' off to a little piece o' land o' yo' own?"

"But I thought you was the gover'ment, suh."

"I ain't exactly the gover'ment; I represent the gover'ment. 'N' I'm gon' be honest with you, boy. We do make a few loans sometimes to niggers on plantations to buy a little farm, but they mostly good ole nigger whut done wore theyselves out 'n' ain't no mo' good. We know from the start they ain't gon' make it, but we make 'em loans to take 'em off the hands o' the plantation owners. But you look strong 'n' healthy; you mus' be one o' the bes' niggers on Mr. Williamson's place. The committee ain't gon' approve no loan fer you 'n' take you 'way from Mr. Williamson, 'n' I couldn't blame 'em."

"The committee, you say, suh?"

"Yes, the committee o' leadin' white farmers 'round here in the county. We jes' can't make you no loan."

"Yessuh," Papa said, and there was a sag in his voice like the sag of a cotton-picking sack you just emptied. Our hopes had been raised by Mr. Amos Ammons, but now they lay on the ground.

I felt water gathering in my eyes, and before I knew it, tears were running down my cheeks, and my mouth was open wide and a fearsome sound was coming out. I ran to Papa and hugged his leg. He picked me up in his arms and I saw tears in his eyes, too.

As we turned away from the counter, Papa said, "Muchoblige, suh."

Papa carried me all the way down the steps and out of the post office. On the stoop he put me down and we walked around back to Mr. Willie's car. I was still crying, but Papa's eyes were dry and his face was hard and dull like a hoe that has been under the house all winter and is no longer bright and shiny.

Mr. Willie, who was standing by the car talking with Mama and Grandma, who were seated inside, saw my tears and read Papa's face. "Whut done happen?" he asked.

Mama looked wildly out of the car. "Whut's the matter, Silas? Whut's the matter with you 'n' River?"

"Oh, it ain't nothin', Becky."

"Did somebody bother my baby?" she asked, getting out of the car and wiping my face with her tiny handkerchief. Her tenderness, plus the sad news Papa and I carried in our hearts, triggered more tears as she knelt by me. "Whut's the matter with River, Silas? I done ast you did somebody in that ole office do something to my baby?"

"Naw, Becky, ain't nobody done nothin' to him; he jes' crying 'cause us ain't gon' git no loan to buy no farm," Papa explained.

"How come?" Mama asked.

"'Cause us ain't old 'n' wore out."

"Whut you mean, Silas?" Mr. Willie wanted to know.

"The gover'ment don' lend no money to niggers on plantations, 'cep'n they old 'n' the white folks wanna git rid o' 'em."

"Oh, go 'way from here, Silas, you is joking, ain't you?"

"Naw, I ain't jokin'. That's whut the man said; 'n' anyhow, Willie, how come you didn't come in like you said 'n' see 'bout gittin' a loan yo'self?"

"By the time I finished with the mail, Becky 'n' Miz Carrie was back, 'n' us already late; gotta go by 'n' see Naomi 'n' all. So I thought I'd see how you made out, 'n' I'd go by some other day when I'm in town."

By now I was in the car with my head in Grandma's lap. She was caressing my hair and face with one hand and patting my back with the other. "My po' little baby," she said, "disapp'inted 'cause us ain't gon' have no farm. Well, the Lawd, He gon' look after us." Then she reached down on the floor and picked up a box and opened it. "Oh, look whut yo' mama done bought you, a new pair shoes."

They were black and shiny and had the smell of newness. I clutched them in both hands, lay back down in Grandma's lap, and went to sleep. When I awoke, Naomi was standing by the car.

"Come on in, y'all," she was saying.

She was thinner than I had ever seen her, and her face and lips were pale and a little wrinkled like Mama's hands after washing our clothes. We all got out of the car and followed her. The houses were close together and seemed to be sitting down in a hole with their porches and little walkways pressed against the hillside like bottom lips forming a path to and from the sidewalk.

Inside, the walls were covered with beautiful paper with pink roses climbing up a white fence, but from part of the ceiling, the paper had come unglued and was hanging loose in places. There were a bed, two small chairs, and a washstand with a shiny tin basin on it, not at all like Mama's china pitcher and bowl, which were never used, except when the preacher came to dinner.

Naomi lived in a little room downstairs. It was so small, we all couldn't get inside. Papa and Mr. Willie and I stood on the steps while Mama and Grandma went into the room with Naomi to get the baby. It had already come. About two weeks ago, my sister said, but she had felt too weak after coming out of the hospital to write and tell us about it.

"Her weigh eight pounds, Mama," Naomi said. "Ain't her a big girl?"

"Her sho' is; lemme hol' her," Mama said. "Unnnnuh hunnhuh, ain't her fine, Silas?"

"Her sho' is 'n' her almos' white, too," Papa said mostly with pride, but with some misgivings, I think.

"That her is, that her is," Grandma added without reservations. "That's 'zackly whut her wanted. Ain't her white 'n' pretty? 'N' her jes' like her daddy."

"Lemme see, Mama?" I asked, tiptoeing and stretching my neck to try to see.

Mama held the baby low so that I could get a good look. To me the baby looked like a little pig fresh from a litter. She was white and withered with red bumps all over her and tried to hold up one hand, which trembled constantly. Naomi, who had been standing proudly with her arms folded, reached over and pulled the baby's blanket up a little.

"Her look like her papa, but I think her got my eyes, don't you, Mama?" my sister asked.

"They big 'n' round jes' like yo's was when you was a baby, ain't they, Silas?"

"Jes' like 'em, Becky," Papa agreed.

"Her sho' is a pretty baby," Mr. Willie said, "as pretty as a little doll."

"Thank you, Mr. Willie," Naomi said, her big eyes smiling and her gold tooth showing.

As I looked at my sister, I thought of the picture of Moses in our Bible showing him standing in the mountains smiling as he viewed the Promised Land after forty years in the wilderness. I knew this bright baby was what she wanted more than anything else in this world. Nobody would ever call her daughter black or rub her with lard and bleach creams, trying to make her bright. And no teacher would ever give her the servant's role in the school play, and the boys would never leave her sitting while others danced. She would never need a gold tooth in the front of her mouth or a straightening comb in her hair.

"Whut the baby name?" Mr. Willie asked.

"Yes, whut her name, Naomi?" Mama joined in.

"I named her after Grandma; her name Carrie Mae," my sister said.

"Ain't that nice, Silas, her named her after Ma."

"It sho' is, ain't it, Miz Carrie?" Papa said.

Grandma started dabbing at her eyes to keep back tears. "Indeed, it is, Silas, indeed, it is," she answered in a muffled voice. "These old bones may soon be gone, but my name gon' be carr'ed on."

We heard the door opening upstairs and someone coming in.

"It's Miz Addie," Naomi said, "her the lady I lives with. "Miz Addie, us down in my room, come on down."

The lady came to the head of the stairs and hollered down, "Why don't y'all come up here, where it's mo' room?"

When we got up the stairs, she said, "Mr. Woods, you 'n' the other gentleman set in the chairs, 'n' Naomi 'n' her mama 'n' grandma 'n' the little boy can set on the side o' the bed. "This yo' little brother you been tellin' me 'bout? Ain't he cute?"

"Yessum, Miz Addie, that's River 'n' this here my papa, Mr. Silas Henry."

"Pleased to meet you, Mr. Henry; you sho' got a nice daughter. I'm so glad to have her here with me."

"Thanky, ma'am; her was always a good girl," Papa replied.

"Miz Henry, how you 'n' yo' ma been?"

"Us been fine, Miz Green, jes' fine."

"Miz Green," Papa spoke up, "us come by to settle whut Naomi owe; us done ginned us cotton."

"You don' owe me a thing, Mr. Henry; the welfare been payin' me fifteen dollars evvy month."

"But they was two weeks late startin', Miz Addie," Naomi said, "so Papa owe you fer ha'f a month."

"Whut is two weeks?" Mrs. Green said. "You don' owe me nothin'."

"That sho' nice o' you, Miz Green, but I gotta give you somethin'," my father said, handing her five dollars and Naomi ten.

Both smiled broadly and thanked him.

"'N' Naomi," Mama said, "us done brought you somethin' fer the baby; got 'em jes' while ago at the Valley. Go git 'em, River; they in a bag in the car."

I ran to the car and returned with the bag. Mama pulled out the things for the baby: diapers, socks, and two little dresses. "Wish I had got 'em pink. The lady said pink was fer girls 'n' blue was fer boys, but I didn't know it was born, so I got blue."

"Blue, pink, whut the diff'ence?" Naomi said. "They sho' pretty."

Then Mama laid out the three pieces of cloth she had bought to make the dresses. "Which piece you like, Naomi? I'm gon' make you a dress."

"They all pretty," my sister said, holding the cloth up to the light, "but I think I like this piece bes', this brown plaid."

"That's whut Ma 'n' me thought you'd like," Mama said. "I really got the black piece fer Ma 'n' the blue stripe fer myself."

"Well, us better be goin', 'cause Willie got to git the mail to the Bend," Papa said, "but us be back befo' Christmas."

"Don' worry 'bout me 'n' the baby, us doin' jes' fine," my sister said. "Soon as I git my strength back, I'm goin' to work. Miz Addie done got me a job right next do' to where her work. "I'm gon' cook 'n' clean up fer the lady 'n' her gon' give me fifteen dollars a week. Bessie Mae, her the girl in the second house, her gon' keep Carrie Mae fer me 'long with her chillun, 'n' I'm gon' give her three dollars a week. That gon' leave me eight dollars 'n' a ha'f after I pay Miz Addie fer the zoom. So you see, I'm gon' be doin' all right."

"'N' her can make ten or fifteen dollars durin' the Christmas, ef her feel like it, jes' helpin' me out where I works," Mrs. Green said.

"Oh, that's wonderful, ain't it, Silas?" Mama replied. "'N' us thanks you fer evvythin' you been doin' fer Naomi, Miz Green."

"Her almos' like my own daughter. Course, I ain't got no chillun."

"Us sho' muchoblige to you, Miz Green," Papa said.

We had started toward the door when Mama turned back quickly. "I almos' fergot. How is Reverend Fisher 'n' his chillun doin', Naomi?"

"Jes' fine. I meant to tell you 'bout them," my sister said. "He visited me while I was in the hospital with my baby 'n' he give me two dollars."

"Reverend Fisher give you two dollars?" Papa asked as if he thought something was wrong with his hearing.

"Yessuh, Papa," Naomi replied. "He give me two dollars 'n' he prayed with me."

"He mus' be doin' all right ef he give you two dollars," Grandma added.

"Yessum, he tol' me he now actin' pastor of a big Baptist church, New Hope, here in Vicksburg."

"A Baptist church 'n' he a Methodist?" Mama asked in disbelief.

"He say he gon' be ordained in the Baptist church," my sister explained. "Said there wasn't no future no mo' fer him in the Methodist church. He already livin' in the parsonage, 'n' jes' as soon as he ordained, he say they gon' make him pastor o' the church."

"Well, ain't that fine? I'm sho glad to hear that," Mama said.

"Me, too," said Papa.

"The Lawd do move in mysterious ways," Grandma added.

"He said all his chillun is fine 'n' is goin' to school," Naomi pointed out, "'n' he said Lilly Mae's trial is comin' up after Christmas."

"After Christmas?" Mama asked.

"Yessum, he tol' me it was set fer January 12. I 'member it, 'cause Carrie Mae'll be two months old on that day. 'N' Papa he said he was gon' git in touch with you befo' then, 'cause he want you to 'pear in court 'n' speak a good word fer Lilly Mae."

"He did?" Papa asked. "Well, he ain't got in touch with me."

"I guess he gon' write you befo' long," my sister said.

"I hope he don', 'cause I don' wanna git mixed in it no further'n I'm already is," Papa said in a quiet voice.

"He said with the NAACP handlin' the case, you was 'bout the only one he knowed whut wouldn't be scared to testify."

"I ain't scared, but us got 'nuff problems o' us own right now without takin' on no mo'," Papa said.

"Whut kinda good word can you say fer that gal, anyhow?" Grandma wanted to know.

"Oh, Ma, don' say that," Mama chided Grandma. "There some good in evvybody. You 'n' me both know that po' chile ain't never had no chance, 'specially since her mama died."

"Well, Silas can git mixed up in this ef he wanna," Grandma persisted.

"I'm gon' think 'bout it, Miz Carrie, 'n' I'm gon' wait fer him to contact me," Papa said, opening the door. "Us better be goin', you know, Willie got to git the mail to the Bend."

Then we all took another look at the baby, kissed Naomi, and said goodbye to Mrs. Green.

"I'm gon' bring yo' dress next time us come," Mama said. "You 'bout the same size, ain't you?"

"Yessum, I'm 'bout the same, maybe a ha'f size smaller. Oh, wait a minute; I saw a dress in the paper." She went downstairs and returned with a wrinkled piece of newspaper. "See this dress, Mama? I'd like it like this," my sister said, tearing the picture out and handing it to her.

"That's cute, Naomi; hope I can make it."

"Oh, you can, Mama; you can make anything."

Mama smiled and we left the house and got into the car. Naomi followed us and said goodbye again. We all waved as the car pulled off.

Mr. Willie hadn't said anything for a while, and his smile was gone. As soon as we were out of the heavy traffic, he spoke up. "Silas, you oughta try to git outa testifyin' fer Lilly Mae. It don' mean nothin but trouble. I'm tellin' you fer yo' own good. Mr. Walter jes' ain't gon' understan' you testifyin' fer the NAACP."

"Willie's right, Silas; that's somethin' to think 'bout," Mama said. "Course us all know Lilly Mae ain't no sho'nuff bad girl, but yet 'n' still yo' standin' up fer her in court could git us in trouble with Mr. Walter, like Willie say."

"Silas, Becky 'n' Willie is tellin' you the truth," Grandma put in. "You can't 'ford to git mixed up with that gal 'n' that N Double-A CP."

"Y'all is right," Papa said. "It don' make no sense fer me to git mixed up in this, but I got to think 'bout 'n' do whut my conscience say."

"Well, I sho' hopes yo' conscience got mo' sense 'n' you got, " Grandma warned.

"Reverend Fisher he off the plantation now 'n' in Vicksburg doin' good," Mr. Willie pointed out. "It ain't no skin off'n his back don' care whut Mr. Walter do to you 'n' yo' family."

"'N' us sho' needs two mo' years at the Bend to save up 'nuff to pay down on a farm o' us own, since the gover'ment ain't go help us," Mama argued.

"I thought o' that, Becky," Papa replied, turning around in the front seat to look at Mama as he spoke. "Jes' give time to think it over." He was firm and determined in his statement, and he said it a little gruffly.

Everyone understood and the car was quiet, except for the purr of the motor and the sound of the tires rolling over the concrete highway.

As we passed the road where we had turned off to go to Mr. Ammons', Papa spoke up for the first time since he had called a halt to the discussion about him testifying for Lilly Mae. "That feller down the road there sho' doin' good," he said. "Own his own farm 'n' got a nice house 'n' it's painted, too."

"Silas, us gon' have a place o' us own one o' these days; I jes' know us is," Mama said. "All us needs is ha'f a chance. A year or two mo' at the Bend 'n' us oughta have 'nuff to git a farm without the ole gover'ment's help."

"Us sho' can, Becky, ef us jes' have ha'f a chancelike you say," Papa agreed.

"But you ain't gon' have no chance a'tall, ef you go testifyin' fer that gal," Mr. Willie warned.

"Now, Willie, I done said I was gon' think 'bout it, ain't I? Jes' give me little time; don' rush me so; I gotta make up my min', Gawddamit," Papa said with finality.

As we near the Bend, I thought of those ole people in the government office and how they had accused him of wanted to sneak off the plantation. "You don' reckon that ole gover'ment man gon' call Mr. Walter 'n' tell him us been there, do you, Papa?" I asked.

"I hadn't thought o' that," Mama said. "You don' reckon that man would do that, do you?"

"I don' know; I don' think so, then he might," Papa said.

"Oh, I don' think he would do that," Mr. Willie put in.

"Naw, I don' think so either," Papa agreed. "Whut reason would he have fer doin' that?"

"White folks don' have to have no reason," Grandma said flatly. "I bet the gover'ment 'n' these plantation folks workin' hand 'n' glove like they always done 'bout the parity checks 'n' 'bout the 'lotments."

"I know, they is, Miz Carrie," Papa said, "but ef us can jes' stay a couple mo' year like Becky say, us gon' git a place."

"But right now us gotta worry 'bout two things, Silas," Mama pointed out. "Us gotta worry 'bout the gover'ment man tellin' Mr. Walter us been there tryin' to git a loan so us can git away from the Bend, 'n' us gotta worry 'bout whut gon' happen, ef you testified fer Lilly Mae.

XIX

Sharecroppers Worried about Owner Losing the Plantation

The government man did tell Mr. Walter. Called him as soon as we left and told him we had been to his office, trying to get a loan to buy a farm. And he told Mr. Walter what he told us and asked him if Papa owed him any money.

That's what Mr. Walter told us that same afternoon when he and Mrs. Rhoda drove down to our house, parked out front, and blew the horn. Papa went out to see what they wanted. He didn't go as casually as Mr. Ammons had come over to Mr. Willie's car, but he didn't exactly rush, either. Mama had cooked and we were eating when we heard the horn, the loud, demanding horn of Mr. Walter's big car. I followed Papa out to the car, followed at a distance until Mrs. Rhoda smiled at me. Mama and Grandma came out, too, seeing Mrs. Rhoda.

"We just drove down to talk with you," Mr. Walter began. "Mr. Warrenton called from Vicksburg 'n' told us you 'n' yo' boy had been down there tryin' to git a loan to buy a little farm."

"Yessuh, I sho' did," Papa said and Mama flinched a little. "I didn't mean no harm, us jes' want a little piece o' land o' us own."

"That's all right," Mr. Walter replied, "but we don' want you to feel pushed in any way. I know there been talk goin' 'round since Mr. Win was killed 'n' I had to buy out Mrs. Susie 'n' the children, 'n' I don' mind tellin' you we're a little up against it right now, but I think we gon' pull through. May be a little tight a year or two, but we gon' make it. So y'all don' have to feel you ain't got a place here."

"Yessuh, thank, suh," Papa said, "us muchoblige to know that."

"Of course, Silas," Mrs. Rhoda spoke up. "We know in the longrun, there won't be a'place at the Bend for all the folks. Once Walter and I get things straightened out, we want to help some of the folks in an orderly way to find places to which to move."

"I sho' hope it ain't to town, Miz Rhoda," Mama said, "'cause us wanna stay in the country 'n' have a farm."

"Naw, Lawd, not to town, Miz Rhoda," Grandma added.

"Well, I don't know," Mrs. Rhoda answered hesitatingly. "I'm afraid some will have to move to town, maybe not you, but some certainly. You saw how the weed killer reduced chopping, and I am sure you have heard about the mechanical cotton picker."

"'N' on plantations where these are used," Mr. Walter cut in, "obviously, fewer people are needed."

"Yessuh, us understan' that, Mr. Walter," Papa said, moving closer to the car, "but still there oughta be some place in the country fer some po' folks like us."

"There will be, Silas, for a few," Mr Walter replied, "but only a few. Take me, for instance, I don' wanna replace the people with chemical weed killers 'n' mechanical cotton pickers, but I don't have any choice. Everybody else is using this new technology to cut costs. 'N' we have to reduce costs, too, not only because of our present financial situation, but also because cotton is in surplus 'n' the price is certain to get lower 'n' lower."

"Yessuh," Papa said quietly with his eyes on the ground, where the toe of his shoe was digging into a small mound of dirt.

"Now, Silas," Mrs. Rhoda said quickly, as if to catch Papa's spirit before it hit the ground, "Walter will not be able to buy machinery this year or maybe next, so you have no real worry about moving for at least two years. By then, we hope to have improved the school, provided some trade school training so that those who may have to leave will be better equipped to earn a living wherever they go."

"Whut 'bout the old folks whut's too old to learn? Whut 'bout them?" Grandma wanted to know.

"Frankly, we don't know the answer, Aunt Carrie," Mrs. Rhoda said, "and that keeps me and Walter awake nights trying to figure out how they can be provided for. Of course, some will move with their children, but for those who do not have children or close relatives, we'll have to find a place for them." Then she looked at Mr. Walter as if she expected him to add something, but he seemed buried in thought.

"Nat'ally, Miz Rhoda 'n' Mr. Walter," Papa said, "Miz Carrie goin' where us go." He paused a little after he said Miz Carrie, as if he wasn't sure he should have said it, knowing how white folks were about colored folks calling each other Mr. and Mrs in their presence. But after the pause, he went on hurridly. "So us ain't worried 'bout that. Whut us worried 'bout is ef us gon' have a place to go us-selves."

"Oh, you gon' have a place to go, Silas," Mr. Walter said, "probably a little farm o' yo' own like you say."

"But I ain't sho' us can save up 'nuff in a year or two to pay down on a farm," Papa replied. "'N' Mr. Warrenton at the gover'ment loan place didn't talk like he was gon' help us buy no farm. He said he made them kinda loans mostly to old wore-out farmers on plantations to take 'em off the hands o' the owners."

As Papa spoke, his eyes began to light up as if an idea had come into his head. "'N' maybe, Mr. Walter, ef you spoke to him, he might make loans to some o' us on the place to help take us off'n yo' hands in a year or two when you git yo' cotton-pickin' machines 'n' add mo' cattle 'n' don' need us no mo'."

"Personally, I don't think the government should be used that way," Mr. Walter replied, "but you're a good farmer, Silas, 'n' I would certainly recommend you. In fact, I told Mr. Warrenton that today when he called."

"Did you, Mr. Walter, sho'nuff?" Papa said, swinging his arms and smiling more broadly than I had ever seen him smile in front of a white man.

"I certainly did. So when the time comes, you don' have to worry about that, I'll recommend you."

"Thanky, Mr. Walter 'n' Miz Rhoda," Papa said with the smile even broadening on his face.

"Us sho' thanks you, Mr. Walter 'n' Miz Rhoda," Mama added. "The Lawd'll bless you, I know He will," Grandma said.

"Thank you, Aunt Carrie," Mr. Walter replied, "but y'all, let's wait 'n' see how things go first." Then he reached down and placed a hand on my shoulder. "You haven't said anything about this, River; I bet you wanna go straight to town."

"Nawsuh, Mr. Walter," I said. "I wanna stay with Papa on the farm 'n' drive his tractor when he gits one."

"You do?"

"Yessuh."

"Well, you don' have to wait until yo' papa's gets one, when you grow up you may be drivin' a tractor for me right here at the Bend. How would you like that?" Mr. Walter asked.

I was afraid not to say, "Yessuh, I'd sho' like that," and yet I wanted to tell him I wanted to drive Papa's tractor on our own farm. So I hesitated and avoided his eyes by keeping mine on the ground where the frost had turned the grass brown. But Mrs. Rhoda understood.

"The boy wants to drive his father's tractor, Walter, on their own farm, not one on a plantation," she said as if reading my mind.

"Well, they'll have their chance one o' these days, maybe," he said as he started up his motor. "But you ain't got nothin' to worry 'bout right now, Silas."

"Yessuh, thanky, suh," Papa yelled as the car pulled off.

They left all of us smiling.

"Did you hear whut Mr. Walter said?" Papa asked in a happy voice. "He said he would recommend me to the gover'ment loan man in Vicksburg so us can git a farm o' us own when the time come."

"Thanky, Jesus," Grandma said with mist gathering in her tired old eyes.

"It's sho' good, ain't it, Becky, Mr. Walter 'n' Miz Rhoda talkin' like that?" Papa said, still standing in his tracks, watching Mr. Walter's car move up the lane.

Mama did not answer immediately. She was quiet as if afraid even to hope for so much, as if afraid to begin counting on it, as if there was something in the back of her mind troubling her. When she did speak, what was troubling her came out. "It might sound good now, Silas," Mama said, "but whut they gon' say when they finds out you gon' testify fer Lilly Mae 'n' that N Double-A CP?"

The joy in Papa's eyes went out like a lamp blown out by the wind. He jammed his hands down in his pockets, bit his top lip, and kicked as clod of dirt as he walked slowly toward the house. Before he reached the steps, he turned to Mama and said, "I ain't finished thinkin' 'bout it yet, Becky, but you know I got to do whut I thinks is right."

All the next week, Papa was a restless as a young colt. He seldom sat down but paced the floor or stood by the fire with his elbow on the mantlepiece. Even when we went pecan hunting over the levee, he didn't pick up many nuts but spent most of his time leaning against the trees. From the middle of the week on, he and Mama were gone all day, helping neighbors kill hogs and clean chittlings. And when they came home late in the afternoon, they brought some of the chitterlings and a little pork sausage. Mama fried the sausage and served it with hot lyehominy, baked sweetpotatoes, and collard greens. This, I thought, was the best food in the whole world, only there never was enough sausage, although she gave me most of what she brought home, while she and Papa and Grandma smacked their lips after gobbling down the chitterlings, which she had recleaned and cooked in a pot out in the backyard so that they wouldn't stink up the house. I never ate any of them.

Friday was hog-killing day at our house. Neighbors were there at daybreak boiling water out in the yard in the big black wash pot to scald the hair off the hogs. Papa killed two shoats and said he was going to kill another one around the first of the year. There were Mr. Tom and Mrs. Luiza, General Lee's folks, Mr. Ben and Mrs. Mary, Mr. Miller Jackson and Mrs. Emma, and Mr. Stock Robinson and Mrs. Viney. By noon they had finished, including the stuffing of chitterlings with sausage and hanging them up in our smokehouse to be cured along with hams and shoulder and sides of bacon. It was my job to help keep the slow fire going for about a week to smoke the meat.

After the hog killing that day, Mr. Ben and Mrs. Mary were the last to leave. I think Papa had held them back purposely so that he could talk with them about his problem. Mr. Ben was a light brown-skin man with curly hair like Mr. Willie's, and Mrs. Mary was black like Papa and Grandma and Naomi. She was plump like Mrs. Ida at Mrs. Rhoda's house, but her face was pleasant and usually carried a smile. Not like Mr. Willie's smile to mask a fear or curry favor, but a generous, friendly smile that her heart seemed to create.

When the others had gone, Papa asked Mr. Ben and Mrs. Mary to come in and sit by the fire. Everybody sat, except Papa. He stood at the corner of the mantlepiece with his elbow resting on it.

"Ben 'n' Mary," he began, "I got somethin' I wanna talk with you 'bout." Then he paused and the room was quiet, except for the cracking of the fire and the steaming of green logs out of which oozed steam and a kind of foam. "You know," he continued, "Reverend Fisher done tol' Naomi he want me to say a good word fer Lilly Mae at her trial next month."

"He do?" Mr. Ben asked in surprise. "After the way that gal done treated y'all?"

"Still 'n' all," Papa went on, "I was they neighbor, 'n' the gal's in a heap o' trouble."

"Whut Mr. Walter gon' say to that, Silas?" Mr. Ben asked.

"I don' 'zackly know, Ben; Mr. Win was his brother 'n' he might ruther I didn't say nothin'," Papa replied.

"Silas, seem like you leanin' with the preacher," Mrs. Mary said.

"I been tryin' to talk some sense in him," Mama cut in.

"I is, too, but it don' do no good," Grandma added.

"Well, you see, Ben 'n' Mary," Papa spoke up, "I ain't fully decided whut I'm gon' do."

"I see," Mr. Ben said doubtfully, looking down at his feet.

"I don' know whut to tell you myself, Silas," Mrs. Mary said, "'cep'n to foller yo' conscience. Lilly Mae sho' did y'all wrong, writin' that note to Miz Susie, tryin' to hurt Naomi. Yet us all knows, the chile ain't had no real chance like the rest o' us. Her po' mama died 'n' left her papa with six chillun, 'n' he don' know no mo' 'bout raisin' cotton 'n' a bullfrog. I don' know whut I'woulda done, ef I hada been in her fix. I mighta been worser 'n Lilly Mae." The smile on her face vanished temporarily and then soon reappeared.

"I know that, too, Mary," Mama said. "The gal ain't had no chance, but still I think Silas oughta try to stay outa this mess ef he can. "Like you 'n' Ben, Mary, us been savin' a little to try to buy a farm o' us own. 'N' like us tol' you us was gonna do, Silas done went to the gover'ment loan man in Vicksburg, but he say he don' make no loans to niggers less'n the white man on the the place where they at say it's all right 'n' speaks up fer 'em. Now Mr. Walter done say he would speak to the gover'ment man fer us. But ef Silas git hisself mixed up in that trial with Lilly Mae 'n' that N Double-A CP, us jes' ain't gon' git no loan. 'N' y'all know, don't care whut no nigger say at that trial, it ain't gon' make no diff'ence nohow." Water was in Mama's eyes when she finished.

"Is Mr. Walter done said he would speak to the man fer you, Silas?" Mr. Ben asked, looking straight at Papa as I poked in the ashes with a stick, feeling the sweetpotatoes I had placed there to see if they were soft yet.

"Yes," Papa answered, "he tol' me that las' Sadday after us come back from Vicksburg."

"Ef he gon' do that," Mr. Ben said with certainty in his voice, "I sho' wouldn't take no chance messin' 'round with that gal's trial."

"'N' nobody else but a fool," Grandma added firmly.

"Hush, Ma, this ain't none o' yo' bizness," Mama said. "It's up to Silas to make up his own mind."

"Becky, did you say the N Double-A CP was handling the case?" Mr. Ben asked.

"Yes, it sho' is, Ben."

"Now you know, that don' spell nothin' but trouble," Mr. Ben said.

"Yes, Ben, I know there a lot at stake," Papa said. "Course, I ain't scared to speak fer the gal nor the N Double-A CP, but I do have to think o' my family. 'N' maybe, like Becky say, it ain't gon' make no diff'ence nohow whut no nigger say."

"Now you talkin' sense, Silas," Mr. Ben responded with a big smile on his face.

"He is that, he is that," Grandma added.

"Course, I ain't definitely made up my min' yet, but I'm gon' keep on thinkin' 'bout it, 'n' like Mary say, I'm gon' foller my conscience."

"'N' I ain't gon' bother you, Silas; I'm gon' let you make up yo' own min', 'cause that's the onliest way," Mama said, pressing her apron with her hand and fighting back tears.

"You right, Becky, it's the onliest way; he gotta 'cide fer hisself," Mrs. Mary agreed, rising to go.

Two days later was the second Sunday, and Reverend Whitten came up from Vicksburg as usual to preach. But when Sunday school let out and we went outside to play before church started, there sat Mrs. Rhoda in her car. And when the services began, she was sitting in the pulpit with the preacher. She added to the whiteness of the sheets, which covered the alter rail and the communion table where trays of wine and bread sat.

There was a quietness in the church that Sunday as if God took second place to Mrs. Rhoda. Nobody shouted, except old Mrs. Louvenia Robinson, Silvester's grandma, and even she didn't seem to shout and holler as vigorously as she usually did. It didn't take but two ladies to hold her, and she didn't sling her hand bag up into the pulpit. And even Grandma didn't say, "Amen, preach the word," as strongly as usual.

Reverend Whitten was quieter, too. He didn't holler as loud or stomp as hard. I thought he was afraid of jarring Mrs. Rhoda or stirring up dust in her face. And his sermon wasn't as long as usual; he preached about Paul and Silas being in jail and angels coming and shaking the jail doors open and setting them free. At first I thought he was talking about Papa; he had been in jail, but no angel had come and shook the doors open. Then I realized he was talking about a man in the Bible named Silas whose picture I had won in Sunday school. After that my mind drifted to Lilly Mae, who was still in jail, and it stayed there with her almost throughout the rest of the sermon. I kept telling myself that an angel was going to Vicksburg and set Lilly Mae free, if she had faith, like Reverend Whitten said as he stood there perspiring and reaching as if trying to touch the garments of the Lord in heaven, and talking about faith to open jails and move mountains. Then I wondered if Papa would suddenly find himself owning a farm, if he had enough faith. Of course, Reverend Whitten didn't say anything about faith to own a piece of land and a painted house like Mr. Ammons, but I just wondered. When he had finished his sermon and the song we all sang had ended, he said we were going to hear Mrs. Rhoda Williamson before we took sacrament.

Mrs. Rhoda rose and walked to the stand where the big Bible lay and clutched it as if she was going to open it, but she did not. Instead, she held it like a support to brace her for what she was going to say. She was tall and graceful, and like some folks said, as thin as a switch. She made a few favorable comments about the sermon and praised the congregation for being so attentive. "Now, I want to talk with you briefly," she said, "about the changes that are taking place on the plantations all around, and sooner or later they are coming to the Bend. These changes are going to alter your lives, and so I want to talk with you about getting ready for them."

Having steadied herself and gotten into her subject, Mrs. Rhoda took her hands off the Bible and walked around the stand and down to the alter rail, where she would be closer to the people. "Mr. Walter," she continued, "wanted to come here and tell you this himself, but he is so much one of you, having been born and reared on this place like most of you that he didn't feel up to talking with you about these changes, which may mean for some of you moving away from the plantation." "Oh, naw, oh, naw; Lawd Jesus, naw," came the wail from the congregation.

"I know how you feel," Mrs. Rhoda said over the continuing whispers of the people, "but it's something that must be faced. Not right away, not right away, but sooner or later, and Mr. Walter and I want you to be ready fort the changes. Of course, we would stop the changes if we could and have Williamson Bend be just like it always was."

"Amen, amen, Jesus," came from the audience, and I think Grandma said it louder than anyone else.

"As much as we all would like that," Mrs. Rhoda went on, "it just cannot be. The world is changing and we must change with it. What you need most," she was saying, but the grumbling drowned out her voice.

Reverend Whitten stood up and held up his arms for order. The grumbling slowly died.

"What you need most," she said again, "for the coming changes is preparation for modern farming for those who will remain and preparation for jobs for those of you who may leave."

The word "leave" brought forth moaning and groaning from the people.

"Lawd, us don' have to leave, do us?" Grandma asked in a loud voice.

Mrs. Rhoda walked back up to the stand where the Bible lay as if she needed the stand and the Bible to steady her. Before answering Grandma's question, she took out a small handkerchief and wiped her eyes and then looked up in the ceiling of the church for a long time. Finally, she said, "I wish you didn't have to leave, especially the older folks, and I hope God will help us find a way to keep you here. But for those who will leave, you will need training for jobs in town. Mr. Walter and I have asked the superintendent of schools to provide a bus to take some of the men to town in the evening to attend a trade school twice a week. There you could learn to be auto mechanics, carpenters, bricklayers, and skilled workers in other fields. The superintendent hasn't said yes, and he hasn't said no, so we are hopeful."

There were a few "amens" mingled with groans as Mrs. Rhoda paused.

"As for the women," she continued, "we are going to convert Mrs. Susie's house into a training school for maids and cooks and nurses and babysitters. You can earn good pay on these jobs if you know the work and can perform well."

There were more groans but a lot of "amens" too. Mrs. Rhoda went on.

"And for all of you, men and women alike, Miss Taylor and I are going to conduct night classes once or twice a week in reading and writing and arithmetic. In town, you will certainly need to know how to read and write and figure. The night classes will start right after the first of the year, as will the training for the women. The trade school training will begin as soon as we can complete arrangements for the bus and work out a few details with the trade school principal. Now, do you have any questions?"

"When us gon' have to move?" Mr. Tom Lee asked.

"Let me make this clear," Mrs. Rhoda said. "All of you will not have to move, but some of you may be moving in two or three years, not right away."

"Is us gon' be paid while us is learnin'?" Mr. Miller Jackson wanted to know.

"I hadn't really thought of that," said Mrs. Rhoda with a puzzled look on her face, "but maybe something can be worked out for those taking the bus to town. But no one will be paid to go to school here on the plantation. We are doing this for your benefit."

"It's fer us own benefit, course, us ain't gon' be paid," said Mr. Hamp Davis, the Sunday school superintendent.

There were no more questions, and Reverend Whitten thanked Mrs. Rhoda for coming and for her interest in the people. "Ef there was jes' a few mo' white folks like you 'n' Mr. Walter," he said, "things would be so much better.

"Thank you, Reverend Whitten," Mrs. Rhoda said with a smile that did not part her lips. On her way out of the church, she shook hands with almost everyone.

After Mrs. Rhoda departed, Reverend Whitten called for order and everybody calmly took his seat and got ready for sacrament. But when communion was over and we began shaking hands with everyone in communion fellowship, many eyes were wet and voices sad and husky. Papa, who was right behind me, was pulled aside by Reverend Whitten; they seemed to be whispering.

When we got into our wagon to go home, Papa told us Reverend Fisher had sent word by Reverend Whitten that he wanted him to testify for Lilly Mae at her trial the next month.

"Whut did you tell him?" Mama wanted to know.

"I tol' him I would have to think 'bout it some mo' but he said ef I don' testify, there ain't gon' be nobody to speak up fer the gal, 'cep'n her folks 'n' he say they word don' count," Papa said, looking straight at Mama and begging with his eyes and with the tone of his voice for her understanding.

But Grandma cut in. "How much you think yo' word gon' count?" she asked coldly.

"Ma, us done been through all this, 'n' you know how Silas is, 'n' you know, us done promised to let him make up his own min'," Mama said firmly.

XX

Plantation Owner and Silas Notified to Testify in Murder Trial

Christmas passed that year with little notice because we all were thinking about Lilly Mae's trial and whether Papa was going to testify. In the chair beside my bed on Christmas morning, there were a new pair of pants, a hat, some socks, a cap pistol and some caps, and the usual bag of apples and oranges. The Christmas before, I had expressed doubt that Santa Claus had brought my things because I could see no sign at all that he had come down the chimney. I had pointed out to Papa that the same old soot was hanging there as always, and I had argued that Santa Claus couldn't have come down the chimney without disturbing the soot. Papa had had no answer, except to say, "River, boy, you don' know how slick Santa Claus is."

So Papa had taken the time that Christmas to brush some of the soot away and leave imprints of his hands at several places in the back and sides of the fireplace to prove that Santa Claus had come down the chimney. But I knew the shape of Papa's hands as well as I knew the shape of my own. For some reason, however, I didn't tell him he had made the imprints in the fireplace, but I did run out of the house into the yard, which I swept clean almost every day to remove the chicken droppings. There were the tracks of the chickens but none of reindeer. "How come Santa Claus' reindeer ain't left no tracks?" I asked.

"Oh," Papa answered in mock surprise, "didn't you know, man, Santa Claus come through the air 'n' land on roofs? Didn't you know that, River?"

He had me there, but I still had my doubts. Two books Mama often read to me planted the doubts in my mind, I think. There were only three books in our house besides my *First Reader* and two of Naomi's books. These three books were Grandma's Bible, another book, *Heroes of the Dark Continent,* which she said she had had for nearly thirty years, and Mama's little book, *Going East by Sailing West.* It was about the discovery of America. It told about Columbus setting sail from Spain in August a long time ago and not landing until October. *Heroes of the Dark Continent* was about Mr. Stanley's long search in Africa for Dr. Livingstone. These two books gave me some notion about the size of the world. For Santa Claus to drive all over it in one night, stopping at every house, seemed impossible to me even at the age of seven.

We had hoped Naomi might surprise us and come up for Christmas, but we found out later that she had worked during the holidays and had made twenty dollars.

The day after New Years', Mr. Walter sent for Papa. He had seen Mr. Miller Jackson at the store and had asked him to stop by our house and tell Papa to come up there. Papa decided to walk, said he needed to stretch his legs. I asked to go with him, but he said, "Naw, I'm goin' on bizness."

"You stay here with me 'n' Ma," Mama said, and I settled down by the fireplace to roast sweet potatoes and parch peanuts in the hot ashes.

When Papa got back home, it was almost night. He said he had walked back down the levee to catch some fresh air and look at the river.

"Whut Mr. Walter want, Silas?" Mama asked.

"It 'bout me testifyin' fer Lilly Mae 'n' the N Double-A CP," Papa replied, not looking at Mama but looking in the fireplace, where he was poking at a log.

"Whut did he say?"

"He say Miz Susis done called him 'n' tol' him ef anybody on the place say a word at the trial fer that nigger gal whut done kilt her husband, her gon' make trouble fer him. 'N' so he tol' me not to testify, said he heard the preacher done ast me to."

"'N' whut did you say, Silas? 'N' don' keep me waitin' while you drag this out; tell me whut you done tol' him," Mama demanded.

"I ain't draggin' it out, Becky. I'm jes' tellin' you like it was."

"Well, don' tell me like it was, jes' tell me whut happen."

"I tol' Mr. Walter I could see his point, but it seemed to me like somebody oughta say somethin' fer the gal."

"Silas, you drivin' me crazy," Mama said. "Please, please, jes' tell me whut done happen."

"Mr. Walter said he done tol' me how it was, 'n' as much as he hated to do, he was gon' put us off the place, ef I testifies fer that gal whut done kilt his brother. 'Jes' be ready to move when you testifies,'" he said.

"Silas, Silas," Mama screamed, "is you gon' put us in the road ag'in? Where us goin'?"

"I wanted to 'splain to Mr. Walter that I hadn't 'zackly made up my mind' 'bout testifying, but he said he done said all he had to say, 'n' he got up 'n' walked outa his office, you know, there in the back o' the sto' 'n' he went up to the front counter. When I was leavin' I looked at him, hopin' he would turn toward me or say somethin', but he didn't look at me or say a word."

"Silas, you jes' a fool," Grandma said flatly, spitting in the fire in disgust.

"Now, Ma, you knows you shouldn'ta said that," Mama protested. Then turning to Papa with tears in her eyes, she asked almost in a prayer, "Silas, ain't there somethin' us can say to change yo' min' 'bout testifyin'?"

"I don' know, Becky; I wish there was; Lawd knows, I wish there was," Papa answered.

"Well, Silas," Mama said, "you know when you testifies, they gon' ast you how come you was in jail, 'n' ef Naomi's there with her baby, they gon' ast you who's the baby's papa, 'n' you gon' have to tell 'em."

"Naomi don' have to be there, do her?" he shot back.

"Naw, her don' have to be there," Mama replied calmly, patiently, "but her might as well be there, 'cause when you 'splain how come you was in jail, evvybody gon' know whut done happen."

Papa stood up; his eyes were glassy. He rammed his hands into his pockets and walked around the room, ending up at a corner of the mantlepiece where he placed his elbow and looked vacantly across the room. "How come the preacher had to ast me to say a word fer Lilly Mae? How come us happen to live next do' to 'em? How come it couldn'ta been somebody else, 'cep'n us?" Papa asked, talking, it seemed, more to himself than to Mama or Grandma.

"Us don' know the answer to them questions," Mama said.

"It look like to me it was the Lawd's will," Papa said, answering his own questions. "'N' Miz Carrie done said many times that the Lawd don' give us mo' burdens than us can bear."

"Yes, Silas, I is done said that," Grandma spoke up, "but the Lawd ain't 'spectin' you to be fool 'nuff to try to pick up a bale o' cotton when you know good 'n' well you can't lif' it."

"He tol' Abraham to sac'fice his own son, didn't He?" Papa asked. "'N' he woulda done it, too, ef the Lawd hadn't showed him a ram. Maybe the Lawd jes' tes'n' me to see ef I'm worthy to own a farm o' my own. Maybe He jes' tes 'n'," Papa pleaded.

"You reckon, Silas?" Mama asked, trying to wipe away the tears that were still running down her face.

"He could be, Becky; the Lawd could be, but whether he tes'in' me or not, I got to speak fer Lilly Mae 'n' try to 'splain that her was tryin' to help her papa 'n' her five little sisters 'n' brothers with no mama 'cep'n her, 'n' her ain't had no chance much like the rest o' us. Becky, please don' ast me how come I gotta do it, 'cause I don' know no mo'n how come I gotta plow my mule up 'n' down the field faster'n anybody else on the place, or how come I couldn't take low that time 'bout the parity check up in Sunflower County. There jes' somethin' in me, Becky, like there somethin' in a dewberry vine that make it have thorns, or like there somethin' in a bird that make it sing." Papa took his elbow off the mantlepiece and walked toward the door. As he opened it and went out, he hollered back in a strong voice, "Us don' have to live at the Bend, us can find a place!"

Two days before Papa was to go to Vicksburg and tetify, Mr. Walter and Mrs. Rhoda drove to our house early that morning and blew their horn for Papa to come out to the car. He opened the door and looked out as if he wasn't certain he had heard Mr. Walter's horn or as if he doubted it could have been Mr. Walter blowing at our door, when a week and a half before, he had refused to look his way in the store.

"Yessuh," Papa yelled, "I'm comin', soon as I git my jumper." He turned back inside with the door still open because he didn't think it proper to shut a door in any man's face, no matter how much cold air it let into the house. "It's Mr. Walter 'n' Miz Rhoda," he said more to Mama than to me and Grandma.

I ran to peep out of the window while he lifted his jumper off a nail behind the door and put it on, and Mama rushed to get her sweater.

"I'm goin', too," she said.

"Can I go, Papa?" I asked.

"Naw, River, you stay inside with Miz Carrie; it's col' out there."

Mama and Papa went out to the car; Grandma came to the door and looked out and then went back to her seat by the fire. I stood at the window, watching. Mr. Walter opened the back door of his car for Papa and Mama to get in. My heart jumped into my mouth. I thought he and Mrs. Rhoda were going to take my parents some place and do them harm, like Grandma said folks in town did, especially in the big cities like Chicago and New York. I thought Mr. Walter may have heard that Papa had been riding from plantation to plantation trying to find a place for us to move to and was angry about it. But the car didn't move, and Mr. Walter wasn't even looking where he was going, if he was going to drive off. Instead, he and Mrs. Rhoda had turned around in their seats and were looking at Papa and Mama in the back seat.

Maybe us gon' have to move today, I thought.

Although we had started getting ready to move, we weren't ready to move today. In fact, Papa was still looking for a place. If Mr. Walter and Mrs. Rhoda had come a little later, Papa would have been gone on ole Salt to another plantation to ask for a house and a few acres of cotton to work.

He had been going off every day since Mr. Walter told him he was going to put him off the place if he testified. But each night until night before last, he had returned empty-handed to soak his tired feet in the wash tub and salve his depressed feelings with silence. Some days he rode ole Salt all the way to whatever plantation he was going, if it wasn't more than ten or twelve miles away. Other days he would ride out near the highway, get permission from a farmer to hitch ole Salt to his fence or a tree with a long rope so that he could graze, and then walk along the highway hitchhiking. Some days he said he hitchhiked as far as Rolling Fork and Anguilla and Delta City. When he returned night before last, however, he told Mama he had found a place.

"On the other side o' Onward," Papa said. "I went to see a man somebody tol' me needed folks, but he don' need nobody. Said he had to let some o' his folks go he already had. He got fo' cotton pickers 'n' I don' know how many tractors. 'N' he got three o' them machines whut harvest soybeans 'n' oats. They great big babies, bigger'n cotton pickers. 'N' there ain't no end to the cattle he got. Out where his pastures was, there wasn't nothin' but white face cattle jes' as fer as I could see. They say he used to have two hund'ered families on his place. Now he tol' me he ain't got but sixteen. The mens 'n' boys drives the tractors 'n' other machines, 'n' the women 'n' chillun set at home," Papa said, dropping his shoes on the floor and putting his feet in the tub of water.

"It look bad, don't it, Silas?" Mama asked.

"It sho do," Papa agreed, "but this here man tol' me 'bout 'nother man out back o' Cary whut still usin' mules. I caught a ride up there 'n' say the man. He is Mr. Holly Samuels, 'n' he say us can move there."

Mama jumped for joy. "How come you ain't tol' me, Silas? How come you ain't tol' me?" she asked. "How come you gotta drag evvything out so?"

"I'm tellin' you now, ain't I'm?"

"Yes, you tellin me now, but it took you so long to git to the main part."

"I'm hoping to find somethin' better, Becky. The house Mr. Holly's bossman showed me sho' ain't much, jes' two rooms 'n' there holes in the flo' big as my hand, 'n' the ceilin' looked worser. But he said he would fix it up some. 'N' 'bout the crops, he say Mr. Holly take one bale outa evvy two after all 'spenses been taken out, 'n' he don' 'low his folks to grow no corn. He grow all that hisself 'n' he sell 'em roastin' ears. 'N' he don' 'low no cattle or stock on his place, 'cep'n they his'n."

Mama had sat back down in her chair and looked straight into the fire with her arms folded in her lap. Her joy of a moment before was all gone. Then she looked at Papa and said, "Us ain't gon' move there, is us, Silas?"

"I don' know, I'm gon' keep on lookin', but it's the onliest place I found, 'n' I didn't wanna turn it down. You know, they say a bird in hand is worth two in the bushes," Papa replied and smiled weakly, hopelessly, as he looked at Mama.

"Whut us gon' do with us cow 'n' us mules?" she wanted to know.

"I don' know, Becky," Papa said, "sell 'em to Mr. Holly, I reckon."

"Well, I guess it's better 'n nothin'," Mama finally said, "'n' us can fix it up; 'n' us don' have to stay there forever, us can keep on lookin' evvy year 'tel us find somethin' better."

"'N' I still got three mo' day to look befo' I have to go to Vicksburg to testify," Papa had said. He went out the next day. Said he hitchhiked as far as Midnight up in Humphreys Countybut found nothing.

This is where things stood that morning early when Mr. Walter and Mrs. Rhoda drove down to our house.

"They still talkin'?" Grandma asked.

"Yessum," I said from my place at the window where I kept peeping.

It was a cold morning, and Mr. Walter had left his motor running to keep warm. White smoke puffed out from under the back of the car and rolled several feet through broken cotton stalks before it rose and scattered like a flock of birds.

I stood there wondering what they could be saying that would take all this time. *Ef he ain't tellin' Papa to move right away,* I thought, *then maybe he givin' him mo' time to find a place. Or maybe it's Papa whut's doin' the talkin'; maybe he done tol' Mr. Walter he ain't gon' say nothin' fer Lilly Mae. But he too much like a mule fer that. Once he say he he gon' say a word fer her, he ain't gon change less'n Reverend Fisher or the N Double-A CP tell him they don' need him no mo.*

So I concluded that Papa hadn't agreed not to testify, but I kept trying to see if his mouth was moving. My face must have been almost against the windowpane because it suddenly clouded up and I had to wipe it off with my hands before I could see through it again.

During the moments that I could not see through the pane, it occurred to me that Mr. Walter may have said something to Papa that had made him angry. *Maybe he gon' jump outa the car 'n' run to the house to git his gun,* I thought.

I had to rub faster and faster to get the glass clear so that I could see if Papa was running to the house. The idea fastened itself so tightly to my mind that I started to run and open the door for him. But I didn't want to run to the door until I had wiped the windowpane clear so that I could see. At last the glass was clear; Papa was not running to the house; the car door was closed and smoke was still coming out from under it like steam from our teakettle.

Later a door of the car opened slowly and Papa and Mama got out, smiling. They stood by our fence until Mr. Walter had turned his car around and headed for the lane. As he was driving off, he rolled his glass down and hollered something to them. Papa and Mama waved to him in reply. Mr. Walter had left the gate to the lane open when he came in. So it wasn't necessary for him to get out and open it. Papa followed the car and closed the gate; Mama stood where she was and waited for him. When he returned, she put one arm around him and he covered her shoulders with part of his jumper to keep her warm. They were both grinning as they walked into the house.

"Whut they say, Papa? Whut Mr. Walter 'n' Miz Rhoda say?" I asked, running to him as they came in.

"Yes, whut the white folks say, Silas?" Grandma joined in.

"They say us ain't gotta move, less'n us wants to," Papa replied with the grin broadening on his face.

"Glory be, Lawd Jesus, You done heard my prayers," Grandma cried out, rising from her seat by the fire and putting her arms around Papa and Mama.

"No'am, Ma, us ain't got to move," Mama said.

"Us sho' ain't, Miz Carrie," Papa added.

"Then you done learnt some sense 'n' ain't gon' testify, hanh?"

"They ain't ast him not to testify, Ma; they say he can testify ef he wanna."

"They say they made 'rangement with the bank, Miz Carrie, 'n' Miz Susie can't cause 'em no trouble."

"Miz Rhoda, her the one," Mama said. "Said her couldn't sleep after Mr. Walter tol' her he done tol' Silas to git off the place ef he testify."

As Papa hung up his jumper, he said, "'N' Mr. Walter said, course, Mr. Win was his brother 'n' he loved him, but he ain't had no bizness foolin' 'round with these gals on the plantation."

"Silas, ain't you gon' have to tell that white man you done talked to over 'round Cary that you ain't gon' be movin' to his place?" Grandma asked. "Some o' these white folks can be awful mean 'bout things like that when you don' show up after you done promised."

"I know, Miz. Carrie, 'n' I done tol' Mr. Walter 'bout it, 'n' he gon' call Mr. Holly 'n' straighten it out," Papa said, sitting down rather than standing with his elbow on the corner of the mantlepiece for the first time in weeks.

"Well, that's good," Grandma said, "'cause I knowed a nigger whut a white man shot to death on a plantation up in Coahoma County 'cause he didn't move to his place after he done give the man his word."

"I know, Miz Carrie, 'n' it all gon' be straightened out. Mr. Walter gon' straighten it out fer me."

"Yes, Ma, Mr. Walter gon' see 'bout it," Mama added.

XXI

Silas and Plantation Owner Testify in Brother's Murder Trial

The day Papa testified, he and Mama got up early. In fact, it seemed that they never went to bed, but I guess they did, although Mama was mending a dress and her coat, pressing Papa's suit, polishing shoes, and washing and ironing way into the night. They had two reasons to be excited: They were going to town with Mr. Walter and Mrs. Rhoda in their big black car, and Papa was going to testify in court as was Mr. Walter.

By the time Mr. Walter blew his horn well before eight o'clock, Mama had milked the cow and cooked breakfast, and Papa had fed the mules and hogs and had brought in a pile of wood for the fire. After we all had had breakfast, they washed up, put baking soda under their arms and dressed.

"Can't be stinkin' up them white folks in they car," Mama said as she slipped her dress over her head. Then she and Papa sat waiting for Mr. Walter and Mrs. Rhoda.

I had begged to go with them, but they turned me down flat.

"You gotta go to school 'n' a trial ain't no place fer a little boy nohow," Papa said.

"Ma gon' be here with you when you come back from school," Mama explained, "'n' us oughta be back befo' night."

At the sound of the horn, Papa and Mama jumped up and rushed out and got into the car. Grandma and I stood in the door and watched as the big car drove off. Mama and Papa were smiling as they waved back at us.

That day at school was one of the proudest in my life. Not only had Papa gone to Vicksburg to testify for Lilly Mae, but he and Mama had gone with Mr. Walter and Mrs. Rhoda in their big car. I couldn't wait to brag.

"Did your father get off to Vicksburg?" Miss Taylor asked with a twinkle in her eyes and a soft smile on her face, which I seldom saw when she was speaking directly to me.

"Yessum," I said "Papa 'n' Mama left early this mornin'; Mr. Walter 'n' Miz Rhoda done took 'em in they fine, big car." I could feel my voice rising. It was like at Easter when I stood up in church and recited a verse from the Bible.

"That's fine," she replied, "fine." And throughout the day, she seemed kinder to me than usual.

And most of the children were kind, too. "Yo' Papa gone to Vicksburg to help Lilly Mae, ain't he?" some whispered. During the recess period, I was the center of attention until Roosevelt Harris hit me. Before that, children had gathered around me to ask about Papa speaking up for Lilly Mae. To which I had replied with pride, "Yes, he gone to Vicksburg with Mr. Walter 'n' Miz Rhoda. He and Mama both. 'N' he gon' help the preacher's girl, Lilly Mae, whut done kilt Mr. Win. They went in Mr. Walter's great big ole Buick."

Most of the children said, "Yo' papa ain't scared o' the white folks. Us glad he gon' help Lilly Mae."

But Roosevelt laughed and said, "Boy, you think you shit on a stick, don't you, jes' 'cause yo' ole crazy pa's ridin' with white folks in they car, 'n' 'cause he crazy nuff to talk up in court fer the preacher's gal?"

"How come yo' papa ain't testifyin'?" I asked. "'Cause he scared, that's how come," I said and poked my tongue out at him.

When he started toward me with his fist balled up, I ran, but he caught up with me and struck me in the back. I never stopped running until I was inside the school, safe at Miss Taylor's side.

"Roosevelt done hit me 'cause my papa's testifyin'," I lied.

"Go tell Roosevelt to come here," she ordered.

I rushed to call Roosevelt, but I went no farther than the safety of the door. "Roosevelt, Miss Taylor say fer you to come here!" I hollered across the yard to the boy.

He came slowly. "Tattler," he said as he passed me in the door. "I'm gon' git you; jes' wait 'tel school let out."

His warning sent a shiver through me. He was a little taller than I and about two years older; however, I didn't back down. "I ain't scared o' you," I said.

"Why did you strike River, Roosevelt?" Miss Taylor asked.

"'Cause he say my pa scared o' white folks, 'n' he stuck his tongue out at me."

"Did you do that, River?"

"Yessum, but he said I thought I was somethin' nasty on a stick."

"He did, did he?"

"Yessum."

"Hold out your hands, Roosevelt," Miss Taylor said and took her strap and stung his hands.

When school let out that day, I played it safe and waited for Miss Taylor on the pretext of helping her carry her books. Roosevelt and his sister, Barbara, were waiting for me when I came out, but when they saw Miss Taylor coming out right behind me, they walked on. Miss Taylor lived with Mr. Hamp Davis, the Sunday school superintendent, and his wife, Mrs. Julia. Roosevelt lived about a half a mile farther down the road toward Mr. Willie's. I thought he and his sister might wait for me, so I walked as slowly as I could, trailing well behind Miss Taylor. This, of course, slowed her down, but she didn't complain; I think she understood. At Mr. Hamp's gate, I handed Miss Taylor her books and looked all around for Roosevelt, but I didn't see him. As soon as the teacher was in her door, I took off as fast as my short legs would carry me over the road across the plantation.

I slowed down before I got home so that I wouldn't be out of breath when I got there and subject to questions from Grandma. She was sitting by the fireplace, stirring a pot of lyehominy, and I jumped for joy because I knew we were going to have hominy and smoked sausage for supper. Next to molasses and biscuits and buttermilk and cornbread, I liked lyehominy best, especially when Grandma put some cracklings in it.

When Papa and Mama came, it was dark. Grandma and I had milked the cow and performed the other chores. The table was set, the hominy was cooling on the back of the stove, and the sausage was frying slowly. We didn't hear the car because Mr. Walter let them out at the lane gate, but we heard our gate slam and footsteps on the porch. I ran to open the door.

Mama and Papa entered silently. She didn't stoop to kiss me or even say a word more than, "Hi, y'all!"

Papa did touch my head as he passed. Then he hung his coat up in the corner and took a seat by the fire, stretching his long legs out until they were almost in the ashes. He kicked a log on the front of the andirons Mr. Joe had made for us at the blacksmith shop, and he settled back in his chair with his legs still stretched out.

Mama, who had walked into the kitchen absentmindedly, returned and began getting an everyday dress to change into.

Grandma looked from one to the other of them and then asked, "Is anybody dead?"

"Naw, Miz Carrie," Papa said, "us jes' had a bad day down there in the courthouse. The man done ast me all sorta questions, 'n' I don' know is I helped Lilly Mae or hurt her."

"It was awful, Ma; they tried to make out Silas was a member o' that N Double-A CP, 'n' thought he was good as white folks," Mama explained. "'N' they brought up all that 'bout Silas bein' in jail, 'n' 'bout Naomi 'n' her baby," Mama sat, wringing her hands and wiping her eyes.

"When I tried to say, like us been saying here, that Lilly Mae was a good girl, but her 'n' them chillun was hongry 'n' her ended up gittin' groceries from the sto' through Mr. Win, which her paid fer in the onliest way her could, that Gawddam lawyer ast me ef I thought all whores was good ladies, jes' 'cause they was hongry. 'N', Ma, you shoulda heard them ole people in that courthouse laffin' at Silas," Mama said. "Ef I hada had Silas' cowhyde whup, I coulda used it, Ma, I mean used it."

"Then that peckerwood ast me ef my own daughter, Naomi, was a good girl. 'N' I tol' him yessuh. Then he ast me didn't her have a baby fer Mr. Win? 'N' I tol' him, I guess so. 'N' he said, guess so? Whut you mean, guess so? Her had a baby, ain't her? The baby is almos' white ain't her? 'N' yo' gal is black like you, ain't her? Now whut you mean, you guess so? 'N' the folks jes' laffed they damn fool heads off, Gawddam they souls to hell." Papa stormed and got up out of his chair and stood at the corner of the mantlepiece with his elbow on it.

"Oh, Silas, don' say that, the Lawd'll take care o' 'em in His own way 'n' in His own time, don't you worry 'bout that," Grandma said and spat forcefully into the fire as if she were spittin' into hell's damnation all the folks who laughed at Papa.

"I started cryin', Ma," Mama said, "when that lawyer ast Silas all them questions. I think I screamed once or twice, but he kept right on questioning Silas."

"Yes, he say you wasn't guessin' Mr. Win had spoilt yo' gal when you runned 'n' got yo' gun to kill him, was you? 'N' I said, nawsuh, I sho wasn't."

"Then that lawyer said to Silas, you one o' them mean, smart niggers, ain't you? How long you belong to the N Double-A CP?"

"I was ready then, Miz Carrie, to grab that sonofabitch and mop up the flo' with him. I got up outa that chair 'n' stood up 'n' he backed back, 'n' two o' them deputy sheriffs rushed over 'n' the judge tol' me to set down or he would put me in jail."

"I was scared, Ma, that Silas was gon' hit that man or kick one them deputies," Mama said, "'n' I holler 'n' tol' Silas not to act no fool."

"When I set back down," Papa said, "that lawyer ast me ag'in, how long I been a member o' the N Double-A CP. 'N' I said, all my life, whose bizness is it? Jes' made me so Gawddam mad. 'Course, I ain't never b'long to it."

"After Silas testified, they called fer Mr. Walter," Mama said. "He said Mr. Win was a good man, a fair man, but a little wild. 'N" they ast him whut he meant by wild, 'n' he said Mr. Win drink some 'n' he runned 'round with some o' the gals on the place. 'N' they ast him how many gals he funned 'round with, 'n' he said fo' five, he guessed, but not at the same time."

"He done runned 'round with mo'n that," Grandma said, "but you got to give him credit, it wasn't but one at a time, 'cep'n when Naomi sneaked in the car."

"When the lawyer ast Mr. Walter ef he was sho' it was only fo' five 'n' not twenty-five, Mr. Walter said he was sho' 'n' that his brother wasn't no worser'n the rest o' the plantation owners 'round here whut go with gals on they place," Mama said with pride in her voice.

"He did?" Grandma asked with a chuckle.

"Did Lilly Mae testify?" Grandma asked.

"Yessum, her had already done testified when us got there. Her testified late yistiddy," Mama said. "So us didn't hear her.

"But Reverend Fisher said her tol' the court jes' like it was, that it was a accident," Papa said.

"'N' that N Double-A CP lawyer proved it was a accident that Mr. Win brought on hisself, tryin' to whup Lilly Mae, 'n' then gittin' his pistol when her held on to the whup," Mama said.

"But ole judge was set on givin' her some time," Papa added. "Ain't no nigger gon' kill no white man down here 'n' not serve some time, don' care ef it is a accident."

"How much time did the judge give her?" Grandma wanted to know.

"Ten to twenty years," Papa said. "But the lawyer he explained to us after the trial that he could git her out in 'bout three or fo' years."

"Po' thing, tse-tse-tse-tse-tse," Grandma said and wiped her eyes on the corner of her apron. "But still I guess her is lucky. I knowed the time the white folks up 'round Friars Point woulda tried her theyselves 'n' kilt her right there on the plantation."

"Reverend Fisher said her was lucky, too," Mama added. "Said her was lucky to be on the Williamson plantation 'n' to have that N Double-A CP lawyer."

"That no count preacher brought all this on that po' chile," Grandma said. "Ef he had jes' made ha'f a crop, that gal might nota got herself in this mess."

"I know, Ma, but maybe he was doin' the best he could here on the place," Mama said. "Reverend Fisher jes' wasn't cut out to be no farmer, but he doin' real good in Vicksburg with his church. Said he wanted us to visit sometime when us in town; Willie 'n' Daisy Lee was with him, 'n' they was clean 'n' had on good clothes. Po' little Daisy Lee jes' cried 'n' cried when they sentenced her sister. Her was still cryin' when us left 'em."

"I wish I coulda said somethin' that mighta made 'em go easier on Lilly Mae," Papa said. "Miz Carrie, I wanted to tell 'em 'bout the preacher's po' cotton crops; 'bout Lilly Mae's mama dyin', 'bout how hongry them chillun got no matter how much us 'n' the other folks give 'em. It jes' wasn't nuff, it jes' wasn't nuff, cause us 'n' nobody else had nuff theyselves to give 'em any mo'."

"Them po' chillun lived on bread 'n' gravy," Mama said, "'n' a little meat once in a while, 'n' the milk 'n' stuff outa the garden us 'n' Mary 'n' Ben give 'em. Lilly Mae took up flour 'n' salt meat at the sto'."

"I don' b'lieve that judge 'n' them white folks on that jury know nothin' 'bout bein' hongry like that," Papa said. "But I jes' didn't git chance to tell 'em; that ole lawyer was astin' me so many questions 'bout Naomi 'n' that N Double-A CP that I didn't have time to tell 'em." Then Papa kicked a log in the fireplace to express his deep regret, and then he stood up and walked around the room. "I wanted to 'mind 'em, too, Becky, that Lilly Mae is bright 'n' good lookin' 'n' face mo' temptation 'n' a lot o' other gals."

"You didn't have to 'mind 'em o' that, Silas," Mama put in. "I bet evvy peckerwood in that courtroom, 'cep'n Mr. Walter, was droolin' over Lilly Mae, I know that ole sheriff can't wait to git his hands on her, ef he ain't already."

"I reckon you right, Becky, but I wish I coulda said it anyhow. But that ole lawyer was astin' me so many questions. How you reckon he know 'bout Naomi's baby; know it's a girl and is bright 'n' evvything?"

"I don't know," Mama moaned, "but he sho' knowed her was bright like Mr. Win."

"My po' baby," Grandma said, "off there in Vicksburg all by herself, her 'n' her chile. Did you see her?"

"Yessum, her come by the courthouse after her got off from work," Mama replied, "but I didn't have the heart to tell her whut that ole lawyer said 'bout her. Course, us know her gon hear 'bout it. Her saw Mr. Walter 'n' Miz Rhoda and they shook her hand. You can say whut you wanna 'bout Mr. Walter 'n' Miz Rhoda, but they the nicest white folks in this world."

XXII

The Plantation Owner's Spouse Training for Jobs in Town

That winter seemed milder than ever, and folks on the plantation said that was a bad sign. They said it wasn't cold enough to kill the boll weevil eggs, and that meant, they said, a heap of boll weevils next spring and summer. They also said there was going to be a lot of sickness, too, because the winter was so mild. But I liked it mild because I didn't get so cold walking to school, and after school Papa and I could visit neighbors more. Mr. Walter had divided Reverend Fisher's four acres between Papa and Mr. Tom, General's father. Papa got two acres, giving him nine again, and Mr. Tom got two, increasing his cotton land to eight.

Papa liked to go about the place talking about the extra two acres Mr. Walter gave him and how much more cotton that was going to make. We had had seven acres the year before, which brought us eight bales. And he told everybody the nine acres were sure to yield at least ten and maybe eleven or twelve bales, if the weather was good and the boll weevils weren't as bad as the folks said they might be.

Mr. Tom bragged, too, when Papa and I visited his house. While he and Papa and Mrs. Luiza talked, General and his two sisters, Lucy and Laura, and I played in the yard for a while and then he and I stuffed our pockets with used salt from salting pork the year before and ran off across the field, trying to catch birds by throwing salt on their tails. Of course, we didn't catch any.

Sometimes when Papa and I went visiting, Mama came along if she knew the ladies would be quilting. Mama didn't like to visit just to sit and talk; she liked to be doing something. Grandma seldom came with us, except when we went in the wagon; said it was too cold. On the very cold days, we sat around the fireplace, roasting peanuts and sweet potatoes, while Mama pieced together squares for quilts or made garments for folks on the plantation.

We visited Mr. Ben Moses and Mrs. Mary and their children, George and Joshua and Ruth and Beulah, often because they lived in the next house down the road. But I didn't like to visit them because they were much older than I, and George liked to tease me about not having any hairs around my "root."

"Ain't you got no hairs, boy?" he would ask me right in front of his sisters.

And I would cover my face with my arms and say, "Yes, I got hairs."

Then he would ask, "Lemme see 'em," unzipping his own trousers and pulling out his hairs in a kind of dare. "I mean hairs like these, River," he would say with his back turned to his sisters.

Ashamed that I had no hairs to show him, I would start crying, and Beulah would make him let me alone. But one time that winter when we visited, I was prepared for George. I took some of Mama's hair out of her comb and tied it to a string and then tied the string around my waist. When

George asked me that day to let him see my hairs, I unzipped my pants and pulled Mama's hair out through my drawers. "See!" I said boastfully, but I had pulled too hard and the string was showing. Both George and Joshua fell out on the porch and rolled with laughter, and their sisters ran into the house, giggling.

Mr. Ben and Papa came out on the porch to see what was going on, and Mama and Mrs. Mary followed them. I was standing there crying with my pants open and Mama's hair hanging out. Everybody joined in the laughter, including Papa, who came and zipped closed my pants and put his arms around me. "Man," he said, "don' pay no 'tention to 'em, cause you a big man like Papa," and I thought my chest would burst with pride.

Before that winter was over, Papa and I had visited almost every family on the place, including Mr. Henry Woodson and Mrs. Nettie and their two girls, Della and Mary Lou. Although Mama knew Mrs. Nettie and some of her neighbors would be quilting, she didn't go because she had heard that Mrs. Nettie had said something about Naomi having a baby for Mr. Win. But Papa, I think, couldn't resist going to let Mr. Henry know that Mr. Walter had given him two more acres of cotton.

Della was almost as old as my sister, Naomi, but Mary Lou was only a year or two older than I. While Papa was inside bragging about his extra acres, Mary Lou and I were on the porch playing "Mary Mack." In the middle of the game, she said, "River, let's go out in the toilet and fonk."

"I don' wanna fonk," I said. "That's nasty; I wanna play Mary Mack."

"Yo' sister didn't think it was nasty when her was fonkin' Mr. Win 'n' had a baby fer him," Mary Lou came back.

"Well, Mama say it's nasty, 'n' I don' wann fonk; I'm goin' in the house," I said and went inside, where Mr. Henry and Papa were arguing about his two additional acres of cotton.

"It jes' some mo' land fer you to work, Silas, 'cause you ain't gon' make no mo' cotton off'n it. 'Cause the boll weevils, bad as they gon' be, gon' sho' eat it up," Mr. Henry said.

"Don' care how you look at it, Henry," Papa replied, "the mo' cotton I plant the mo' cotton I'm bound to make."

"Not ef the boll weevils gits it," Mr Henry shot back.

"Whut 'bout yo' seben acres, Henry? Ain't the boll weevils gon' git that, too?"

"Naw, 'cause I can fight boll weevils better on seben acres, Silas, 'n' you can on nine."

"But you know good as I do, Henry, that Mr. Walter done said he was gon' use planes to dust the cotton this year; 'n' a plane can dust nine acres easy as it can seben," Papa said.

"But Silas, where Mr. Walter gon' git the money?" Mr. Henry asked. "This place is mortgaged to the hilt."

"'N' him testifyin' at y'all's trial in Vicksburg ain't done him no good, 'cusing all the white mens in the county o' goin' with nigger gals on they place," Mrs. Nettie added.

"Nettie, whut you mean talkin' 'bout y'all's trial?" Papa asked in a voice that was growing angry.

But before Mrs. Nettie could answer, Mary Lou, who had had her hand on my thigh ever since we came inside, grabbed my penis, and I jumped up and screamed, "Mary Lou done grabbed my privates 'n' squeezed it, Papa!"

"You jes' lyin', River," she said with a straight face. "I ain't grabbed his thing."

"You is," I insisted.

"Hush, River," Papa ordered.

"But her hurt me, Papa."

"Gal, whut you doin' hurtin' that boy?" Mr. Henry asked.

"I didn't go to hurt him," Mary Lou replied. "I jes' had my hand on his leg."

"You come back here," Mr. Henry said to her, rising and starting toward the kitchen. "I'm gon' teach you 'bout grabbin' boys in they privates."

"Now wait, Henry," Mrs. Nettie spoke up. "Us got company; you can whup her after they leave."

"Well, us goin' anyhow," Papa said, getting to his feet.

"Ain't no need to rush off, Silas," Mr. Henry said. "I was jes' 'bout to git you straightened out 'bout this here little extra land Mr. Walter done give you. I could have mo' acres, ef I wanted to, but I got too much sense fer that."

"Say whut you want to, Henry, but when ginnin' time come, I'm gon' have mo' cotton'n you," Papa said, moving toward the door.

I was holding his hand with one of my hands and my privates with the other.

The next day at school, Mary Lou tried to make up for hurting me. She shared her lunch with me after Roosevelt grabbed mine and ran and dared me to tell Miss Taylor. "You jes' tell Miss Taylor," he warned, "'n' you better spend the night with her, 'cause I'm gon' wait fer you, nigger."

Instead of telling Miss Taylor, I ran after him. When he saw me coming, he stopped dead in his tracks as if this was what he had been hoping for. I wanted to stop or at least slow down, but I knew everyone was looking. So I ran headlong on straight into his fists, but not before I had gotten in a blow of my own. But I was no match for Roosevelt; in a moment he had me on the ground. But Miss Taylor appeared in the door before things got worse. Mary Lou, who had called the teacher, came over and helped me to my feet, brushed me off some, and offered me part of her lunch, after pointing out that mine had fallen out of the small shoe box it was in right in the dust of the schoolyard. At first I refused; Mama didn't allow me to eat other children's lunch or accept food at anybody's house, except when we were invited there to eat.

Mary Lou had a good lunch. Next to us and Mr. Willie Woods and his family, and Mrs. Ida and Mr. Tobe, and Mr. Ben and Mrs. Mary, the Woodsons were the best livers on the place. In her box she had fried chicken, baked sweet potatoes, cornbread, and a stick of candy. I continued to refuse, although a little weakly, until she dragged a chicken leg across my lips slowly. I found my mouth opening and my tongue crawling out, getting a taste of the gravy in which it had simmered. I caught her hand and she released the chicken and handed me a piece of bread and a potato. The food made me forget my anger as well as my shame.

"Yo mama sho' is a good cook," I said, running my tongue around my lips to gather in any crumbs that might be left there.

"Her sho' is," Mary Lou replied, smiling broadly with two big buckteeth standing in the middle of her mouth.

"I had chicken in my box left over from yistiddy, but it got throwed on the ground by that ole Roosevelt," I complained.

"Roosevelt is bad, River, 'n' my papa say, ef Mr. Joe 'n' Miz Lucinda don' do somethin' with him, he gon' sho' wind up in jail," she said.

"I'm gon tell my papa on him ef he bother me ag'in; I'm sho' gon' tell him," I said, "'n' he'll fix him 'n' Mr. Joe 'n' Miz Lucinda, too."

"He sho' will, 'cause yo' papa's the baddest nigger on the place, River, 'n' evvybody know it," Mary Lou said with fire in her eyes.

"Naw, he ain't scared o' nobody," I added with pride.

"He sho' ain't," she agreed. "They say he don' take no foolishness off'n nobody, not eben white folks."

"Naw, he don' take no foolishness off'n nobody," I repeated her claim.

"I'm sho' glad he didn't git mad at me yistiddy at us house fer squeezin' yo' thing," Mary Lou said in a whisper, looking at me with big bright eyes. "River, I thought you knowed 'bout fonkin'."

"I know 'bout fonkin," I insisted strongly, "but I done tol' you yistiddy Mama say that's nasty." Not wishing to be pressed further on the subject, I jumped up and ran across the yard to where General and Silvester were firing their cap pistols at each other.

Usually, the plantation was quiet in winter. No tractors puffed up and down the fields; no mule-drawn plows sliced through the ground with the drivers yelling "Gee" and "Haw" to the animals as flocks of birds following in their wake to harvest the bugs and worms uprooted from their homes.

No hoe hands were in the field fighting grass and singing songs about Heaven and rest and sundown and tomorrow. And no cotton pickers dragged long white sacks through seas of snowy fiber, looking up every time they came to a turnrow, wondering why the sun was so hot, or speculating with every handful of cotton how many bales they were going to make, or praying fervently on some plantations for a settlement without mean words and dashed hopes and having to move in the night.

At the Bend in winter as elsewhere the fields were silent as if resting from long months of toil, and from the houses dotting the fields came lazy breaths of smoke that meandered skyward or down among the naked cotton stalks waiting to be plowed under in the spring. Overhead flew birds and geese and from the woods came sounds of shotguns as farmers hunted. Usually, the women stayed close to home, patching the family's clothes or making quilts.

But the winter of 1955 was somewhat different at the Bend. Beginning in late January streams of women in half-day shifts made their way to the house where Mr. Win and Mrs. Susie used to live. There, Mama said, Mrs. Rhoda taught them to be maids and cooks and babysitters and waitresses and laundry workers. And at night women and men went to school at Mount Olive just as we children did in the day. Mrs. Rhoda and Miss Taylor taught them to read and write and figure.

The trade school training project in Vicksburg fell through. Papa said that after Mr. Walter testified at the trial, everything in the county dried up for him like shallow sloughs in late summer.

Papa said the school superintendent refused to let the high school shop be used for training the men, saying he didn't have the funds to pay the teachers for night work. When some of the teachers volunteered to teach free of charge, the superintendent said he couldn't let the plantation men use the equipment because they would break it up. Mr. Walter then went to the chairman of the school board and tried to get him to override the superintendent, but Papa said he told Mr. Walter he didn't have time to call a board meeting. And from the very beginning, the superintendent refused the use of school buses to the farmers, telling Mr. Walter the buses were for white children only, and he wasn't going to have niggers smelling them up.

Papa said Mr. Walter had some hope of working something out to provide training for the men until he went to the bank to get his regular loan for making a crop and was turned down. He then went to the Production Credit Association of which he had been a member of the board for some time, and he was turned down again. Papa said without money to furnish the folks at the store and money for fertilizer and weed killer and poison and gas for the tractors, Mr. Walter was going to have a hard time.

The Williamsons had always been disliked by the other plantation owners around, Papa said, because they settled fairer, and because they delayed buying cotton pickers so they could continue keeping their people on the place when the others were putting them off, although they and their fathers before them had promised, too, "You can stay here as long as you live."

Papa said Mr. Walter's actions bothered the white folks' conscience because they showed they had gone back on their word. It made them unfortable, too, Papa explained, because Mr. Walter could take care of his folks, and the other planters couldn't, if they were going to pay for all the machinery they had bought. And white folks hate to admit to niggers they can't do anything they want to, Papa said.

Crushing Mr. Walter would solve these problems for the other plantation owners, Papa figured. And he said now was their chance while Mr. Walter was knee-deep in debt at the bank and couldn't get credit anywhere.

Realizing that it was unlikely that they would be able to hold on for much longer than the remainder of the year, Mr. Walter and Mrs. Rhoda, Papa said, were racing against time to get their tenants ready for jobs in town after they were put off the place, which was sure to happen if the Williamsons lost it.

It seemed funny seeing Mama and Papa going to school just like me and coming home at night trying to work arithmetic problems, and reading about Bob and Nancy, and questioning each other about Europe or Asia or the Cape of Good Hope.

Grandma didn't go to school. Said she was too old to learn, and wasn't anybody going to hire her anyhow at her age, if she did have to go to town. There she would pause and look straight into the fire with its blaze shining in her eyes showing a little dampness in the corners. "Have mercy, Jesus," she would say. "Lawd, jes' let me die right here on the place, 'cause I sho' don' wanna go to town."

Mama and the other women continued in training until cotton-chopping time, but they complained every day. "Miz Rhoda 'n' Ida done showed us how to put two sheets on the bed," Mama grumbled, looking up from her book. "Did you ever hear o' such a thing? Two sheets. Folks feeeze to death with two sheets on they bed. 'N' her come talkin' 'bout the right side and wrong side o' sheets. Said the hem is sewed on the wrong side."

"Shucks," Grandma added, "they ain't no right 'n' wrong side o' no sheets. "It's all the same."

"That's whut I say, too, Ma, but you can't tell Miz Rhoda that. 'N' her almost had a fit yistiddy when her saw Viney wiping her little girl's mouth on a dishrag. Her screamed like her been shot; 'n' her tol' Viney don't you never do that nomo' Then her call all us in the kitchen 'n' tol' us whut Viney had done, 'n' warned us not to never let her catch us wiping us chilluns face on no dishrag. That ain't sani something, her said."

"I always knowed white folks was crazy," Grandma said. "Sleepin' 'tween two col' sheets, scared to wipe they face on a dishrag."

"It's the onliest way to git a little grease on a child's face 'n' keep 'em from being so ashy," Mama said, slamming her book shut.

"I wish I had a nickel fer evvy time I done wipe yo' face with a dishrag. Yo'n 'n' Naomi's, too," Grandma boasted.

"N" Miz Rhoda don' 'low us to soak no pans," Mama said, "don' care how hard stuff stick to 'em. Her got some steel wool or somethin', 'n' her want you to clean all the pots 'n' pans right away."

"Shucks, all I can say, white folks is sho' crazy. Evvybody know pots 'n' pans is easier to wash after they done soaked; 'n' Miz Rhoda don' know that?" Grandma said.

"Sho' seem her don't," Mama agreed.

But for all of Mama's complaining, she was absorbing Mrs. Rhoda's instructions. I noticed that my bed was made up better, the sheets pulled tighter and tucked more neatly at the corners. And before the year was out, two sheets appeared on my bed. And even that same spring, she stopped wiping my face with the dishrag every morning before I went to school. Instead, she dipped a finger in the lard bucket and greased my face and hands.

Papa, like most of the other men on the plantation, put aside his books in the late winter, shortly after Mr. Walter found out for sure the bank wasn't going to furnish him. With no fuel for the tractors, Papa and the other men went back to breaking the ground with the two-mule turnplows. Papa was too tired in the evening to go to school. He tried for a few nights but found himself asleep as soon as he sat down in class.

"Silas, I ain't never seen nobody whut could set us straight as you do 'n' snore so loud," Mama charged jokingly.

"I didn't snore," Papa protested.

"You snored so loud you woke up Gus Hawkins, who been sleepin' in school long befo' y'all started plowin'," Mama insisted.

XXIII

Difficulties and Sacrifices Because of the Unproductive Cotton Crops

Ground breaking led to garden planting. We had always had a fairly large garden, but that year Papa doubled it after Mr. Walter explained there wasn't going to be much furnishing. Everybody, he said, was going to have to live mostly out of his own garden and smokehouse. There would be a little flour and coffee and sugar maybe, but little else. Papa and Mama shook their heads when they heard this, not because they were accustomed to taking up a lot of groceries at the store, but because they thought it was a bad sign. A sign that Mr. Walter might lose the place and we would have to move again.

What made things worse was the rain at cotton-planting time. It rained almost every day for weeks. It was nearly a month after school closed in early April before Papa and the other farmers got their seed in the ground. And about the time it sprouted, the rain set in again and drowned it out. In late May, Papa planted again, but just as we were ready to start chopping, it began raining again, sending up Johnson grass and Jimson weeds and dandelion to choke out the young cotton.

Every day it wasn't too muddy to go into the field, we were there with our hoes, fighting the weeds and grass that seemed to be trying to get even with us for using weed killers the year before. And the extra two acres Mr. Walter gave Papa seemed to get larger and larger. There was no layby time that year and no revival or association meetings. The rain had made everybody late, and so it seemed the Lord would have waited another year for His crop of sinners.

With no poison to kill the boll weevils, we returned to the old custom of picking the insects out of the squares with our fingers and putting them into cod-liver oil, 666, turpentine, and black draught bottles. Mr. Walter promised a dollar a hundred for the boll weevils, but it was never paid.

We hunted boll weevils and fought grass almost to cotton-picking time. The stalks were stunted by the weeds and grass and the lack of fertilizer. They were back-breaking for Papa and Mama and Grandma. They padded their knees with old burlap bags and rags and crawled up and down the rows harvesting the white fiber. The bolls were few and far apart, a sign that the boll weevils had gotten theirs first despite our hunting them down and taking them to the store, where Mr. Lige counted them and threw them in the stove.

Papa stood up one day to rest his knees. As he looked across our field of dwafted cotton, he turned to Mama and said, "Us sho' ain't gon' make much cotton this year. Us be lucky to gin fo' bales."

"That all you think us gon' make, Silas?" Mama asked, pausing to view the scanty crop.

"Maybe a little mo', but not much mo'," he replied, sinking back to his knees and reaching for the lean white bolls on the two rows he carried.

The cotton was so thin that Grandma and I could each carry a row instead of sharing one as we did in the past. But she often had to stop and sit on her sack and rest. We missed Naomi again that year because when she was home, she and Mama both would reach over and pick a few stalks to help us keep up. Mama still did, but it wasn't like having two of them to help us out.

In breaking the ground that year, Papa had followed the long rows laid out by a tractor the year before. Trying to carry one of these long rows wasn't easy, and Grandma and I often fell well behind. Mama and Papa, too, would turn around and meet us on our rows. Papa boasted of being the best cotton picker on the place. Said he could pick four hundred pounds a day in good thick cotton. And I bet he could, too, because his hands moved like lightning from boll to boll, gouging each empty with a single grasp. Mama usually picked two hundred, Grandma, eighty to a hundred, and my tally was usually around forty.

In less than three weeks after we started, we had picked over our whole nine acres the first time and had only three bales. We knew from the scattering of unopened bolls, there wasn't going to be much scraping.

"Maybe ha'f a bale," Papa said.

Every night Mama and Papa figured up what they thought they might get at settlement time. For the first time, as a result of night school, they were actually figuring with pencils and paper. The short staple cotton we were harvesting wasn't bringing but twenty-six to twenty-eight cents. They figured the three and a half bales we were likely to have plus the seed would bring no more than four hundred and fifty dollars. Mr. Walter's third, they said, would be about one hundred fifty dollars, and what they owed at the store for flour and sugar and coffee and two pairs of overalls, nine yards of gingham, and the cloth for our cotton-picking sacks would come to around fifty dollars, leaving them, they figured, barely two hundred fifty dollars. Although they had seventy dollars from last year and the year before, they knew that what they could add to it from this year's crop wasn't going to be enough to pay down on a farm of their own.

"Maybe Mr. Walter ain't gon' lose the place 'n' us can stay here another year or two," Papa said, trying to comfort Mama and Grandma, who were worrying about having no place to move to.

"Miz Rhoda talk like this might be they last year," Mama argued.

"But Mr. Walter ain't said that," Papa persisted bravely, "'n' even ef he don' make it, he done promised to speak to that gover'ment farm loan man in Vicksburg."

"I hope he do, Silas, but you know as well as I do his word don' go fer nomo'," Mama said, looking straight at Papa almost as if to dare him to challenge her reasoning.

"Course, it don't," Papa shot back, "but Mr. Walter still a white man, don' fergit that, 'n' he still hol'n on to a big chunk o' land, 'n' that little peckerwood in Vicksburg gon' think twice befo' he turn him down."

When we finished scraping in early November, like Papa had said, we didn't have but little over half a bale, giving us a total for the year of about three and a half bales. But this was more than anybody else on the place made, Papa said. Our picking boll weevils and fighting grass and weeds so hard had made the difference, he thought. Nobody else on the place made more than two bales, and the whole thirteen hundred acres of cotton on the plantation didn't produce but three hundred five bales, Mr. Willie told Papa.

When Papa came from settlement, he had only fifty dollars, but he said Mr. Walter had admitted owing him more—about one hundred fifty dollars more. "Mr. Walter he say he gon' give me the rest jes' as soon as he git straight," Papa explained. "He say the gover'ment talkin' 'bout rentin' a lot o' cotton land next year fer some kind o' bank—soil bank, I think he said. Ef that go through in time, he say he gon' rent some o' his land to the gover'ment, 'n' that gon' give him money to pay the bank in Vicksburg.

"He say ef all the folks on the place coulda done as good as us done, or ef the price coulda been a little better, he would be in pretty good shape. But now he say 'less he can rent some cotton land to the gover'ment 'tween now 'n' the first o' the year, he might lose the place. So, he goin' to Washington next week to see whut he can do. He say Washington is the capital where the gover'ment at."

"Silas," Mama said with fear and doubt in her voice, "did you ast Mr. Walter 'bout a letter to that gover'ment loan place in Vickeburg?"

"I didn't have to ast him, he ast me ef I had any plans fer next year, in case he los' the place."

"Mr. Walter ast you that?" Mama questioned with the beginnings of a smile on her face, although she didn't take her eyes from the fireplace. It was as if she was afraid the devil was watching to dash her hopes if she hoped for too much.

But Papa wasn't afraid to hope. His answer was quick and boastful. "He sho' did, 'n' he done already give me a letter."

"Shonuff? Shonuff, Silas?" Grandma cut in. "Mr. Walter, Gawd bless his soul, is sho' a good white man," she added prayerfully.

"Yes, Miz Carrie, you can say whut you want to 'bout Mr. Walter, but like you say, he sho' is a good white man," Papa said, pulling the letter out of his jumper pocket. "Here the letter he done give me after I tol' him I wanted to go back to that loan place 'n' ast 'em to help me buy a little piece o' land."

"Lemme see it, Silas," Mama said, reaching for the letter Papa was holding proudly. What had been the beginnings of an uncertain smile broke across her face like a wave, forcing her lips apart and washing her eyes until they were shiny with happiness.

"Whut do it say?" Grandma asked.

"I don' no'am, it sealed."

"Course, it sealed," Papa said, "but Mr. Walter read it to me befo' he sealed it. It say Mr. Walter would be muchoblige to Mr. Warrenton. That's the man's name, Mr. Warrenton, ef he would consider makin' Silas Henry a loan to buy a small farm."

"Ain't that nice, Ma?" Mama said, smiling more broadly than before. "Ain't that nice o' Mr. Walter?"

"It sho' is, Becky, Lawd help us, it sho' is," Grandma replied with water gathering in her eyes.

"When you goin' to Vicksburg 'n' see the man?" Mama asked, getting up out of her chair and walking about the room with her hands rolled up in her apron. I think she was walking about the room trying to shake off the fear that was always there when good news came, that the devil was going to ruin this, too.

"After Mr. Walter come back from Washington," Papa said. "I don' wanna go to that peckerwood 'less'n I have to. And ef Mr. Walter can hol' on, 'n' us can stay here a year or two mo' us'll have enuff to pay down on a farm without that little ole peckerwood having a thing to do with it."

At church that Sunday, all the talk was about Mr. Walter's trip to Washington to try to save the plantation. Mr. Hamp, the Sunday school superintendent, who conducted the covenant meeting, prayed a long prayer for Mr. Walter, and most of the folks included in their "determination" something about the Lord helping Mr. Walter.

I remember what Mama said in her "determination" after singing two stanzas of "His Eye Is on the Sparrow." "Lawd," she said, "I thank You that I'm able to stan' here once mo' 'n' erg'n 'n' tell all y'all I set my feet on the road to glory many years ago 'n' I ain't never turn back, 'n' I ain't 'bout to turn back now."

There was a loud "Amen" from all over the church. I was sitting on the front bench with General Lee and his two sisters and Sylvester and Mary Lou. I looked back at Mama, who was standing about halfway the church. She looked smaller standing there all alone. Her brow was knit, her eyes closed, and her lips trembled as she spoke.

"Lawd," she said, "life ain't never been easy fer us 'n' it seem like it gittin' tougher 'n' tougher. There was a time when us didn't have nothin' to worry 'bout but rain 'n' grass 'n' boll weevils 'n' settlement time 'n' leaks in the roofs o' us houses. But now, Lawd, us worried 'bout havin' a roof a'tall over us head."

"Amen, amen, sister; tell Gawd 'bout it," Mr. Hamp cried out and others joined in with loud "amens."

"Lawd," Mama continued, "Mr. Walter done gone to Washington to try to save this place. Please, suh, won't you go with him 'n' stan' by him. 'N' us know, Lawd, ef You do that evvything gon' be all right."

Again, everybody said, "Amen, amen."

And Mrs. Emma Jackson screamed, "Lawd, Lawd, where is You at? Where is you at, Lawd?" and began to shout.

Mrs. Nettie Woodson and Mrs. Mary Moses tried to hold her, but she broke loose from them and ran to the front of the church, hurling her hat and her pocketbook as she ran. At the altar rail, she stopped and turned around and stood there with her arms outstretched like Jesus on the cross. Then she bellowed again, "Lawd, Lawd, where is You at?"

Her husband, Mr. Miller, and Mr. Hamp put their arms around her and walked her back to her seat, where she sat limp, staring vacantly toward the pulpit.

Mama was still standing; Papa, who had jumped up from beside her to go and help hold Mrs. Emma, sat back down. Although Mama was biting her lip as she usually did to hold back tears, her eyes were wet and drops of water ran down her face. "All y'all know," she said, "my determination is fer heaven 'n' I wanna make heaven my home. Y'all pray fer me 'n' pray fer Mr. Walter so us can have a home here on the place 'tel the Lawd call us home to us reward."

There were more "Amens" as she sat down, and there were tears, too. The uncertainty about the plantation lay bare on the faces of the people. They sat there frozen in their fear for a long time. Then Mr. Riley Jones stood up, gripping and regripping the back of the seat in front of him with his short, knobby fingers. He didn't say a word at first. Finally, in a low voice, he began singing "He's Got the Whole World in His hands."

This opened the floodgate. All the pentup fear and sorrow and doubt came rushing out in plaintive wails that merged with Mr. Riley's strong voice. There were more tears and more outcries, but slowly the assurance of the song spread over the congregation and brought calm. Tears dried, screams quieted, and the covenant meeting was over.

XXIV

Plantation Owner's Failure to Get Credit and Government Help

The next Wednesday, Mr. Walter came home from Washington. But since he didn't ring the bell and call the folks to his house to tell them how he made out, everybody was whispering that he must not have got any help. And Papa said Mr. Willie told him Mr. Lige said that Mr. Walter found out the government was going to rent some cotton land to improve prices, but this wasn't likely to happen until spring. That was going to be too late, Mr. Lige told Mr. Willie, unless the bank gave Mr. Walter more time.

At first as word seeped out over the plantation about the government's delay, fear that Mr. Walter was going to lose the place cast gloom. When folks came to our house, everyone talked in whispers, except Grandma, who said loud and strong that she would rather die than have to move to town.

But the gloom thinned when Mr. Willie started telling everybody, although in a whispered voice, that the bank might wait and give Mr. Walter a chance to rent some of his land to the government. So at church on that second Sunday in Decembe,r many were smiling, and a few had on new shoes like Papa and Grandma and me. Mama had new shoes, too, but she didn't wear them. Over her vigorous protest, Papa had gone to Vicksburg and bought the shoes and a bottle of whiskey on the strength of what Mr. Willie said he had heard.

"How come you don' hol' on to us money, Silas, 'n' wait 'n' see whut Mr. Walter say?" Mama asked.

"'Cause Willie say Mr. Lige done tol' him the bank gon' wait," Papa answered.

"But Silas," Mama protested, "it wouldn't hurt to wait 'tel us sho.'"

"Woman, my feet's on the ground 'n' yo'n, too, 'n' River 'n' Miz Carrie need shoes bad as us do," Papa argued. "Ef Mr. Walter lose the place or keep it, ef us stay here or ef us move, us gotta have some shoes."

The next morning, Papa had walked out of the house, turned down the side road, and headed for the main road to catch Mr. Willie. When he came back late that afternoon, he had new shoes for all of us, including Grandma. I grabbed mine and tried them on; they hurt a little, but I didn't say a word about it because I wasn't going risk not wearing them to church the next day. Mama not only refused to try her shoes on, she hurled the shoes, box and all at Papa's head and just missed. Papa laughed and laughed. Then he reached in a bag a pulled out a bottle of whiskey and took a drink.

"Us could do without shoes," Mama stormed, "'n' you sho' could do without that ole booze."

"Woman, I done worked all year, do you hear me? All year!" Papa bellowed. "'N' ef after that I can't have a pair o' shoes 'n' a little drink, well, whut the hell, Gawddamit."

Mama knew she couldn't win an argument against Papa and piecing and started humming as she sat back down and began sewing. As Mama hummed and sewed, Grandma took her shoes out of the box quickly and placed them in her lap as if she were stealing them. I think she was afraid Mama might grab them in her anger and skin them up throwing them at Papa. At first Grandma covered them with her apron and let them lie in her lap. As she noticed Mama's anger dying, she slowly uncovered one of the shoes and looked at it carefully and smiling as she rubbed dull places with her apron to make the shoe shine more brightly.

Papa had gone into the kitchen, opened the pots, scooped up his supper, and sat eating and washing it down with buttermilk. When he had finished, he went out into the backyard, slamming the door as hard as he could. Mama jumped up and ran and opened the door, hollering to Papa, "Silas Henry, us gon' have to move outa this house soon enuff without you knockin' it down." Finally, she herself slammed the door and came back and sat down and resumed her sewing without saying a word. And she still wasn't speaking to Papa when we left for church that Sunday. He pleaded with her to wear her new shoes, but she didn't even answer him.

I limped about the church in my new shoes both because they hurt a little and because I wanted everyone to notice them. Sylvester was the only other child who had new shoes; he limped, too. Although no others were limping in new shoes, most were smiling because there was hope for the plantation.

Reverend Whitten was up from Vicksburg to preach and preside over the fall drive. His sermon was about a little boy with a basket containing five loaves of bread and two fish. He and thousands of others followed Jesus out into the countryside. Then everybody became hungry, but nobody had any food except the little boy. Reverend Whitten said the Lord took the boy's bread and fish and fed all the folks. This, he said, showed that God could take care of everybody. "So don't you worry," he screamed, "the Lawd gon' take care o' y'all."

Everybody yelled, "Amen, amen."

And Mr. Hamp said, "Tell the truth, Reverend; preach the word."

But I kept thinking how generous the little boy was to give his bread and fish to Jesus so that he could feed the people. And I kept wondering what would have happened if he had refused to give Jesus his lunch, of if he, like the others, had forgot to bring his lunch.

Before Reverend Whitten had finished, Mrs. Viney and Mrs. Mary and General Lee's mama had shouted. It took nearly half the church to hold them. Then regular collection time came, and we all marched up to the table and put down our money. Papa and Mr. Hamp stood at the table, counting the money. They smiled when I put a dime in the plate; I had another dime for the drive. Papa started it off with a dollar bill, which he held high in the air before he laid it down. Both Mama and Grandma gave a dollar in the drive. Altogether, the church raised twenty-nine dollars and forty-five cents that day. Out of their meager funds, the people were paying the Lord to take care of them like the preacher said He would. Reverend Whitten was all smiles.

But as things turned out, the money didn't buy anything from the Lord. Mr. Walter lost the place anyway. Mr. Willie told Papa two plantation owners on the board at the bank refused to agree to give Mr. Walter any more time.

This final decision was made by the bank two days before Christmas, but Mr. Walter didn't say a word about it until after New Years'. As usual on Christmas Day, he and Mrs. Rhoda and Frank, Mr. Tobe's son, visited every house on the plantation delivering "Merry Christmas" and bags of apples and oranges. Frank sat in the back seat, bagging up the fruit according to the size of each family. I thought Frank had the best job in the whole world, handling all that fruit and eating as much as he liked.

We all went out to the car, including Grandma to exchange Christmas greetings with Mr. Walter and Mrs. Rhoda. When Papa attempted to ask if everything was going to be all right on the place, Mrs. Rhoda cut him short. "Now this is Christmas," she said. "It's time to be merry."

She said it with a broad smile, but her eyes weren't smiling. They seemed a little dull, a little vacant, staring straight at us with all their blueness, and yet seeming not to really see us.

"Naw, it's Christmas," Mr. Walter added, "it's time for us to be merry." Then he pulled off slowly, waving and yelling back, "Merry Christmas, y'all!"

We waved and hollered back, "Merry Christmas!" and then stood there by the side of the road until the car turned in at Mr. Ben's.

Papa handed me the bag of fruit, and I ran into the house ahead of them and spread all the apples and oranges out on the bed. There were four of each. To these, I added the two apples and two oranges Santa Claus had brought me. Spread out on the bed slick and shiny, they seemed like all the apples and oranges in the world. I put all the apples in one row and all the oranges in another and looked at them for a while. Then I made one long row, alternating an apple and an orange. The row stretched from the pillows more than halfway to the foot of the iron bed.

While the fruit was still on the bed, I looked out of the window and saw General walking down the lane toward our house. I hurridly gathered up the apples and oranges and put them back in the bag and hid it under the bed so that General wouldn't see it and start begging me for my fruit.

"Whuuuuuuut Santa Claus donnnnnnnnnnne brought you?" he asked after scraping the mud off his shoes and coming into the house.

"This cap pistol 'n' some caps 'n' a sweater 'n' some socks 'n'," I was about to say a heap o' apples 'n' oranges, but I paused and repeated, "a cap pistol 'n' some caps 'n' a sweater 'n' some socks. Whut did he bring you?"

"Heeeeeee ain't brought meeeeeeee 'n' my sister nothththin' but a stick o' cannnnnnnndy a piece."

"How come he ain't brought you 'n' yo' sisters nothin' but a little ole stck o' candy? Y'all musta been bad," I said.

"Ussssssss wasn't bad. Paaaaaaapa say Mr. Walter wouldddn't let Santa Claus taaaaake up nothin' at the sto'."

"How come?"

"Heeeeeee say Mr. Waaaaaaaaalter done tol' Mr. Lige not to let noooooooobody have no creeeeeeeeedit 'til he goooooooooo to town 'n' talk with the bank ag'in," General replied.

"Whut the bank got to do with Santa Claus?" I asked.

"River, don' ast so many questions," Mama ordered as she walked into the room.

"Givvvvvvvvve some o, yoooooooooo' fruit, River."

"Didn't Mr. Walter 'n' miz Rhoda bring y'all no fruit?" I asked.

"Theyyyyyyyy brought us some, buttttttt us done et it up."

"I done et mine, too," I said.

"Youuuuuuu done et 'em all?"

"Evvy last one."

"River, you stop tellin' stories 'n' give General one o' yo' apples 'n' one o' yo' oranges," Mama commanded.

"Naw, Mama, Naw," I pleaded.

"Do you want me to give him ha'f o' 'em?"

"No'am, Mama; please, Mama."

"Well, you git under that bed 'n' git that fruit 'n' give General a apple 'n' a orange like I tol' you."

"Yessum, Mama; yessum," I said, slowly crawling under the bed to get the fruit.

While I was still under the bed, I opened the bag and felt over every apple and every orange in search of the smallest ones to give General. As soon as I handed him the fruit, he bit into the apple, engulfing nearly half of it. While he was eating the orange, peal and all, I suggested that we go outside and shoot my cap pistol. He agreed and I put my fruit back under the bed.

XXV

Plantation Is Lost and There Is a New Owner

Christmas and New Years passed, and although Mr. Walter hadn't said whether he had been able to save the place or not, the people started putting two and two together. No credit at the store, sale of all the cattle that had been grazing along the levee, and trips and trips to Vicksburg almost every day by Mr. Walter and Mrs. Rhoda led just about everyone to conclude that the plantation had either been lost or was about to be. Soon the bad news was confirmed by the presence of the surveyors.

They surveyed the south line of the plantation down by Mr. Miller Jackson's and word soon spread everywhere. When I got home from school that day, Papa had gone down to Mr. Miller's to find out about the surveying. He returned just before night so depressed he didn't stop to clean the mud off his feet before walking into the house, mumbling, "Mr. Walter done los' the place."

"Is you sho', Silas?" Mama asked with disbelief in her voice.

"Well, they sho'nuff been measurin' down by Miller's 'n' they done put stakes all the way out to the road below Willie's. That mean Mr. Walter done los' the place to the bank," Papa said almost in a moan.

"Have mercy, Jesus; have mercy, Jesus," were all the words Grandma could find to express her sorrow.

"Did Miller talk with the mens?" Mama wanted to know.

"Yes, Becky, Miller say he talk to 'em 'n' they tol' him the bank done forelosed 'n' the sheriff's office done sent them to check the south edge o' the place."

"Miller hisself tol' you that, Silas?" Mama asked sadly, her face breaking into furrows of grief.

"That's whut he say, Becky; that sho' is whut he say. He say at first he thought the mens was takin' pictures when they set down a three-legged thing 'n' started lookin through it right in front o' his house. He say he was scared they was gon' take a picture o' him like some other mens did years ago and came back at ginnin' time 'n' was gon' charge him almos' a bale o' cotton fer the picture in a fancy frame 'til Mr. Walter's daddy threatened to have 'em put in jail. 'N' he say Mr. Williamson tol' him not to never let nobody take his picture, he didn't give a damn who it was.

"So Miller say he went out 'n' begged the mens not to take his picture, 'n' he say they jes' laffed 'n' laffed 'n' then tol' him they wasn't takin' no pictures; they was measuring the land fer the bank, 'cause it was fo'closin' Mr. Walter."

Mama stretched across the bed crying for a long time. Papa lay by her side, patting her and telling her everything was gon' work out all right, that as bad as he hated to, he was going to Vicksburg the next day and see that government man about a loan to buy them a small farm.

"I'm gon' take that letter Mr. Walter done give me," he said, "'n' I bet the man'll make me a loan, 'cause he done said he make loans to niggers whut bring letters from the plantation owners."

"Silas, you reckon it gon' make any diff'ence that Mr. Walter done los' his place?" Mama asked in a voice muffled by tears.

"I don' think so, Becky; I don' think so," Papa said.

"You shoulda gone a long time ago when I tol' you," Mama complained.

"I didn't wanna jump the traces, Becky; I wanted to wait 'n' see how Mr. Walter was gon' come out."

"I sho' hope you ain't too late," Mama moaned.

"I'm goin' firs' thing in the mornin', Becky."

"Yes, Silas, don' wait no longer," urged Grandma, who had been sitting by the fireplace all the while staring into the fire, whose flickering reflection showed streaks of tears on her face.

"Yessum, Miz Carrie, I'm goin' firs' thing in the mornin'."

"Can I go with you, Papa?" I asked.

"Naw, River, you got to go to school," he reminded me.

"But I could miss jes' this one time couldn't I, Papa?"

"Naw, you stay here; 'member that ole man made you cry befo'," Mama added.

"Yessum," I said slowly, recalling when I went with Papa before to that old government office.

Mama and Papa and Grandma talked on about the prospects of getting a loan to buy a farm of their own, but I didn't half listen after they turned me down. I did, however, hear Mama tell Papa to be sure and ask Willie to take him by where Naomi worked so he could see her. We hadn't seen her since just before cotton-picking time, when she and her boyfriend drove up and brought little Carrie Mae. She said they were going to get married, and it seemed she could eat him up without any salt, but he didn't say much. He was yellow like Roscoe and had good hair.

Grandma winked her eye at him and said, "Naomi can sho' pick 'em."

At Christmas time, we received a box from my sister. She sent me a sweater, Papa a shirt, and Mama and Grandma some yard goods for dresses. Although we hadn't seen her since late last summer, she was seldom off Mama's mind. Often she said, "I would sho' like to see little ole Carry Mae." But money was too short and things too uncertain for a couple of dollars to be spent riding to town with Mr. Willie to visit them.

Just before Papa went out of the door early the next morning to catch a ride to town with Mr. Willie, however, Mama reminded him again not to forget to go by and see Naomi.

Papa had barely left the house when the plantation bell rang. Everybody knew its sound, which was different from our church bell or the Baptist church bell. Their sounds were thin and came through the air like a sparrow, light and swift and begging. But the plantation bell, which hung between two tall poles in front of Mr. Walter's barn, had a heavy, demanding sound. It rang four times every day, except in winter and during layby time. It rang at five in the morning to get the folks up and into the fields by six; it rang at noon to bring them home for dinner and the work-stock to water and rest; it rang at one to send the families back to the fields; and at six it rang again to bring them home for the night.

To hear the bell ring in the dead of winter was very unusual, but everybody knew what it meant. It called them to Wilmyra for special instructions. Sometimes it was for Mr. Walter to tell them to break and burn cotton stalks to kill boll weevil eggs, sometimes it was to remind them to open all gates and gaps and let the Williamson cattle graze the fields, and once in a while it was to warn the people not to tear down their fences and pull up their steps for firewood, but to go into the woods and cut trees.

When the bell rang that day, hearts fluttered because everybody knew it wasn't about boll weevils or cattle grazing or firewood, but about the plantation itself—whether it had been lost or saved.

When Papa heard the bell, he turned around and came back home. In a little while he had hitched up the wagon and we wore on our way to Mr. Walter's. Back down the lane, we could see others coming. Some were in wagons, some on horseback, and others on foot. At Mr. Walter's, Frank and his papa, Mr. Tobe, directed everyone to the hitching area off to the side of the road near the Williamson family cemetery. Mr. Walter and Mrs. Rhoda were standing on their steps, and Mr. Lige was out by the gate, waving to the folks to come on over. A large heavy table made out of rough planks was sitting across the walkway near the gate. A chair to serve as a step stood with its back against the table on which sat two other chairs. Grandma remained in our wagon, but Papa and Mama and I walked over and stood right up against the white picket fence, which enclosed Wilmyra. By tiptoeing, I could look between the top of the pickets, where they were trimmed to a point like a church steeple, and see the table. It was a cold day and almost all the people had quilts around their shoulders. Papa and Mama had theirs in their arms.

Soon Mr. Walter and Mrs. Rhoda walked out and mounted the table. Frank held the chair, which was used as a step. Mrs. Rhoda sat down, but Mr. Walter remained standing. He looked out over the crowd and waved. Then he took out his handkerchief and wiped his face, holding it to his eyes for what seemed like a long time.

Still holding the handkerchief in one hand, Mr. Walter said, "I have called you here today to tell you how things stand with the plantation. Mrs. Rhoda and I have done everything we could to save the place, which has been in my family for almost a hundred years. As you know, I went to Washington to see if I could get them to hurry up with the so called soil bank program, but I wasn't successful. Also, we have been negotiating with the bank in Vicksburg for weeks, trying to work out some way to save the place, but we were unable to do so. Now, as much as it hurts us, we must tell you that the plantation has been lost."

"Naw, naw, naw," came from the crowd. "Lawd, naw, naw," some said.

Other cried out, "Lawd, Lawd, have mercy, Jesus!" while many were crying and screaming.

Papa leaned against the fence and bit his lip, and tears rolled down Mama's face. Then we heard Grandma scream and looked and saw her standing up in the wagon with her arms reaching toward the sky. The quilt had fallen from her shoulders and from her lips came a deep and mournful, "Lawd, Jesus, is you fergot us?"

We rushed to the wagon; Mama and Papa climbed in and helped her to sit back down in her chair, which had turned over. Mama picked up the quilt and put it around her again and sat down by her, patting her heaving back.

After a while, Mr. Walter held up his hands for quiet the way Miss Taylor did at school, and Mrs. Rhoda stood up beside him as if to give him strength. As the murmuring died down, Mr. Walter continued.

"It's true that we have lost the place, but you are not going to have to move, least not for a year." He said it quickly, like the firing of an automatic rifle aimed at a rattlesnake. He, too, must have been trying to kill something—fear, I guess.

Having fired on the basic fear, having to move, Mr. Walter proceeded more slowly. "The man who is going to take over the place from the bank, Mr. Holly Samuels, has promised that no one will be put off the place this year," he said firmly and somehow managed a weak smile. "Mr. Samuels already has one place over near Cary in Sharkey County," Mr. Walter continued. "With the two plantations, he says he's gon' start mechanizing like the other plantations 'round here, 'n' he's sure to put some of his cotton land in the soil bank, if that program is ever enacted, but no matter what, he has promised definitely not to put anyone off this year," Mr. Walter repeated. Then the handkerchief went up to his face again and he stood there, wiping his eyes.

Doubting that Mr. Walter would be able to go on at the moment, Mrs. Rhoda spoke up: "So you have a year, a whole year to make plans for moving elsewhere if you have to. Mr. Walter and I saw the possibility of this a year ago; that is why we held school to teach some of you to read and write and figure better, and to train some of the womenfolks to cook and do housework and wait tables and do other work in town."

At the mention of town, Grandma screamed, "Naw, naw, Lawd, please, haw, naw!" She was joined by others who also cried out, expressing their doubts and fears.

But Mrs. Rhoda went on: "I am sorry the crops prevented us from devoting more time to this training last spring. You have made a start, however; I hope you will build on it and find jobs with good families. I have some back copies of women's magazines showing pictures of city homes with proper furnishings and modern conveniences. You can learn something about the care of homes from these magazines. I gave you some of these last spring; I'm going to give you the rest of them now. Frank and Tobe and Ida will pass them out. Exchange them among yourselves so that you can see as many of them as possible."

Frank and Mr. Tobe and Mrs. Ida passed out the pretty magazines. Mama got one and let me hold it. It had pictures just like our mail-order catalogue, but not as many. The magazines seemed to ease the people's fears or at least take their minds off of them. The moaning and crying and sighing had subsided when Mr. Walter stood up to speak again.

"You will forgive me," he said, "but the loss of this plantation affects me deeply as I know it must also affect you. I'm hopeful that things are going work out better than you think, but if there is anything you think Mrs. Rhoda and I might be able to do for you, please let us know. We are going to be living in Memphis, and I am going to be working with my cousins, who are cotton buyers there. We have a home in Memphis, which my mother-in-law left us years ago." As he finished, the handkerchief went up to his eyes again and he merely stood there.

"We are leaving at the end of the week," Mrs. Rhoda said as if to fill the void. "We'll be seeing most of you before we leave. God's blessings upon all of you." Then water gathered in her eyes, too, and spilled down her face.

Catching Mr. Walter's arm, Mrs. Rhoda stepped down from the table. He followed and they both walked back toward their house. Mr. Walter's shoulders were shaking; he never looked back, but Mrs. Rhoda turned around at the steps and waved.

XXVI

Sharecroppers Apply for Government Loans to Buy Six Hundred Acres

After Mr. Walter and Mrs Rhoda had gone into the house, the people slowly drifted back to their wagons or horses. We were already at our wagon, keeping an eye on Grandma. Mr. Ben and Mrs. Mary stopped a moment to talk.

"Whut you gon' do, Silas?" Mr. Ben asked with fear in his voice.

"I'm gon' try to git off this place jes' as soon as I can," Papa replied.

"You is?"

"I sho' is, 'cause I don' like that Mr. Holly. His folks say he don' like to settle. You know, I went to his place year befo' las' when I thought us was gon' have to move."

"OmyGawd, ef he don' settle, I'm gon' try to move, too. But Silas, I sho' hates to leave the Bend; been here most o' my life."

"I hates to move, too, Ben, but us ain't got much choice. I'm goin' to Vicksburg tomorrer 'n' see that gover'ment loan man I tol' you 'bout, 'n' ef I have any luck, I'm gon' tell you 'bout it," Papa promised.

"You goin' to see 'bout movin' there?"

"Naw, Ben, you know I ain't thinkin' 'bout movin' to no Vicksburg. I'm goin' to see 'bout gittin' a little piece land o' my own to move to through the gover'ment. You know, I tol' you 'bout it."

"Oh, yeah, I 'member now. Silas, you be sho' 'n' let us know, ef you have any luck."

"Yeah, Silas, you let us know soon as you git back so Ben can go 'n' see 'bout a loan," Mrs. Mary added. "'Cause us would like to move wherever y'all moves to."

"That would be nice, Mary," Mama said, "ef us could find a place together."

"It sho' would, Becky; it sho' would."

Then Mrs. Mary gave Grandma a little hug, and she and Mr. Ben went on their wagon. George and their other children weren't with them; they must have stayed home.

"I sho' hopes that gover'ment loan place gon' be able to help us, Silas," Mama said quietly, almost in a whisper as Papa pulled off toward home behind three or four other wagons.

"He shoulda done gone down there to see 'bout it weeks ago, soon as Mr. Walter give him the letter, 'stead o' sittin' 'round here 'tel the last minute," Grandma fussed.

"Oh, Ma, hush yo' mouth," Mama ordered. "This is me 'n' Silas business."

"Let her talk, I don' give a damn," Papa said with a knife in his voice and struck old Salt with the slack in the reins.

"Ef y'all gon' start arguin' 'n' talkin' like that, me 'n' River gon' git out 'n' walk," Mama warned.

"I'm jes' tellin' the Gawd's truth," Grandma said.

"Now, Miz Carrie, you know damn well I was goin' to Vicksburg today, ef that bell hadn't done rung, Gawdamit," Papa swore.

"I'm tellin' y'all," Mama warned again, "I'm gon' git outa this wagon, ef y'all keeps on."

Although Grandma kept on fretting quietly that we were going to be put off the place with no place to go, except to town to starve to death, Papa didn't say another word. Early the next morning, he got up and walked across to the main road to meet Mr. Willie and go to town with him. I made one more attempt to get him to let me go along.

"You gon' let me go with you, ain't you, Papa?" I asked feebly.

"Naw, man, you stay here 'n' go to school like I tol' you yistiddy."

"Ain't nothin you can do, River, but be in the way," Mama added.

"Yessum," I said, smiling a little because Papa had called me man.

"Now Silas, don't you fergit to go by where Naomi work at 'n' see her, but don' tell her nothin' 'bout us might have to move, 'cause her be worryin'," Mama said.

"Becky, I won't fergit," Papa promised, putting his jumper on over his Sunday coat. When he finished buttoning it up, he ruffled my hair as he passed, pausing long enough to stoop down and ask me, "River, you is Papa's little man, ain't you?" This completely melted my disappointment like a pat of butter inside a hot biscuit.

As Papa went out of the door, I hollered after him, "Us gon' have a farm o' us own, ain't us, Papa?"

"I sho' hope so, man," he replied, slamming the door behind him.

When I came home from school that day, Grandma was sitting by the fireplace rocking and smiling, and Mama was in the kitchen, cooking supper and singing her favorite song, "His Eye Is on the Sparrow." As soon as she heard me speaking to Grandma, she rushed into the room, wiping her hands on her apron. "Yo' Papa done had good luck," she said, joyously pressing her hands together. "The gover'ment gon' help us git a farm o' us own."

"It is?" I screamed, running to her and wrapping my arms around her legs as far as they would go.

"It sho' is, it sho' is," she repeated, "'n' it gon' help a heap o' other folks, too; 'bout nine or ten families, Silas say. He gone to tell 'em; that where he is now."

I jumped up and down, screaming, "Us gon' have a farm! Us gon' have a farm!"

"Silas say the man in Vicksburg say there 'bout six hund'ered acres in the hills the other side o' Red Wood, out pas' that Mr. Ammons' place that he gon' try to git fer us 'n' some o' the other folks here on the place. That'd be 'bout fifty or sixty acres apiece," Mama said excitedly.

"Lawd, Jesus," Grandma moaned prayerfully, "I sho' hopes us gits it." Joy and fear mingled in her eyes, and she dabbed at them with the corner of her apron.

"Ma, Silas say the gover'ment man say us sho' to git, less'n some o' the rich white folks from up North gits it firs' fer bird huntin'," Mama explained.

"Us gon' have a farm, us gon' have a farm!" I sang, skipping through the house.

It was after dark when Papa came home. He was so excited he didn't want any supper. "I done tol' 'em, you know, the nine families us 'greed on, 'cep'n I done added Henry 'n' Nettie, after Willie say he gon' stay on here 'n' carry the mail; 'n' I don' blame him 'cause he doin' pretty good."

"Yeah, but it ain't like ownin' a piece o' land o' yo' own," Mama said with assurance.

"Well, you know how Willie is; he ain't gon' take no chances, long as he can grin at white folks 'n' keep his job carryin' the mail."

"I sorta wish Henry 'n' Nettie wasn't goin', Silas, but I guess it'll be all right, long as they ain't livin' next do' to us."

"Oh, it'll be all right, Becky, 'cause us can make sho' there some families like Ben 'n' Mary, 'n' Tom 'n' Luiza 'tween us 'n' them," Papa said.

"Y'all goin' tomorrer, ain't you, like the white man said?" Mama asked.

"Course, us goin' firs' thing in the mornin' 'n' 'ply fer loans to buy that land Mr. Warrenton tol' me 'bout," Papa said, walking up and down the floor.

"Ain't the Lawd wonderful," Grandma said. "When it was darkest 'n' us didn't know where to turn, He done come with His blessin's."

"You is sho' right, Ma; you is sho' right; He done come," Mama agreed with tears of joy in her eyes.

The next morning, when Mr. Willie left with the mail, ten men, including Papa, had crammed themselves into Mr. Willie's car and Mr. Tobe's truck and we were headed for Vicksburg. I was sitting in Papa's lap. He had tried to leave me behind, but I had cried so he and Mama gave in. The Lord had been so good to them, opening the government man's heart and getting him to help us get a farm that they were not prepared to deny me the trip.

In Mr. Willie's car were Mr. Ben, Mr. Tom Lee, Mr. Stock Robinson, Papa and I, and in the truck with Mr. Tobe were Mr. Hamp, Mr. Miller Jackson, Mr. Henry Woodson, Mr. Riley Jones, and Mr. Joe Jones.

When we passed the turnoff to Redood, Mr. Willie pointed to the road and said, "The place must be right back in there 'bout three fo' miles, ef it out by Amos Ammons."

"The man said it was jes' 'bout ha'f a mile the other side o' Amos Ammons' place," Papa added. "Y'all oughta see it; it pretty back there."

"I ain't never lived in the hills, do they grow much cotton back in there?" Mr. Ben asked, leaning forward toward Papa's ear.

"You 'member I tol' you 'bout Amos Ammons; he grow a little cotton, but mostly he raise hogs 'n' chickens 'n' cows, 'n' sell milk 'n' eggs," Papa explained.

"'N', Papa, he live in a pretty white house," I said, "white like Mr. Walter 'n' them's houses."

"He do?" Mr. Tom asked.

"He sho' do," Papa replied.

"I ain't never growed nothin' but cotton 'n' corn myself," Mr. Stock said, "hope I ain't too old to learn 'bout raisin' cows 'n' chickens."

"Us all gotta learn," Papa said, looking back at Mr. Stock as the car shot up a steep hill.

In Vicksburg, Mr. Willie drove straight to the post office with Mr. Tobe right behind him in his truck. They turned off the main street, where Mama bought her stove, and pulled in behind the post office. But Mr. Willie got out of his car and went back and explained to Mr. Tobe that only government cars and trucks could park there. Mr. Tobe backed out and parked on the street. Then we all got out and went around to the front of the building. Seems that everybody turned to look at us as we walked up the steps.

"You boys want to see Mr. Warrenton, don't you?" one of the white ladies in the office asked. "Well, he's waiting fer you. Mr. Warrenton!" she called out. "Silas 'n' some other boys from the Williamson plantation is here!"

We all lined up at the counter and in a few minutes, Mr. Warrenton appeared, looking at his watch. "Silas," he said, "I thought you 'n' these boys was gon' be here firs' thing this mornin' like you said, instead o' nine o'clock. You boys keep bankers' hours, don't you?"

"Nawsuh," Papa spoke up quickly. "Us thought you didn't open 'tel nine 'n' us wanted to be here right after you open."

"I see," he said in a short dissatisfied kind of way. "Well, I been here thirty minutes waitin' fer you."

"Yessuh, us sorry, suh, fer bein' late," Papa apologized, "but us jes' didn't know."

"Nawsuh," Mr. Hamp added, "us woulda been here right on time ef us had knowed.

"Well, try to be on time next time," Mr. Warrenton said coldly.

I couldn't see Mr. Warrenton's face because he was standing too close to the counter, and I was looking up through the fence, which enclosed the rest of the office, but I could see the two ladies who sat with their backs partly turned to the counter. They kept whispering and giggling secretly with their hands over their mouths, like Mama and Grandma did at church when they mere poking fun at some woman's hat or dress.

Mr. Warrenton was telling Papa and the other men about the big farm out back of Redwood. "As I tol' Silas yistiddy," he was saying, "there 'bout six hund'ered acres fer sale back in there. Now ef I can buy this land befo' some rich Yankee from up North buys it up fer huntin' fer hisself 'n' his rich friends, I might be able to sell it to you boys."

"Yessuh, yessuh," everybody said.

"But you ain't gon' git ahead o' no Yankee, dragging in here at nine o'clock," Mr. Warrenton warned.

"Us ain't gon' be late nomo', Mr. Warrenton," Papa promised again.

"Nawsuh, nawsuh," everybody joined in.

"Well, see that you don't," he said firmly and then turned and picked up some papers offa table. I could just see his hands. But the ladies kept on giggling with their hands up to their mouths.

"Now I have some application forms fer you boys to fill out. Can all y'all write?"

"Yessuh, us can all write a little; Miz Rhoda learnt evvybody on the place to read 'n' write las' year," Mr. Hamp explained.

"Whut's yo' name, boy?" Mr. Warrenton asked.

"Who, me?" Mr. Hamp replied.

"Yes, you. Whut's yo' name?"

"I'm is Hamp Davis, suh."

"Here the forms," Mr. Walter said, passing them out. "Now y'all fill 'em out 'n' leave 'em here with Miss Harkness."

"Mr. Warrenton," Mr. Miller Jackson spoke up, "would you tell us a little mo' 'bout the land us might be able to buy? Course, Silas done tol' us somethin' 'bout it, but us would like to hear a little mo, ef you don' mind, suh."

"Mainly, Mr. Warrenton, all us wanna know is how much the place gon' cost 'n' how much us gon' have to pay down, 'n' how much evvy year," Papa said, trying, it seemed, to regain his leadership from Mr. Hamp and Mr. Miller.

"Silas, I aim to offer one hund'ered per acre fer the land, 'n' that's whut I'm gon sell it to you fer. You don' have to pay nothin' down, 'n' you'll have forty years to pay off the loan at fo' percent interest. Ef we divide the six hund'ered acres up 'mong you ten boys, you'll have sixty acres apiece. At one hund'ered per acre, that come to six thousand dollars fer each o' you boys. Of course, you gon' have to have a house 'n' some farm buildings; these will cost 'bout five or six thousand dollars mo'. So yo' total debt would be 'round leben or twelve thousand dollars. Now ef you take forty years to pay it off, the interest would run around two hund'ered dollars a year. In round figures, you gon' have to pay 'bout three hund'ered dollar a year plus the interest."

"That all it gon' be?" Mr. Ben asked.

"That's all, ef I can buy the farm fer that price. Ef it's mo' I won't be able to buy it, because it will be overpriced," he explained.

"Lawd, Mr. Warrenton, I sho' hopes you can git that land fer us," Papa said. His hopes were reinforced by a smile on every face and muffled comments from every man, making the office sound like our church on prayer meeting nights.

"Now, you boys, hurry up 'n' fill out yo' applications so I can see 'bout buyin' the place. But don' count yo' chickens. Any day some Yankee can come in here 'n' buy that land right out from under us. I hear they payin' much as two hund'ered dollars a acre fer hill land jes' so they can bring their friends down in the fall to hunt quail 'n' other game."

"Thank you, Mr. Warrenton, thank you, suh," Papa said.

And they joined in with, "Yessuh, thank you, suh."

"Jes' leave those applications with Miss Harkness 'n' y'all will hear from me jes' as soon as they are approved by the committee, ef I can git the land, of course."

Slowly, laboriously, Papa and the other men filled out the applications, frequently consulting with one another. While they were writing, I spent part of my time watching them and the other part watching the two white ladies. They still had that funny grin on their faces, looking mostly at each other, but occasionally sneaking a look at Papa and the other men. I wondered if they were just two silly white ladies, or if there was some secret between them. A secret that had something to do with Papa and the others.

When the applications were finally filled out and given to Miss Harkness, Papa and all the others left the office smiling.

"It seem too good to be true," Mr. Ben said.

"It sho' do," Mr. Stock agreed.

"I tol' you it sounded good," Papa spoke up, "but this the way the man in jail tol' me they did out the other side o' Yazoo City. He said they helped hund'ereds o' colored folks 'n' po' white folks, too, to buy farms o' they own."

Mr. Willie loaded up his car and took us by to see Naomi while Mr. Tobe and the men who came with him waited by the post office. My sister worked up the hill from the post office about a mile or so at a pretty brick house with trees and green bushes all around it. Papa went to the back door and knock, and Naomi came out screaming with joy when she saw who it was. She threw her arms around him and then stooped down and kissed me after I ran to join her and Papa.

"Let me run 'n' git a sweater befo' I catch cold in this here weather," my sister said and went back into the house and returned wearing a heavy green sweater.

She and Papa and I walked back to Mr. Willie's car, where she shyly greeted Mr. Willie, Mr. Tom, Mr. Stock, and Mr. Ben.

"Whut all y'all doin' in town?" she asked, looking first at Papa and then at Mr. Ben.

"Us 'bout to git farms o' us own," Mr. Ben boasted.

And although Papa had promised Mama he wasn't going to tell Naomi anything about it, bursting with pride, he proceeded to explain that they might be able to buy sixty acres apiece through the government out of some land out back of Redwood.

"That's good, I'm glad you done found a place," Naomi said. "I saw Reverend Fisher the other day 'n' he said he had read somethin' in the paper 'bout Mr. Walter losin' the place or somethin'; 'n' he ast me ef I had heard anything."

"Yeah," Papa said slowly, painfully, "Mr. Walter done los' the place 'n' a man name Mr. Holly Samuels done bought it from the bank. So us been lookin' 'round tryin' to find a place to move to, jes' in case Mr. Holly might put some o' us off."

"'N' us done had good luck due to yo' papa's gumptions," Mr. Ben said. "You see, he done gone to the gover'ment fer help with a note from Mr. Walter 'n' it look like us gon' git a place."

"Oh, it wasn't nothin'," Papa said cooly, but he couldn't hide the smile of satisfaction that broke over his face like a wave in pond when a big catfish jumps up. "Ef I hadn't went to jail I never woulda heard 'bout gover'ment credit."

"Out 'round Redwood you gon' be closer to Vicksburg 'n' y'all can come to town most anytime 'n' see me 'n' little Carrie Mae," my sister said, pointing across the yard in the direction of the community.

"Yeah, that gon' be fine, ef us gits the place," Papa said with just a trace of doubt in his voice. Then catching himself and smiling a little, he asked, "How is little Carrie Mae?"

"Her fine; jes' as fat as her can be. The girl next do' to me on Third North, her keep her fer me with her chillun while I'm at work," my sister explained carefully, with a smile that showed her gold tooth all the way up to her gums.

"Y'all oughta see her," Mr. Willie said boastfully. "Her jes' as pretty as her can be. Bright, too; almost white with good hair, ain't her, Naomi?"

"Yessuh, her sho' is," my sister replied with pride in her voice.

"Next time us come to town to see Mr. Warrenton, I'm gon' git Willie to drive us by there so y'all can see," Papa added proudly. And there was that look of satisfaction on his face like when we layby or when he comes home after a good settlement.

"I sho' wanna see her," Mr. Tom said, "us missed her last summer when you brought her up to the Bend."

"Us got to see her then, though," Mr. Ben cut in. "Her the prettiest child I ever seen."

"Oh, go on,' Mr. Ben," Naomi said coyly, smiling more broadly.

"I ain't jokin'; Carrie Mae is a pretty chile," Mr. Ben insisted.

"Us all gon' see her the next time us come to town," Mr. Willie assured the group.

"Naomi, you mentioned Reverend Fisher; how is he?" Papa asked.

"Yeah, how is the preacher?" Mr. Stock wanted to know.

"He fine, jes' fine, 'n' doin' real good," my sister said.

"You been to his church?" Mr. Ben asked.

"Yessuh, I been there once; you know I works on Sunday, so I don' git to go to church much. But he got a big church," Naomi said. "He Baptist now, you know," she added.

"How the chillun?" Mr. Tom asked.

"The chillun is fine, too, but he say they need a mama, so he say he gon' git married," Naomi reported.

"Yeah, he sho' do need a wife," Papa put in.

"'N' Papa I'm gon' git married, too. George 'n' me. You 'member George? He the one whut drove me up to the Bend," my sister explained.

"That's good, baby," Papa said.

"I was gon' write y'all next week 'n' tell y'all 'bout it. Had a letter from George yistiddy. He in Chicago; went up there right after Christmas 'n' done found a good job drivin' fer white folks like he was here. Say he gon' come back befo' summer 'n' git me."

"Yo' mama gon' be glad to hear that; her worry 'bout you bein' down here by yo'self."

"Oh, I have a pie in the stove," Naomi squeeled and ran back into the house.

"Us gotta go anyhow!" Papa yelled after her.

"Wait a minute, I'll be right back!" she hollered to us.

In a moment, she was back in the yard. "It hadn't burn; it was all right," she said.

"Well, us gotta be goin'," Papa repeated. "It sho' been good seein' you, baby; yo' mama 'n' yo' grandma gon' sho' be glad I seen you 'n' you doin' all right."

"Yessuh, Papa, give 'em all my love," my sister said, stooping to put her arms around me and kiss me. After a quick squeeze, she stood up, patted my father's arm, and kissed him. "Give 'em all my love, Papa, 'n' tell Mama I'm gon' write," she said as we got into the car. Then she waved to us all and stood watching and smiling as Mr. Willie turned his car around and headed back to the post office.

My sister seemed happier that day than ever, except the first time she showed us her baby. I knew it was because of George, who had said he was going to come back and take her to Chicago and they were going to get married. Of all the things in this world, I think Naomi likes bright people with good hair best, and George was bright, almost half-white, and had good hair.

At the post office, Mr. Tobe and Mr. Hamp and the other men were gathered around a stranger when we returned.

"Y'all git out 'n' come over here!" Mr. Hamp yelled to us.

Mr. Willie parked his car and we got out.

"This Mr. Burton Mackey," Mr. Hamp said as we walked up. "He the colored county agent 'n' he know 'bout that land us might buy."

"He do?" Papa asked.

"Yeah, he travel all over the county in his work," Mr. Hamp replied.

"Yes, gentlemen," the stranger spoke up. "It's pretty good land; used to be a dairy farm, but the man died and his widow move into town here. It's been growing up in weeds and brush. I heard she was going to sell it, but I didn't know she had already put it up for sale." There was no guessing in his voice; he spoke with assurance like Mr. Walter.

"Didn't they never grow no cotton on the place?" Mr. Stock asked.

"Years ago, perhaps, but not recently," the stranger replied. "Of course, a few farmers around there grow a little cotton now, but a half to three-quarters of a bale to the acre is about all you can make on that land."

"Us ain't never raised nothin' but cotton 'n' corn," Papa explained, "'n' us don' know nothin' much 'bout cows. Some o' us got a cow fer milkin' jes' fer us families, but that's all."

"I understand," the man said, "but on that land you can make a whole lot more off milk than you can off cotton."

"Sho'nuff?" Mr. Ben asked.

"Yes, you certainly can," the man replied. "You see, one fairly good cow will give about five gallons of milk a day, if she's on good pasture, maybe more."

"Us don' git nothin' like that much," Papa said, moving closer to the man who was leaning against Mr. Tobe's truck.

"I'm sure you don't, if you have poor stock and no pastures," the man said, "but better cows on good pastures would give you five gallons or more a day. At a milk plant where they make canned milk or cheese five gallons of milk will bring you about a dollar and a quarter. If you had five cows, you'd get six or seven dollars a day, or around two hundred dollars a month. Of course, high-protein feed and medication plus hauling might run you forty to fifty dollars a month, but you'd still have a hundred and fifty to a hundred and sixty dollars left for milking and looking after your cows. In a year, you would clear around eighteen hundred dollars off your five cows. Now isn't that more than you ever made off five acres of cotton?"

"Hunh, it sho' is," Papa said and all the others agreed. There was the beginning of a smile on his face that he seemed to be trying to hold back.

"Did you say eighteen hund'ered dollars a year off 'n five cows, mister?" Mr. Tobe asked.

"I certainly did," the man replied.

"Eighteen hund'ered a year off 'n five cows, did you hear that, Miller?" Mr. Tobe exclaimed as if he couldn't quite believe it.

"I sho' did," Mr. Tobe answered.

"How much land y'all figure on having apiece out of the six hundred acres?" the man wanted to know.

"There ten o' us," Papa said, "'n' us figurin' on havin' 'bout sixty acres apiece."

"Out of your sixty acres, you would need but about fifteen for pastures for five cows. And you'd have about thirty left, not including your woodland, for corn and hogs and chickens and vegetables and even some cotton if you wanted to grow some. If y'all farm that land right, y'all can clear four or five thousand dollars a year apiece," the man said.

"Us can?" Mr. Hamp asked. "Did y'all hear that?"

"Now if you could build grade A barns so you could sell grade A milk," the man went on, "you could make a lot more off five good cows. And what's gon' keep you from saving heifer calves and raising them up. In time you could be milking ten to fifteen head o' cows apiece or even more."

"This been us lucky day," Mr. Tom said with a smile so broad I could see the whole chew of tobacco in his mouth.

"It sho' is, Tom," Mr. Hamp agreed. "That gover'ment man done said us might git to buy us a piece o' land, if some Yankee don' git it firs', 'n' then us done run into you, mister, whut say us can make fo' or five thousand dollars a year off a few cows."

"That's true," the man said, leaning up off Mr. Tobe's truck and moving a step toward Mr. Hamp, "y'all can make a good living on that land. But what's this you saying about some Yankee getting the land first?"

"Yessuh," Mr. Hamp replied, "that whut Mr. Warrenton said, didn't he, Silas?"

"Yessuh," Papa spoke up. "Mr. Warrenton tol' us us might sho' git the land, ef some rich Yankee from up North don' buy it firs'."

"He told you that?"

"Yessuh, he sho did," Papa said.

"Well, doesn't he have an option on the land?" the man asked.

"Us don' know, suh; whut is that?" Papa inquired.

"It's an agreement or bargain, or a contract to have first choice at buying something at an agreed upon price," the man explained.

"He didn't talk like he had one o' them, did he, Ben?" Papa asked, turning to Mr. Ben.

"He sho' didn't, 'cause he kept on sayin' some Yankee might buy it fer huntin'," Mr. Ben replied.

"Yeah, he talk like some Yankee might buy the land any day," Mr. Tobe agreed.

"Well," the man said slowly with his face twisted up in a question, "I'll look into it and let you know."

"When you fin' out 'bout it, you can send word to 'em by me," Mr. Willie offered. "I come here evvyday to bring the mail."

"Fine," the man said, "I'll find out about the option just as soon as I can, and I'll send you word by this gentlemen." The man had his hand on Mr. Willie's shoulder.

"I'm Willie, Willie Woods, mister," Mr. Willie said with a grin and left his mouth hanging open.

"Whut gon' happen ef he don' have one them things you talkin' 'bout?" Papa asked with a pleading look on his face.

"Just what Mr. Warrenton said could happen. Anybody might come in here today or tomorrow and buy that land, if he doesn't have an option on it," the man explained.

"Sho 'nuff?" Papa asked in a sagging voice.

"But don't worry right now, I'm gon' look into it for you."

"You reckon how come he ain't got one them things?" Mr. Tom wanted to know.

"Maybe he got one, but jes' didn't tell us," Papa said hopefully with a weak smile on his face.

"At any rate, I'll find out and let you know," the man said, moving to go.

"Where is you at, ef us wanna come 'n' see you, mister?" Papa asked, "'n' whut is yo' name ag'in, suh?"

"My name is Burton Mackey; I'm the colored county agent. My office is next door to the colored YMCA," he replied. "Now the Y is right back over there about three blocks; you can't miss it."

"Yessuh," Papa said.

"Oh, I know where the YMCA is at," Mr. Willie spoke up. "I was there once."

"I wouldn't say anything about this option business," Mr. Mackey warned. "You know how white folks are; Mr. Warrenton may have an option on that land, but he may not like you questioning him about it. He may smile at you, but he's a mean peckerwood just like his brother, Sheriff Jack Warrenton."

"The sheriff's his brother?" Papa inquired as if to make sure he had heard right.

"He sure is, don't you see how they favor?" Mr. Mackey said.

"I hadn't noticed, but now that you mention it, they sho' do favor," Papa agreed.

"Well, just don' say anything about the option to anybody, and I'm gon' look into it and let you know in a few days," Mr. Mackey said and began walking off.

"Nawsuh, us ain't gon' say nothin'," Papa said, "'n' thank you, suh."

All the men joined in the "thank you, suh," and I found myself saying it, too.

"That's all right," the county agent hollered back, "I certainly hope you'll get that farm."

"Thank you, suh, us gon' be countin' on you!" Papa yelled to Mr. Mackey.

On the way back to the Bend, there was talk and laughter about owning five, ten, or even fifteen cows and clearing anywhere from eighteen hundred dollars a year to five or six thousand dollars, about raising a few acres of cotton on the side just to keep their hand in, if, of course, they could get allotments. And Papa kept talking about building a home and painting it white with a white picket fence around it, and about being his own boss.

There were moments of quietness, too, when nobody said a word. It was as if their quietness helped them hold on to their newfound dreams in the face of some doubt and fear raised by the county agent. During such periods, Papa sometimes broke the silence with questions about Mr. Warrenton. "Reckon Mr. Warrenton mean like his ole brother, that Mr. Jack Warrenton, the sheriff?" he once asked.

"I don' know, Silas," Mr. Ben replied, "but I sho' hopes he ain't."

"That sonofabitch slapped Becky that time they 'rested me," Papa said. "I sho' hopes Mr. Warrenton ain't nothin' like him."

"I don' b'lieve he is," Mr. Tom added, "'cause he was nice to us in his office."

"Naw, he can't be like that ole sheriff," Mr. Stock spoke up.

Back home Mama and Grandma were glad we had seen Naomi and she and the baby were all right, but they were shocked when I added, "Naomi gon' marry George 'n' move to Chicago, ain't her, Papa?"

"That whut her say," he said dryly. I think he wanted to break the news to Mama more gently.

Mama looked dazed for a moment. Then she asked, "Move to Chicago?"

Her say George done gone up there 'n' done found a job jes' like the one he had in Vicksburg," Papa explained. "'N' her say he gon come back fer her jes' befo' summer 'n' they gon' git marr'ed 'n' he gon' take her back."

"Lawd, I don' want my chile goin' way up there where it git so cold her freeze to death," Grandma said.

"Whut her gon' do with that baby? I know her ain't gon' take that little baby way up there where us ain't gon' see it nomo'," Mama complained.

"I don' know, her didn't say, but her say her gon' write soon," Papa said.

"Well, ef that whut her wanna do," Mama yielded, "I guess us ain't got no right to try to stan' in the way."

"Naomi been lookin' fer somethin' evver since her was born," Papa said, "her ain't never been satisfied."

"Her been lookin' fer herself mostly, like her think her oughta be," Mama said in whispery voice, "'n' Ma, you partly to blame fer some o' it, talkin' so much 'bout bein' black."

"Well, Gawd knows, her is black, jes' like you, Silas," Grandma shot back.

"Gawddamit, Miz Carrie, can't you never think o' nothin' but black?" Papa stormed and walked into the kitchen.

"Don't you be cussin' me, you black nigger, you!" Grandma yelled after him.

"Now, Ma, you jes' shut yo' mouth 'n' stop meddling with Silas," Mama ordered.

"Lawd, have mercy," Grandma moaned, "I know you 'n' Silas 'g'inst me; y'all always been 'g'inst me. All I got is River, my little baby. Come here, River, come here, baby."

I walked slowly over to her side; I wanted to go to her, but I didn't want her to call me baby. She put one arm around me and patted my back in a soothing rhythm. Mama walked into the kitchen, where Papa was and began getting supper ready. Grandma leaned her face against mine. It was wet; she was crying.

I could hear Mama and Papa talking in the kitchen about how he and the other men made out in Vicksburg. In our rush to tell about my sister, we hadn't said anything about the government loan man.

"Evvything went all right," he told Mama, "the man say he gon' try to buy the six hund'ered acres 'n' 'vide it up 'mong us." But there wasn't much enthusiasm in his voice. He seemed to be trying hard not to build Mama's expectations up too high until he was more certain they were going to get the land, or until Mr. Mackey told him Mr. Warrenton was on the square.

But Mama had known Papa too long not to know that he was holding something back. "There somethin' you ain't tellin' me, Silas," she said straight-forwardly.

"Naw, there ain't, Becky; the only thing, us ain't sho' Mr. Warrenton gon' be able to get the land befo' some rich man from up North grabs it fer huntin', like I tol' you befo', but us gon' know in a few days."

Mama accepted that, but there were reservations in her voice. Papa didn't say anything about Mr. Mackey, and neither did I, nor did I mention the way the two ladies in the office kept giggling in a sneaky kind of way.

XXVII

Sharecroppers Fail to Acquire the Loans

Two days after our trip to Vicksburg, Mr. Willie came by our house shortly after I got home from school. He jumped out of his car, leaving the door open, and rushed into our yard and up the steps. I was at the woodpile picking up chips to make a fire in the kitchen stove for Mama to cook supper. Mr. Willie was in such a hurry, he didn't notice me or hear me holler to him, and there was no smile on his face. As soon as he was in the house, I picked up my small bucket half full of chips and ran into the kitchen, poured them into the firebox through an eye of the stove, and skipped into the room where Mr. Willie was talking excitedly to Mama and Papa.

"Mr. Warrenton ain't had no opshun or whutever you call it on that land," he was saying almost out of breath, "but a rich man up North do, 'n' he done hired a lawyer in Vicksburg to buy it fer him fer huntin'."

"How you know, Willie?" Papa asked.

"Mr. Mackey done tol' me; he was waitin' at the post office when I drove up, 'n' he tol' me."

Papa stood up as he usually did when he was worried and leaned against the corner of the mantle-piece. "You sho', Willie?" he asked quietly as if trying hard not to get excited or to excite Mama.

"That's whut Mr. Mackey say. You 'member Mr. Mackey, Mr. Burton Mackey, the colored county agent who said he was gon' fin' out fer us," Mr. Willie explained.

"Who is Mr. Mackey?" Mama asked. "You ain't said nothin' 'bout no Mr. Mackey."

"He the colored county agent, 'n' he done said he was gon' fin' out ef Mr. Warrenton had one them things on that land so he be sho' he'd have firs' crack at buyin' it," Papa explained quickly.

"You ain't tol' me nothin' 'bout no Mr. Mackey," Mama complained accusingly. "I knowed there was somethin' wrong when you tol' me how y'all made out."

"I jes' didn't want you to worry, honey, ef there wasn't nothin' to whut Mr. Mackey said," Papa replied calmly.

"Well, there was sho' somethin' to whut he said," Mr. Willie cut in, "'cause it look like y'all ain't gon' git the land."

Mama and Grandma sat with their heads bowed, while Papa stood numbly leaning on the mantle-piece.

Standing by him, I looked up and said, "Maybe that's whut them ladies was laffin' 'bout."

"Whut ladies?" Mama asked.

"The ladies in the gover'ment office. Miss Harkness 'n' that other lady."

"When was they laffin'?" Papa wanted to know.

"When y'all was talkin' to Mr. Warrenton 'n' while y'all was writin' on them papers, them ladies was gigglin' in a sneaky way all the time."

"They was?" Mama asked. "Is you sho'?"

"Yessum," I said.

"Maybe they was jes' laffin' at the way us looked or somethin'," Papa said hopefully. Then he paused a long time. "You don' reckon that peckerwood would look us dead in the eye 'n' tell us he gon' try to buy six hund'ered acres fer us, knowing all the time the Yankee up North already had one them things on that land?"

"Don' seem like he would," Mr. Willie said, "but then ag'in, I don' know. His brother, that ole sheriff, is mean as a dog."

"Mr. Warrenton's the sheriff's brother?" Mama asked.

"That whut Mr. Mackey say, 'n' they do favor," Papa replied.

"Well, ef he that ole mean sheriff's brother; the one whut slapped me when they 'rested you, Silas, he might do anything," Mama said with a new sharpness in her voice.

"Lawd, is you with us, Lawd?" Grandma moaned.

"Willie, is you tol' the rest o' 'em 'bout this?" Papa asked.

"Naw, I come straight here firs'," Mr. Willie replied.

"Well, ef you got the time, let's go tell 'em 'n' see whut us can do," Papa said.

"Oh, I got time," Mr. Willie said, and Papa put on his coat and jumper and they left.

"Be back afterwhile," Papa said at the door.

It must have been late in the night when he returned because I was asleep and didn't hear him. But the next morning early he was dressed in his Sunday clothes and ready to go back to Vicksburg to see Mr. Warrenton. The others had chosen him and Mr. Hamp to go.

"Now Silas, you let Hamp do the talkin' 'cause you might git mad 'n' say too much," Mama advised.

"I ain't gon' say too much, less'n that cracker tryin' to pull somethin' on us, Becky."

"'Member, Silas, that man got somethin' us need, 'n' us gotta take low to try to git it."

"I know, Becky; I know," Papa said slowly.

When I was ready for school, Papa and I walked across to the main road over by Mr. Hamp's, where he was going so that they could catch Mr. Willie and go back to town. We walked along silently for a long time. I knew he was worried and I didn't want to bother him.

Finally, he said, "Boy, I thought fer sho' us was gon' have a farm o' us own, but I don' know now. Look like some Yankee done beat us to it."

"Yessuh, I hope he ain't," I said with as little concern as I could to keep Papa from feeling bad.

"Me 'n' Hamp gon' talk with Mr. Warrenton; us gon'beg him to help us."

"Yessuh, but ef he don't, us can stay here can't us?" I asked more to let him know I was willing to stay than to find out if we could.

"I sho' hope so, River," he said hopefully in a quiet but determined voice.

At the main road, I said, "Goodbye, Papa," and walked on toward the church, where school was held.

"See you when us git back, man," he said as he turned into Mr. Hamp's yard. His shoulders sagged and his stride was not long and sure as it usually was.

Seeing Papa so worried and feeling more and more that we might not get a farm like Mr. Amos out back of Redwood, I started crying. I stumbled along for a while, and then I sat down on my books by the side of the road. I was early for school, and no other children passed until little Willie Woods and his sister, Martha, came along and stopped and asked me what was wrong.

"Ain't yo' papa tol' y'all it look like us ain't gon' git to buy a farm o' us own?" I asked through my tears.

"Yeah, he tol' Mama 'n' us," Martha said, "but ain't no use to cry."

"Us want a farm o' us own," I persisted, crying more than ever.

"Don' cry, River," Martha pleaded, kneeling by my side.

"Babies cry," little Willie chided. That plus the pleading of Martha made me feel ashamed, and I wiped my eyes on my hands and sleeves and got up.

"Come on, River, don' worry 'bout that ole farm," Martha said, pulling me by the arm.

I fought back tears and walked on to school.

When I got home from school that day, Papa hadn't come back from Vicksburg. But Mama said Mr. Willie had come by and told her he had left Papa and Mr. Hamp at the government office and was going back for them around four. Said they had gone by Mr. Mackey's office first and he had taken them to see the lady who owns the land, and she had agreed to hold up on the sale to the Yankee and sell it to the government office, if Mr. Warrenton can work it out with the Yankee. The price, she said, was one hundred dollars an acre, just exactly what Mr. Warrenton had said he was willing to pay.

Then Mama said Mr. Willie told her papa and Mr. Hamp had gone to the government office to see Mr. Warrenton, but he was out. So he left them there to wait for him.

"Willie say things look real good," Mama said with a twinkle in her eyes.

It was night when Papa came. Mama was all smiles.

"Whut Mr. Warrenton say, Silas?" she asked as he walked in.

"Us didn't git to see him, but us went by Miz Morris. Her the lady whut own the farm 'n' her want us to have it, ef Mr. Warrenton can work things out with that Yankee, 'n' Miz Morris think he can, 'cause her done talked with his lawyer. Her say he say Mr. Johnson, the Yankee, don' wanna buy no land that farmers wanna buy 'n' farm. Don't that sound good?" Papa asked. The smile that had been in his voice all along broke out over his face.

"It she' do, Silas," Mama squealed, "us gon have us own farm."

"Hallalujah, Jesus!" Grandma cried out.

"All us gotta do is see Mr. Warrenton 'n' git him to buy the land fer us. Us waited fer him all day, but the ladies said he was visitin' farmers whut owe him to see how they comin' 'long with they plans fer they crops this year. Us goin' back firs' thing in the mornin', me 'n' Hamp, so us can ketch him." Papa had never sat down. He had been walking up and down the floor, telling us how well he and Mr. Hamp had done.

"Us gon' have a farm, ain't us, Papa?" I said in a loud happy voice.

"It look that way; look diff'ent from this mornin', man?"

"Us was scared that Yankee was gon' grab that land right out from under us," Mama said, "but look like he a good white man 'n' gon' let us have it."

"Yeah, ef Mr. Warrenton will buy it, 'n' he done tol' us he would, ef some Yankee didn't git it firs'," Papa said, still walking the floor. "So now it up to him."

Papa was up earlier the next morning than the day before. He didn't wait for me but ate his breakfast hurriedly and rushed off over to Mr. Hamp's to go to town with Mr. Willie. They didn't want to take any chances being late and missing Mr. Warrenton.

I skipped to school that day, proud and happy that we were going to have our own farm and our own house, and Papa was going to be his own boss like Mr. Amos Ammons, and one day we would have a tractor, which I would drive puffing up and down the field.

When school was out, I ran all the way home to find out if Papa had caught Mr. Warrenton and got him to buy the land. But Papa wasn't home when I got there; Mama was trying to piece a quilt, mostly she was running to the back window to see if she could see Mr. Willie's car bringing Papa home with the good news. Grandma sat close to the fire, poking in the ashes with a stick from time to time to see if the sweet potatoes she was roasting were soft. Occasionally, she, too, went to the back window and returned, saying, "I don' see him yet."

It was well after sundown when he came. Mama had milked and cooked supper and was just waiting for him when we heard the car pull up. She rushed to the door, and I was right behind her.

Both Mr. Willie and Mr. Hamp were with him. They were holding him by the arms and guiding him toward the steps. Papa's Sunday suit was all muddy and he staggered like Mr. Tom did sometimes when he was drunk.

"Whut happen?" Mama screamed.

"He been wallowin' on the ground," Mr. Hamp said.

"Seem like he done gone crazy," Mr. Willie added.

"Bring him on in, y'all; where he wallow?" Mama asked desperately.

"Over Hamp's," Mr. Willie said.

"Silas, Honey," Mama sobbed as they set him down in a chair. "Honey, this yo' Becky."

Papa said nothing; he merely stared into the fire. I was at his side with my hands around his arm.

"Papa! Papa!" I shouted as loud as I could, but he did not respond.

"Whut done happen to him?" Mama asked wildly.

"Us don' know," Mr. Hamp replied.

"When I stopped to let Hamp out while ago," Mr. Willie said, "Silas got out, too. I tol' him he wasn't home yet, but he didn't act like he heard me. He mumbled somethin' 'n' then set down on the ground right in the mud 'n' started wallowin' 'round like a hog 'n' hollerin' jes' loud as he could. I don' know whut was wrong with him."

"Us finally got him back in the car," Mr. Hamp added, "'n' he ain't said a word since."

"Help me git his clothes off 'n' git him in the bed," Mama asked.

They peeled off his muddy coat, Mama unbottoned his shirt; I unlaced his shoes and pulled them off. Mr. Hamp and Mr. Willie got his pants off and stretched him out in the bed. Mama covered him up, and Grandma brought a wet cloth and wiped his face. Then she wet it again and placed it on Papa's forehead.

"Whut done happen in Vicksburg, Hamp?" Mama inquired.

"The farm been sold," he said sadly.

"Sold it yistiddy while they was waitin' fer Mr. Warrenton," Mr. Willie added.

"Sold? Sold?" Mama asked in a voice that broke into a heartbreak. With arms flailing, she ran through the house, screaming and weeping. Grandma tried to hold her, but she broke away and ran into Naomi's room and fell across the bed, moaning and sobbing.

Finally, Mr. Willie and Mr. Hamp and Grandma quieted her. I grabbed one of our Sunday towels, starched and stiff on the washstand, and wet it with a dipperful of water and wiped her face.

When she was composed, she got up and went to see how Papa was, then she took a seat by the fireplace and asked, "How come Mr. Warrenton didn't buy the place fer us?"

"I don' know," Mr. Hamp replied. "Miz Morris say her tried to git him to buy it fer us, but her say he tol' her us wasn't qualified. 'N' then her said he laffed 'N' laffed. When Silas heard her say Mr. Warrenton laffed, he shouted, 'No'am! No'am! Mr. Warrenton wouldn't do that to us 'n' us ain't never did nothin' to him.'"

"Po' Silas," Mama whispered.

"When he shouted like that, Miz Morris jes' looked at him 'n' shook her head 'n' dabbed at her eyes with her pocket handkerchief. Then her said, 'I'm sorry, so sorry.'"

"Her must be a good white lady like Miz Rhoda," Mama said with a little smile that barely parted her lips.

"Her is, her is," Mr. Hamp agreed. "Then me 'n' Silas 'n' Mr. Mackey left. Miz Morris come to the door 'n' waved goodbye."

"Us had walked up on Cherry Street to see Miz Morris," Mr. Hamp continued, "after us done waited near 'bout 'tel noon in Mr. Warrenton's office to see him, but he ain't never come. Mr. Mackey walked by there with us; he had come to the post office to git his mail 'n' seen us standin' by Willie's car.

"After us left Miz Morris 'n' started back to the post office to meet Willie, Mr. Mackey kicked a rock 'n' said it was a shame us didn't git to buy that land, 'but there ain't nothin' you can do now,' he said.

"When he said there wasn' nothin' us could do, Silas was walkin' 'long hittin' his fis' in the palm o' his hand 'n' sayin', 'Naw, naw, he can't do that; he can't do that.' 'N' right after Mr. Mackey say wasn' nothin' us could do, Silas started runnin' 'n' hollerin'. Us took off after him 'n' Mr. Mackey caught him jes' befo' he was 'bout to run out in the street where all them cars was comin'.

"'Lemme go,' he shouted, 'I'm gon' kill that sonofabitch.' It was all us could do to hol' him. 'N' ef Mr. Mackey wasn' young 'n' strong, Silas woulda got away fer sho'."

"Us been disapp'inted so many times," Mama said slowly, looking straight at Mr. Hamp. "I guess this was jes' too much fer Silas."

"I know, Becky; us been disapp'inted a heap, too, me 'n' Minnie."

"Ain't nobody on this place or any other plantation whut ain't been disapp'inted sometime or other; I know me 'n' Birdie is," Mr. Willie added.

"But Silas was so set on havin' a place o' us own; us been savin' fer it off 'n' on since befo' us come to the Bend," Mama explained.

"Us tried to save some once, too, hopin' to buy a little farm, but us give up after the chillun come so fas' 'n' Minnie was sick a long time," Mr. Hamp said in a kind of misty voice of defeat. "Us thought at las' us had a chance when Silas come 'n' tol' us 'bout the gover'ment loan man 'n' the six hund'ered acres out back o' Redwood." Then his voice trailed off and then there was silence for a long time, except Papa's occasional grunt or groan.

"Po' Silas," Mama said. "How did y'all ever quiet him down?"

"Us took him to Mr. Mackey's office; by then, Mr. Mackey done talked some sense in him. Tol' him things wasn't always gon' be like this, 'n' his gittin in a whole lot o' trouble wasn't gon' help nobody, 'n' was gon' cause his family a heap o' grief.

"At firs' Silas didn't listen. He kept talkin' 'bout killin' Mr. Warrenton 'n' sayin' he shoulda knowed any sonofabitch whut was kin to that Gawddam sheriff couldn't be nothin' but a mean bastard. 'N' he tried hard two three time to pull way from us, but Mr. Mackey held on. He strong. Don' look like no man whut ain't been plowin' 'n' pickin' cotton like us is could be that strong, but he sho' is. 'N' I'm glad he was with us, 'cause ef he wasn't Silas woulda got away 'n' done kilt that white man or been kilt tryin'."

"Thank Gawd Mr. Mackey was 'long with you," Mama said just above a whisper and got up and went to the bed again to see about Papa.

"Yeah, Gawd was in the plan," Mr. Hamp said.

"He sho' was," Grandma added.

"Y'all waited there 'tel Willie got back?"

"Yeah, Becky, us waited there 'n' Mr. Mackey he sent the lady in his office out to git some food fer us 'n' her come back loaded down with fried chicken 'n' cornbread 'n' greens 'n' black-eyed peas, but Silas wouldn't touch a thing but a bottle o' pop."

"Whut you reckon got in him after he got back to the plantation to make him wallow in the mud the way he did?" Mama asked with a puzzled look on her face.

"I don' know, Becky," Mr. Willie said, "but Silas acted funny all the way back from Vicksburg, didn't he, Hamp?"

"Yeah, been talkin to hisself, saying, 'You right, you 'zackly right.' Been sayin' it all the way back," Mr. Hamp said.

"He was sayin' it when he set down on the ground 'n' started rollin'," Mr. Willie added.

"Po' Silas; he was worried," Mama said. "Worried mo' 'cause y'all ain't gon' git no land 'n' he was 'bout hisself, bad as he want a farm o' us own. I know Silas; he was blamin' hisself 'cause y'all been so disapp'inted by that peckerwood." There was rising anger in Mama's voice.

It was the next afternoon before Papa came to himself. Mama and Grandma had kept cold cloths on his forehead all night, and Dr. Boyd had come during the night and injected something into Papa's arm and said he was going to be all right. Mr. Willie and Mr. Hamp had gone for him, and they must have stopped along the way and told everybody because it seemed that everybody on the plantation came by. First, Mr. Ben and Mrs. Mary, and then Mr. Stock and Mrs. Viney and Mr. Tobe and Mrs. Ida and Mr. Miller and Mrs. Emma and even Mr. Henry and Mrs. Nettie and Mary Lou and Della. I stayed close to Mama because I thought Mary Lou might grab my privates again.

After Dr. Boyd said Papa was going to be all right, the talk turned to Mr. Wrrenton and what a low-down mean man he was And everybody wondered why he would do a dirty trick like that, pretending he was going to help Papa and them buy six hundred acres and divide it up.

"Whut mo' you 'spect? He that old mean sheriff's brother," Mr. Miller said, "'n' a leopard can't change his spots."

"I bet he had somethin' 'g'inst Silas," Mama said. "I bet that old sheriff done tol' him Silas was a smart nigger 'cause he spoke up fer hisself when they 'rested him 'n' slapped me."

"Reckon he'd be hol'in' that 'g'inst Silas all this time?" Mr. Stock asked.

"Chile, you don' know white folks," Grandma said, "they can hol' somethin' 'g'inst you a thousand years 'n' never breath it 'tel they git the upper han'. You know how they is."

"You sho' right, Miz Carrie," Mrs. Viney agreed.

"Then that peckerwood could have somethin' 'g'inst Mr. Walter 'cause he ain't no cracker like they is," Mr. Tobe added.

"Naw, these peckerwoods don' like no white man whut treats niggers ha'fway right," Mr. Miller said.

The conversation drifted on, but I was too sleepy to listen.

The next morning, just before I left for school, Papa sat up in the bed and asked for a drink of water. I ran and got a dipperful and brought it to him; Mama held the dipper while he gulped the water down and asked for more. I got another dipperful for him and handed it to Mama.

"Want somethin' t'eat, Silas?" Mama asked.

Papa stared at her and then at me as if he had never seen us before, and he said, "Hunh? Hunh?"

"Silas, this me, this yo' Becky, honey."

Papa squinted his eyes and looked closely at Mama and then at me. Finally, he said, "Becky? Becky?"

"Yes, honey, this yo' Becky."

Then he lay back down and went to sleep again without recognizing me. But when I came from school, he was sitting by the fire. He spoke to me as if I was way off, and his voice was hollow and lifeless, and he looked as if he had been sick a long time.

Beginning that day, I divided Papa into two parts: the part I knew before this great disappointment about having a farm of his own, and the part I have known since. The first part was strong and brave and confident of himself—a man who could plow a mule until the animal tired and dropped in the field, who could pick more cotton than anyone else on the plantation, who talked straight to everyone, black and white, and who aimed his life like a rifle toward a goal he felt sure of reaching one day, however distant.

The second part was not as strong or as brave or as confident as the first. It revealed a man who seemed to have gone through a terrible storm and been left broken. Plowed acres and picked cotton were no longer important to him. He seemed to have lost the aim toward which he had pointed his life and had lowered his gun forever.

When Papa went to bed that night, he didn't get out again, except twice to go to Vicksburg to the doctor, until cotton-planting time. And the fees for Dr. Boyd and the doctor in Vicksburg took just about all Papa and Mama had saved. The thought of ever saving up more for a farm of our own seemed hopeless after Papa came back from the store, where he had gone to talk with Mr. Holly about furnishing us to make a crop.

We had heard that Mr. Holly had changed the sharing arrangement from a third of the cotton and a fourth of the corn to half of everything, but we didn't know for sure until Papa came back.

"Us ain't gon' git but ha'f the cotton," Papa said, "'n' outa that gotta come ha'f the cost o' the tractor work, ha'f the cost o' the weed killers, 'n' ha'f the cost o' the fertilize 'n' poison."

"That ain't gon' leave us nothin', Silas," Mama complained.

"I know it ain't," Papa agreed, "'n' side from that Mr. Holly say ef that soil bank thing come through, he gon' put ha'f the cotton acres on the place in that thing 'n' us can farm the res'."

"Us ain't got but eight acres now, Silas, 'n' he gon' put ha'f o' that in that bank thing?" Mama asked, looking straight at Papa.

"That whut he say."

"Well, is Mr. Holly gon' give us ha'f the money he gon' git from the gover'ment?" Mama wanted to know.

"I don' know, Becky; he ain't said a thing 'bout that."

"You 'member, Silas, befo' Christmas Reverend Fisher tol' us ef that soil bank thing come through, Mr. Walter was suppose to give us a third o' the money he got fer puttin' part o' us farm in that thing, 'cause us was farmin' on third 'n' fourth. Seem like Mr. Holly oughta give us ha'f, since us farmin' on ha'ves."

"It sho' do, 'cause I 'member Reverend sayin' that, but Mr. Holly ain't said nothin' 'bout it," Papa said slowly, uncertainly.

"Ain't you gon' ast him 'bout it, Silas?"

"I don' know, Becky; I jes' don' know. You 'member I ast 'bout the parity check up in Sunflower County mo'n twenty years ago 'n' you know whut done happen."

"Yes, yes, I 'member," Mama said with a moan. Then she bowed her head by the fireplace and said no more.

Grandma, who had been sitting quietly by the fire smoking her pipe, asked Papa, "Whut is this here soil bank thing y'all been talkin' 'bout, Silas?"

"Seem like the gover'ment think us growin' too much cotton, Miz Carrie."

"Too much cotton?" she asked in astonishment. "'N' I ain't got drawers to wear, 'n' ain't had but one new gingham dress in a year, 'n' Naomi sent the cloth fer that one, 'n' us needs sheets 'n' you 'n' River needs shirts 'n' overalls, 'n' you say they say they say there too much cotton?"

"That whut they say the gover'ment say, Miz Carrie, course? I don' know myself," Papa replied.

"Hunh, hunh," Grandma moaned.

"Well, anyhow," Papa continued, "the gover'ment want us to grow less cotton right now 'n' save up the land in that soil bank thing 'tel us need mo' cotton ag'in."

"The gover'ment don' make no sense to me," Grandma said. "Talkin' 'bout puttin' land in some kinda bank to keep us from growin' cotton fer us clothes 'n' things; whoever heard o' such a thing?"

"You sho' right, Miz Carrie," Papa agreed, "the gover'ment sho' don' make no sense a'tall. Look at how they let that little ole peckerwood do us 'bout that land over back o' Redwood."

"Well, whut is po' farmers gon' do, Silas?"

"I don' know, Miz Carrie, 'n' I don' know whut us gon' do if Mr. Holly put mo' land in the soil bank thing like he say he might do next year 'n' git rid o' some o' his tenants. He already bought one cotton picker fer his place over at Cary, 'n' they say he gon' git two mo' fer this place."

When Papa mentioned that Mr. Holly might get rid of some some of his tenants, Mama raised her head and wiped her eyes. "Did you say Mr. Holly say he might git rid o' some o' us next year, Silas?"

"That whut he said, Becky," Papa replied as slowly as he could to hold back the dreaded truth.

"Silas, you reckon us gon' be one o' the families Mr. Holly gon' put off?" Mama asked in a quiet but desperate voice. Her hands were trembling a little, and her eyes, still moist, looked dark and fear-ridden.

"Baby, now don' you go worrying 'bout that, evvything gon' be all right."

Then he got up and walked to the door and looked out as if he was expecting someone. He stood in it for a while as if to let fear out or hope come in. When he sat down again, Mama snuggled up to him. She seemed comforted by his faith. There were no more questions.

XXVIII

Silas's Daughter Leaves Her Baby with Family and Goes to Chicago

A few weeks later, one Sunday in late April, just before school closed and cotton chopping began, my sister had a man to drive her up to the Bend. We had just come from church when they arrived with little Carrie Mae.

"Oh, my!" Mama screamed and ran into the yard to meet them. "The baby's walkin', the baby's walkin'!" she said, scooping the child up in her arms.

Papa and Grandma stood by grinning while I caught my sister by the hand.

She stepped back to get a good look at me. "River," she cried out, "whut a big boy you is."

I swelled with pride. "Papa gon' let me plow some," I boasted, "when it's cultivatin' time, ain't you, Papa?"

"Yeah, man," Papa replied, looking down at me. "You a big boy now; he goin' on nine," he said to Naomi.

The man who had driven Naomi up followed her into the yard with a large box.

"This Mr. Jim Willis," she said. "He live right down the street from Miz Addie, 'n' he drove me up."

Papa shook his hand, Grandma nodded, and Mama said, "Please to meet you; y'all come on in 'n' let me put dinner on the table; it's already fixed."

"No'am, us jes' et, 'n' Jim gotta git back."

Then Papa and I brought chairs out on the porch and they all sat down, but I stood beside my sister's chair with my chin resting on her shoulder.

Naomi looked first at Papa and then at Mama and Grandma. Her mouth was open slightly and part of her gold tooth was showing, but she really wasn't smiling. Finally she said haltingly, "I'm goin' to Chicago."

"When is George comin' fer you, baby?" Mama asked.

"He can't come right now, so he want me to come up there 'n' us gon' git married up there," Naomi said with a broad smile that did not linger on her face.

Mama was suddenly quiet, but Grandma said, "Us gon' sho' miss you, Naomi; 'n' us hates to see you go way up there."

"But you gon' write us, ain't you, baby?" Papa asked anxiously, dragging his chair a little closer.

"You know I'm gon' write, Papa," she said, reaching over to pat his knee.

"When is you goin', baby?" Mama wanted to know.

"Next Sat'dy night on the bus after I git paid."

Grandma wasn't ready to talk about going away up to Chicago, so she turned to little Carrie Mae, who was sitting in Mama's lap. "Lawd, this is a pretty baby, sho' as you born. I b'lieve her prettier than Becky was when her was a baby. These long curls, ain't they pretty? 'N' her clear bright skin. Gal this baby almost white 'n' jes' as pretty as her can be."

"Thank you, Grandma; say thank you, Carrie Mae," my sister ordered gently, catching the child by the hand.

Carrie Mae look at Grandma but said nothing.

"This baby is a angel," Mama said, rubbing her nose against the child's face.

"No two ways 'bout it, her pretty all right," Papa added.

"'N' her look mo' 'n' mo' like Mr. Win evvyday," Grandma said with pride.

Everyone was quiet for a minute and then Mama asked, "Whut you got in the box?"

"They Carrie Mae's things," my sister said, looking from Mama to Papa and back again. "I wanna leave her with y'all fer a while 'tel me 'n' George git settled."

"You gon' let us keep her? Thank the Lawd," Grandma said with a new sparkle in her old eyes.

"Us been longin' to have a chance to see mo' o' this baby," Mama said. "Us glad you gon' leave her with us fer a while 'tel you 'n' George find a place 'n' git settled."

Papa was all smiles. He picked up Carrie Mae out of Mama's lap and walked out into the yard with her. She went to him more willingly than she had gone to Mama and this pleased him. "This Grandpa's baby," he said, walking on toward the lane.

When he had gone with Mr. Jim walking along with him, Mama asked my sister, "How is George doin', Naomi?"

"Fine, jes' fine, Mama," my sister said hurridly, almost too hurridly to convince Mama, I think.

"Is you sho', baby?"

"Yessum, he doin' all right; woulda come after me, but can't git off right now," my sister explained with a smile that stopped short as if caught on a nail.

"I jes' wanna make sho' y'all gon' be all right, 'n' you ain't gon' be all the way up there in Chicago cold 'n' hongry," Mama said, enveloping Naomi's hand in her own.

"Lawd, now don't y'all go without no somethin t'eat up there," Grandma warned. "Y'all jes' let us know 'n' us'll send y'all some greens 'n' potatoes 'n' a side o' meat."

"Us ain't gon' git hongry; George got a good job, 'n' I'm gon' find somethin' to do."

"Well, that's good," Mama said. "I hope things gon' be all right."

"Us might be up there with y'all," I cut in, "ef Mr. Holly put us off the place after he put mo' o' his land in the bank."

"Hush yo' mouth, boy," Mama ordered.

"That whut Papa say, ain't it?" I persisted, not wanting to be hushed up in front of my sister, who had just said I was a big boy.

"Didn't I tell you to hush?" Mama said harshly, catching me by the arm and giving me a shake.

"Yessum," I said quietly, seating myself on the floor beside Naomi's chair and trying to conceal my crushed feeling.

"Us gon' be all right," Mama assured my sister, "don' pay no 'tention to whut River say. Yo' Papa done talked with Hr. Holly 'n' he say us gon' make out all right," Mama lied, looking straight at Naomi without blinking an eye.

"I'm sho' glad, 'cause I was gittin' scared," my sister said. "I'm shó sorry y'all didn't git to buy a piece o' that land y'all was talkin' 'bout out back o' Redwood."

"Us all sorry 'bout that, but I guess the Lawd He know best," Mama replied.

"Yes, my Gawd 'n' my Jesus, He wanna do fer the folks, but the gover'ment stand in the way," Grandma moaned.

"But Grandma, maybe it best like Mama say," Naomi said.

"Maybe so, maybe so," Grandma agreed, "only the Lawd He know."

"Well, me 'n' George gon' be straight by Christmas, 'n' ef things don' work out here on the plantation, y'all can come on up 'n' live with us," Naomi offered.

"Whut? Chicago? Way up there, where it git so cold? New indeed, us ain't coming way up there," Grandma said.

"Naw, baby, evvything gon' be all right," Mama assured my sister again.

"Well, y'all would be mo' 'n' welcome," Naomi said, getting up and walking to the end of the porch. Then she sat back down and turned to Mama. "Mama, I ain't been able to save much recently 'cause Carrie Mae been had a bad cold 'n' the doctors they so 'spensive. One time they charge me eight dollars, mo 'n ha'f I make. Then, you know, I have to pay the girl fer keepin' Carrie Mae, 'n' I have to buy milk 'n' baby food. Course, I got my bus fare to Chicago 'n' a little mo, but I'd like to have 'bout ten dollars mo' when I git there."

"You need 'bout ten dollars mo'?" Mama asked, more to give herself time to think than to find out how much my sister needed.

"Yessum, that's all, 'bout ten dollars mo'."

"Lemme see whut us got," Mama said, rising to go into the house and look between the homemade cotton mattresses, where she and Papa kept their money. "You know yo' Papa been sick a heap 'n' that took most o' us money," she added as she went inside. She came back holding some dollar bills and a little change in her hand. "Ma, you got a dollar? I ain't got but nine 'n' some change," Mama said.

"Yeah, I'm most sho' I'm is," Grandma replied, reaching down through the placket hole in her skirt and pulling out her money sack into which she thrust her hand and brought out two crumpled five-dollar bills and three ones plus thirty cents in change. "Here, Naomi, you take this money," Grandma ordered. "I don' need nothin' but the thirty cents to buy a little tobacco now 'n' then. 'N' Becky you keep yo' money fer you 'n' Silas."

My sister took the two fives and left the rest of the money in Grandma's hand. "I don' need but ten, Grandma, 'n' I'm gon' send it right back to you soon as I git to Chicago 'n' find a job."

"You better take a couple o' mo' dollars, baby," Mama said, taking two of the bills out of her hand and reaching them to my sister.

"No'am, Mama, I don' need no mo'," Naomi said.

Papa, who had walked all the way out to the lane with Carrie Mae, was returning to the house with the man who had driven my sister up from Vicksburg at his side.

"Naomi," Mama warned, "don' say nothin' to yo' Papa 'bout this. You know he would give you the shirt off his back, but I jes' don' want him to know you a little short. It might cause him to worry mo' 'bout you being up there in Chicago; 'n', you know, he ain't been too well."

"Yessum," my sister said hastily, crushing the bills Grandma had given her in her hand and putting them in her pocketbook.

Papa led little Carrie Mae into the yard, and then he picked her up in his arms and whirled around with her while she giggled with delight. "Naomi," he said, "you got a little lady 'n' her jes' as pretty as her can be."

"Thank you, Papa; her is a good girl," my sister said, rising to go. "I tol' Mr. Jim I wasn't gon' stay long, 'cause he gotta git back 'n' go to work."

"Us sho' hates to see you go, but you take care o' yo'self 'n' write us 'n' let us know how you is," Mama said, hugging my sister for a long time.

Then Naomi hugged and kissed Grandma and Papa and me before she took Carrie Mae in her arms and walked the length of the porch with her. Suddenly, she thrust the child into Mama's arms and ran and got into the car; tears were streaming down her cheeks. Mr. Jim followed her and pulled off. My sister waved back blindly, holding a handkerchief up to her eyes.

When little Carrie Mae realized that her mother had gone, she cried for hours. Finally, Grandma patted her to sleep.

It was around the middle of July, after Mr. Holly had plowed up half our cotton and put the land in the soil bank, before we heard from Naomi. In the envelope with the letter was a five- dollar bill for Grandma. She said she had found a steady job at a laundry ironing sheets after weeks of looking for work. Said she was making twenty-seven dollars a week.

"Twenty-seben dollars a week," Grandma exclaimed with pride, "that gal's making all the money, but ironin' sheets with a smoothing iron, her sho' workin' fer evvy cent her gits. Po' little thing, ironin' all them sheets," Grandma lamented.

But the next sentence explained that my sister wasn't ironing sheets with a smoothing iron like Mama and Grandma did, but with a big machine called a mangle.

She said she had mailed a doll for Carrie Mae and a cap pistol for me. I jumped up and down in happiness. The letter didn't mention George, and Mama kept wondering what had happened to him. "Maybe her jes' forgot to tell us 'bout George 'n' the weddin'," she said in a worried voice.

"Jes' so her got a good job 'n' a place to stay," Papa said, "is all right."

"Thank the Lawd, her got a good job," Grandma added.

She also said that she was rooming with a lady on the Westside not far from the laundry where she worked. And she said she felt at home in Chicago because there were so many people there from Mississippi.

Within a few days the package came, and Papa picked it up at the store. It contained a doll for little Carrie Mae and my cap pistol. I was overjoyed and ran all the way up to General Lee's house to show it to him. He snapped it so much, I thought he was going to break it. When I began crying, Mrs. Luiza made him give it back to me.

Little Carrie Mae's doll was beautiful. It was snow white with blonde hair like one Naomi herself had had and had kept on the mantlepiece until somebody stole it. Naomi always thought Willie Fisher stole it to put himself between its legs the way he did the pictures of underwear models in the catalogue. Carrie Mae pulled at her doll's hair and beat its head on the floor when she didn't have one of its legs or arms in her mouth. Mama would take it from her sometimes and put it away, but Grandma would sneak it out again and give it to the child.

We heard regularly from my sister. Sometimes her letters contained money and sometimes they didn't. I did most of the writing to her for Mama and Papa because they didn't write so well, and Grandma couldn't read or write at all. My writing was mostly printing, and sometimes I left out one of the letters in Leavitt, the street on which she lived. I thought that was the strangest name I had ever heard. All we said in our letters was that we were well and hoped she was the same and that Carrie Mae was doing fine and growing every day. Sometimes we mentioned the church, and during cotton-picking time, we told about the crop and how nearly we were to being finished. Finding something to say seemed like the hardest thing in the world.

It was a long time before my sister mentioned George. Then in one of her letters she said he had taken up with another woman when he got to Chicago. She said she had thought so because he had stopped writing shortly after he had left Vicksburg. That was why, she said, she had wanted to go to Chicago and see. Said she had a new boyfriend named Roosevelt, who was better looking than George. He worked in the same laundry where she worked.

"I thought there was something' funny 'bout George," Mama said, "'n' the way Naomi went up there talkin' 'bout marryin' that slick-headed, shifty-eyed, yaller nigger."

"He wasn't all that slick-headed, Becky," Grandma said with a chuckle. "I thought he was good lookin'."

"You would, Miz Carrie, jes' 'cause he was yaller," Papa said.

"Well, since you ast fer it, I don' mind tellin' you, Silas, I don' like big black rusty niggers."

"Did you ever look at yo' own black self in the looking glass?" Papa shot back.

"I sho' is 'n' I spit at it," Grandma replied. "I know I'm black, but it wasn't none o' my doin, chile. Ef I had had anything to do with it, I sho' wouldn'ta come here my color."

"Ma, you 'n' Silas stop that kinda talk, 'n' I mean it," Mama said in an angry voice.

XXIX

Sharecroppers Evicted while Houses Are Torn Down

We finished picking cotton in early November. Could have finished sooner, but it rained a lot in October, and even on good days Papa didn't pick like he used to, and Grandma spent more time playing with little Carrie Mae and complaining about her back than she did picking. Of course, we had only four acres after Mr. Holly put the other four in the Soil Bank, and that didn't bring but five bales.

When Papa came from settling with Mr. Holly, he walked up and down the floor cursing just as he had done some years in the past when we came out shorter than he expected. But this time the old fire wasn't there. His curses soon settled into a low grumble that grew quieter and quieter as he sat down with his feet under his chair and not stretched out almost to the ashes as he had placed them in years past.

"How much did us git, Silas?" Mama asked in a low voice that was almost a whisper as if she was afraid to know.

"Twenty-six dollars," Papa cut it as short as he could.

"You mean outa us five bales, us ain't cleared but twenty-six dollars?"

"That's whut Mr. Holly say. Said it didn't bring but twenty-eight cents, 'n' after he took out fer fertilize 'n' poison 'n' that weed killer stuff 'n' the tractor work plus whut us took up at the sto' plus his ha'f that's all was left," Papa explained and sank deeper in his chair with no fight left.

"Twenty-six dollars," Mama repeated, "Naomi make a dollar mo'n that in a week up in Chicago, 'n' us done worked all year."

"Gawddamit, twenty-six dollars," Papa said with revived anger. Then he was quiet for a long time.

Finally, Mama asked, "Is us gon' stay here with Mr. Holly next year?"

Papa cleared his throat twice. I knew he was delaying because the answer he had was not good. When he did speak, he said, "Naw, I don' think so." He said it slowly and indifferently in a useless effort to ease Mama's anxiety and Grandma's stark fright.

"Silas, you mean Mr. Holly gon' put us off the place?" Mama asked in a voice of panic that lay bare all her fears.

"Don' worry, Becky, honey, us gon' find a place. Me 'n' Ben 'n' Tobe 'n' Tom gon start lookin' to-morrer," Papa rushed the words out of his mouth as if they were first-aid. "Mr. Holly said ef I was a little younger 'n' could drive a tractor, he might keep me. Tol' Ben 'n' Stock 'n' Tom the same thing. Jes' 'bout evvybody gon' have to move: Henry Woodson, Hamp, Miller Mose Johnson, Riley Jones, evvybody 'cep'n Jim Harris 'n' Luke Mason 'n' Joe Jones. They can stay with they boys who drive the tractors 'n' the cotton pickers 'n' them combine things whut gathers oats 'n' soybeans. 'N' Mr. Holly say he gon' bring some o' his young niggers from his other place at Cary to help work this place. 'N' he say he gon'put 'bout three hund'ered acres mo' in that soil bank thing," Papa explained, talking on and on as if to prevent Mama and Grandma from asking more questions.

But it was useless. Mama's question was waiting. "Where us goin', Silas?"

"I tol' you me 'n' Ben 'n' Tom 'n' Tobe was gon'look fer a place tomorrer, honey."

Grandma, who had been rocking quietly with little Carrie Mae in her lap, said, "Lawd, Jesus, I sho' hopes you find a place. There gotta be a place some where on a farm fer us."

"There is, Miz Carrie, I know there is; all us gotta do is find it."

"When do us have to move, Silas?" Mama wanted to know.

"Us got plenty time," Papa said boldly.

"'Tel after Christmas?"

"Almos', honey; us have 'tel December 15," Papa said as calmly as if it were a year or more.

"December 15? That ain't but a month off," Mama said in a desperate voice.

"I know," Papa said reassuringly, "but us oughta find something long befo' then."

"But ef y'all don' find a place by then, you reckon Mr. Holly'll let us stay on 'tel after Christmas," Mama asked.

"I don' know, Becky; Mr. Holly say he gon' move some o' the best houses out to the levee 'n' rent 'em to folks whut come 'round here to fish, 'n' he say he gon' use fo' or five fer his tractor drivers 'n' other workers, 'n' he gon' use some fer hay, but the rest, he say, he gon' tear down, 'n' us house is one o' them," Papa said as calmly as taking a drink of water, trying hard to keep Mama from getting too upset.

But he might as well have struck Grandma with an axe.

"Gon' tear this house down in the dead o' winter!" she screamed, frightening little Carrie Mae, who climbed down out of Grandma's lap and started crying.

Mama drew Carrie Mae to her side and patted her back gently while drying her tears. Then she turned to Grandma and said, "Ma, Silas gon' find us a place, don't you fret, Ma."

I got up and eased in between Mama and Papa. When Mama turned to see what I was doing, I asked, "How come us don' go up to Chicago 'n' live with Naomi?"

"Boy, is you crazy? Us ain't stud'in' 'bout goin' to no Chicago to live off'n Naomi. Her hardly got enuff fer herself, 'thout us goin' up layin' up on her," Mama said.

"But you 'n' Papa might be able to git jobs at the laundry where her work," I added.

"Us wanna live on a farm, boy, where us can 'leas' raise us own food; us ain't goin' to no Chicago," Papa said stoutly.

"Naw, Gawd," Grandma put in, "us sho' ain't goin' way up there to starve 'n' freeze to death. Bad enuff starvin' to death 'thout freezin', too."

For the next three weeks, Papa and Mr. Ben 'n' Mr. Tom 'n' Mr. Tobe went from plantation to plantation in Mr. Tobe's truck looking for a place to move but found nothing. All the plantations, Papa said, were growing less cotton and more cattle and putting more land in pastures and in that soil bank. And what cotton they were growing, he explained, wasn't worked with mules and hand labor anymore. Some of the plantations, he said, had as many as ten to fifteen tractors and three or four cotton pickers. "These white folks jes' don' need niggers nomo'," he said one night when he came home empty-handed again. Tears were in the corners of his eyes that did not roll down his cheeks but stood there like ponds in the moonlight as the light caught his face.

A week before our house was to be torn down, Papa still hadn't found a place. Mama had stopped asking him what we were going to do because she knew he didn't know and felt hurt and ashamed when she asked. She wasn't as restless as she usually was. When we had finished supper and the dishes had been washed, she sat quietly beside Papa, totally idle, except for the movement of her eyes that crossed and recrossed the fireplace in a restless motion. No half-finished quilt was in her lap, or garment to be patched; she was not whipping butter in a crock, or churning with perpetual strokes.

Finally, she turned to me and said, "River, write yo' sister, Naomi, 'n' tell her us gon' be put off the place, 'n' us can't find nowhere to move to. Tell her us got 'bout forty dollars."

Papa sat silently as I wrote, but Grandma prayed out loud, "Lawd, Jesus, You know us needs Yo' help; have mercy, Jesus," she repeated over and over.

We got a letter right back from my sister, saying she was going to send for us as soon as she got paid. The same day her letter came, the man in charge of tearing down the houses on the place came by our house to see when we were going to move. "Mr. Holly ordered me," the white man said, "to have this house tore down by thesixteenth. That gives you two mo' days."

"Yessuh, had a letter from my daughter today 'n' us gon' be outa here soon as her send us some money," Papa said. "'N' I'm goin' up to see Mr. Holly this evenin' 'bout buyin' us cow 'n' mules 'n' us new stove."

"I ain't got nothin' to do with that, boy; all I wanna know is ef you you gon' be outa this house in the next couple o' days."

"Yessuh, us gon' be out; I'm goin' up to see Mr. Holly right now 'bout the cow 'n' the mules," Papa replied. He had told us that Mr. Holly had said he would give him twenty-five dollars for our cow and five dollars apiece for the mules. Of course, Miss Lady was old and worn out, but Ole Salt could pull a plow or a wagon as well as he ever did.

When Papa came back from Mr. Holly's, he had only twenty dollars. Said that was all he would give him for our cow and stove and had refused to buy the mules altogether. "Tol' me he ain't got no use fer no mules, and ef I didn't need 'em where I was goin', to take over the levee 'n' shoot 'em, but don' leave 'em live on the place."

After Mr. Holly sent a man to get the stove and put the cow in one of his pastures, Papa got his pistol and put it in his pocket and then went out in the lot and put halters on Miss Lady and Ole Salt and led them toward the levee.

I ran after him, pleading for the mules, but Papa said, "Us can't leave 'em here to starve, can us, man?" Then he walked on leading the mules.

I wondered why he didn't ride Ole Salt and lead Miss Lady, but I guess he didn't have the heart to ride the mule.

I stood on the porch crying until I saw Papa lead the mules over the levee. Then I ran into the house in the hopes that I would not hear Papa's pistol, but I heard it anyway. It fired twice.

When Papa came back, he and Mama scraped together all the money in the house, except Grandma's, and spread it on the bed to see if they had enough to get to Chicago, if the money Naomi was sending didn't arrive in time. There was twenty-two of the twenty-six dollars from the cotton, Papa had spent four for gasoline for Mr. Tobe's truck, and there were twenty dollars for the cow, fifteen Mama had saved out of the money Naomi had been sending, and the thirteen Grandma had in her sack. Mama and Papa counted it, too, although it wasn't on the bed, and they didn't ask her for it. I think they were afraid she would start crying again. She had been crying off and on ever since I wrote my sister and repeating, "I ain't goin' to no Chicago, no indeed."

When Mama and Papa had finished counting, they had seventy dollars and thirty-five cents, including Grandma's money.

"This ain't enuff," Mama said. "The fare for me 'n' you 'n' Ma is twenty-fo' dollars 'n' ten cents apiece. That come to sebenty-two dollars 'n' thirty cents. River he can ride fer ha'f fare 'n' that come to twelve dollars 'n' a nickel. So us fo'teen dollar short."

"Fo'teen dollars short," Papa said, repeating the figure Mama had given. "You ain't figurin' in no fare for little Carrie Mae, is you?"

"Naw, us don' have to pay nothin' fer her," Mama replied.

"But I ain't figured in nothin' fer Willie takin' us out to Sixty-One to catch the bus, 'n' I ain't figured nothin' fer food all the way up there."

"Us jes' can't leave 'tel Naomi's money come; it oughta be here tomorrer or the next day," Papa said. "But jes' as soon as it come, us can leave. Evvything packed, ain't it?"

"Yeah," Mama answered, "us ain't carryin' nothin' but us clothes 'n' some quilts 'n' Ma's Bible 'n' the nine jars o' fruit 'n' stuff left over from whut us put up las' summer."

The next morning we could see trucks and trailers down on the low end of the plantation by Mr. Miller Jackson's. Mama stood on the porch, wondering what they were doing, while Papa and I walked across the field in that direction.

"Us be back afterwhile!" Papa hollered back.

When we got there, they had jacked the house up and were loading it on a low-built moving trailer. Mr. Miller and Mrs. Emma were standing on the edge of the yard beside their few belongings.

"Us waitin' fer Willie, Silas," Mr. Miller said, "to take us out to Sixty-One; us goin' to Memphis, where Esther is."

"That's good," Papa replied, "us jes' waitin' fer Naomi to send us a little mo' money so us can go there where her is."

"Y'all goin' to Chicago?" Mrs. Emma asked almost in a whisper and then turned away to watch them finish loading on the trailer what had been home to them for many years. Tears rolled down her face, which she wiped away with her hands.

"They gon' use us house to rent to folks what come here to fish," Mr. Miller explained. "'N' Stock's house over there been boarded up fer hay."

"It sho' is," Papa replied. "Where is they gone?"

"They gone to St. Louis; left yistiddy," Mr. Miller said.

"That's right, Joe he live in St. Louis, don't he?"

"Yeah, he sent fer 'em Tuesday."

"St. Louis. That ain't fer from Chicago, is it?" Papa asked.

"Naw, they all up North," Mr. Miller said.

"Here come Willie now," Papa said, looking up the road.

Mr. Willie's car pulled up and stopped just as the truck and trailer were pulling off with Mr. Miller's house. He got out of his car and walked over to where Mr. Miller and Mrs. Emma and Papa were gathering up the things on the ground to take them to the car. He picked up a bag.   "Sorry, I'm a little late, Miller," he said noisily as if to drown out the puffing of the truck, and there was no smile on his face.

When Mr. Miller and Mrs. Emma were loaded into the car, Papa shook their hands and held me up so that Mrs. Emma could kiss me goodbye. I don't remember what they said to Papa or what he said to them, but I remember the sad look on Mrs. Emma's face. Her deep-set brown eyes in her tan face looked even darker as she sat there waiting for Mr. Willie to pull off. There were no tears in them; they were dry as if all the tears they ever had had already been shed. And this seemed to make her sadness more stark and real. As the car drove off, she began looking back at the site where her house had stood. She was still looking back when the car pulled around a clump of trees and was out of sight.

Papa and I looked around, Mr. Gus Hawkins' house had been torn down as had Mr. Amos Johnson's, and Mr. Isaac Taylor's was boarded up. We stopped by Mr. Ben's; he and Mrs. Mary were packing up to leave.

"Us goin' to New 'Leans," Mrs. Mary said. "Got us money from George day fo' yistiddy."

"Us hope to git us money from Naomi in the mornin'," Papa said.

"Us leaving this evenin'," Mr. Ben explained. "Willie gon' take us to Vicksburg to catch the bus."

"Us comin' up there to see Becky 'n' Miz Carrie befo' us leave," Mr. Mary promised, and Papa and I walked on home.

Mrs. Mary and Mr. Ben did come up to our house before Mr. Willie came for them. All I can remember are the tears. For the first time since we had been told that we had to move, Mama let down completely and cried as if her heart would break. Papa tried to quiet her without success, and she and Mrs. Mary had out their cry. Then they embraced and Mrs. Mary kissed me and Grandma and little Carrie Mae, and she and Mr. Ben were gone.

More than two hours before noon the next day, Papa and I walked up to the store to wait for Mr. Willie to see if Naomi's letter came. We knew we were going to have a long wait, but I think Papa preferred to wait at the store to waiting at home and witnessing the sadness of Mama and Grandma. When we passed Mr. Tom Lee's house, he and Mrs. Luiza and General and the other children were loading their things into their wagon.

"Hey, Tom," Papa called out, "where you movin' to?"

"I don' know, Silas," he replied, "us jes' gon' load us things in the wagon 'n' us gon' drive 'tel us find a place."

"Which way is you goin'?"

"Us goin' to the hills, Silas," Mr. Tom replied. "You know there ain't nothin nomo' in the delta."

"Yeah, cause us done drove evvywhere in the delta 'n' us ain't found nothin'," Papa agreed. "Plantations all done put part they land in that soil bank 'n' the rest they farmin' with tractors 'n' cotton pickers, or they done planted grass 'n' is raising cattle."

"That's how come us goin' to the hills. Tobe already done gone. Said he was goin' down below Vicksburg somewhere," Mr. Tom explained.

"You mean Tobe already done left?"

"He sho' is; he left yistiddy, goin' South," Mr. Tom replied, pointing in the direction Mr. Tobe had gone. "Where y'all goin', Silas?"

"Us goin' to Chicago, I guess. Me 'n' River on us way to the sto' to meet Willie 'n' see ef us got a letter from Naomi.

"I hear Miller goin' to Memphis where one o' his chillum is," Mr. Tom said.

"Yeah; left yistiddy evenin'," Papa added.

While Papa and Mr. Tom finished talking, I walked over to where General Lee and Laura and Lucy were helping to load the wagon.

"Y'all goin' to the hills?" I asked.

"Yeahhhhhhhh," General replied, "whhhhhhhere y'all goooooooooin'?"

"Us goin' to Chicago, I reckon, ef Naomi send us the money."

"Chhhhhhhhhicago?"

"Yeah, ef us git the money," I repeated.

"IIIIIIIIIII sho' wish ussssss was goooooooooin' to Chhhhhhhhicago."

"Me, too," Laura said with her finger in her mouth.

"Chhhhhhhhicago is wayyyyyyyy up North, ain't it, River?"

"Yeah, that's whut Mama 'n' Grandma say."

We did not get to talk any further because Mrs. Luiza came out on the porch with an armful of things and called General to help her.

"How, y'all!" she said to me and Papa.

We hollered back, and then Papa said to Mr. Tom, "Us know you in a hurry, so us goin' on. Sho' hopes y'all find a good place in the hills."

Then Papa and I started off, but he stopped and turned around and went to the porch and shook hands with Mrs. Luiza and Mr. Tom.

"Goodbye!" he hollered back as he rejoined me in the road.

I hollered, "Goodbye!" to General and Papa and I walked on to the store.

When we came back by Mr. Tom's house, after waiting for Mr. Willie, who brought no letter from my sister, they were gone. I haven't seen them since and that's been twelve years now. Someday I am going back though; going back to Vicksburg and on south of it to see if I can find General.

Long before we got home, we could see two large trucks at our house.

"The mens musta done come to tear us house down," Papa said, increasing his pace.

"You don' reckon they gon' tear it down befo' us gits back, do you, Papa?" I asked.

"Naw, they wouldn't do nothin' like that," Papa assured me.

But as we neared the house, they were tearing it down. We could see the men loading something into the trucks. By the time we got to the gate leading from the lane to our house, we could see that they had taken down the doors and removed the windows. Inside, Mama and Grandma and little Carrie Mae were huddled close to the dying fire in the fireplace while the wind whistled through the house.

"How soon you gon' be outa here, boy?" the man asked Papa.

"Jes' as soon as I can git Willie to take us to Vicksburg," Papa replied gruffly.

"Well, make it snappy, boy; Mr. Holly want this house tore down befo' night."

Papa looked at the man but did not reply. Then he turned to me. "River, you run down to Willie's 'n' tell him to come right away 'n' git us 'n' take us to Vicksburg."

I ran as quickly as I could. I was all the way past Mr. Ben's before I realized that his house had been torn down. Only piles of bricks marked where it had stood. I looked back but kept on running toward Mr. Willie's, passing other houses that had been torn down or boarded up for hay. And I passed other places where houses used to stand, but they had been moved.

When Mr. Willie and I got back to my house, Carrie Mae was sitting on a box among our few things on a grassy spot in front of the house, and Papa and Mama were pleading with Grandma to come on out.

"Come on, Grandma, they tearin' the house down," I said, joining in the plea, but she did not budge. Finally, Mama and Papa tried to drag her out, but she held on to the framing of the door.

"Let me 'lone, y'all, I ain' goin' nowhere!" she said. Tears were running down her face and her boney old fingers dug into the boards around the door.

"Come on, Ma, they tearin' the house down," Mama pleaded. "You can't stay here."

"I done tol' y'all, I ain't goin' nowhere!" Grandma insisted.

"But you gotta go, Miz Carrie," Papa urged.

"Now, don' act like this, Ma; me 'n' Silas tryin' to help you; us goin' to Chicago, where Naomi is."

"I an't goin' to no Chicago; I ain't goin' nowhere 'cep'n righ here, les'n Silas gon' shoot me like he done his mules!" Grandma answered with a sharpness in her voice. But it wasn't sharp enough to cutaway the sadness in her eyes.

By this time the men were on top of the house, taking off the roof. I caught Grandma's dress and started pulling on it.

"Please, Grandma, don' let the roof fall in on you, the mens is tearin' it off!" I pleaded.

"I don' care, I ain't goin' nowhere!" Grandma stood firm.

"Willie," Mama called, "come help us git Ma to yo' car!"

Mr. Willie came running. "Now Miz Carrie, this is Willie." There was a smile on his face and in his voice. "Come on, Miz Carrie, I'm gon' take you fer a nice long ride in my car 'n' then I'm gon' bring you back."

"Naw, you tryin' to fool me, Willie."

"No'am, I ain't tryin' to fool you, I'm gon' bring you back."

"Willie, is you sho' you ain't foolin' me?"

"No'am, I ain't foolin', Miz Carrie."

Grandma's fingers slowly let go of the frame of the door, and Papa and Mr. Willie carried her to the car and put her down by the side of little Carrie Mae. Mama got in on the other side. Mr. Willie had already loaded our two boxes and the quilts into the trunk of his car. Papa and I got in the front seat with Mr. Willie. He started the motor up and was about to pull off when Grandma jumped out of the car and started back to the house.

Papa and Mr. Willie overtook her.

"I don' wanna go to no Chicago; it's too cold up there. Please don' make me go," she pleaded.

"But us gotta go, Ma, cause us ain't got no place else to move to," Mama explained.

"Yeah, Miz Carrie, you gon' like it up there with Naomi," Papa said.

As they held her, the wild look went out of her eyes, the tears dried on her cheeks, the moan in her voice died, and and in a strange way, she yielded and walked back and got into the car with little assistance.

"Where y'all goin', out to Sixty-One to catch the five o'clock bus?" Mr. Willie asked.

"Naw," Papa said, "us goin' to Reverend Fisher's to wait 'tel Naomi send us the rest o' us bus fare. You know where he live don't you?

"Course, I know where he live," Mr. Willie said. "I was by there las' week."

As Mr. Willie turned on to the main road that led from the plantation to Vicksburg, Grandma started crying, then she began screaming, and she cried and screamed almost all the way to town. Mr. Willie stopped the car when she first started crying, and Papa got in the back seat with Mama with Grandma sitting between them. Little Carrie Mae and I had the front seat with Mr. Willie.

At Reverend Fisher's house, we all had supper, except Grandma. She went straight to bed still crying. When I went to bed, I patted her until I fell asleep. The next morning when I called her, she did not answer. I shook her, but she did not move. Then I rose up in the bed and looked into her face. Her eyes were wide open, frozen into a sightless stare. Tear stains marked a trail all the way down her face into the wrinkles around her mouth, and on down under her thin chin. She was dead.

After the undertaker came and took Grandma away, little Carrie Mae and I played with Woodrow and Addle Lou; Willie and Daisy Lee and Lucy were at school. I tried to ride Woodrow's tricycle, but I was too large for it. Then he tried to show me how to skate, but after I fell twice, I gave it up. When Willie came home from school, he rode me around the block several times on the handlebars of his bicycle. I thought it was the best ride I had ever had.

The next day Mr. Willie came from the Bend to bring the letter from Naomi. It contained thirty-two dollars. This was more than enough for our bus fares; we had needed only fourteen, including Grandma's. We didn't need a ticket for her anymore, but there were the funeral expenses.

"Us got a hund'ered 'n' two dollars 'n' thirty-five cents," Papa told Reverend Fisher. "Now us don' need but fifty-five dollars to git to Chicago, 'n' us can put the rest on Miz Carrie's funeral."

"Whut about Naomi's fare down here for the funeral 'n' back?" the preacher asked.

Papa paused and looked at Mama, who spoke up slowly. "Reverend, me 'n' Silas thought us wouldn't tell her 'bout Ma 'tel us git there; us don' see no need fer her to come 'n' spend all that money."

"I guess you right," Reverend Fisher agreed. "Anyhow, you gon' need all the money you got to git to Chicago 'n' git things straight when you git there," he added.

"But whut 'bout Miz Carrie's funeral?" Papa asked.

"Don't you worry 'bout that, Brother Henry 'n' Sister Henry; me 'n' my church gon' look after that," Reverend Fisher said with a quick smile. "I ain't gon' never fergit whut y'all did fer me 'n' my chillun when I had to git off the place. Naw, Gawd, the Lawd knows I ain't gon' never fergit that," he said almost as if he were preaching, and his eyes became a little misty.

"Yeah, Sister Henry 'n' Brother Henry," his wife, who had come into the room, said, "Reverend done tol' me 'bout y'all many times, 'n' how y'all helped him git off that plantation. 'N' I was at Lilly Mae's trial 'n' I heard Brother Henry speak up fer her, 'n' he was the onliest one. Reverend tol' me it was at the risk o' bein' put off the place yo'self. So don't y'all worry 'bout nothin'."

Mrs. Fisher was a large woman like Mrs. Ida, Mr. Tobe's wife, but she was friendlier and carried a smile almost like Mr. Willie.

That Sunday the church raised ninety-four dollars toward Grandma's funeral, and Reverend Fisher announced that they would raise something every Sunday until it was paid out. The goodness of the people brought tears to Mama's eyes.

"Ain't they wonderful?," she said in a voice that was muffled by her handkerchief, "'N' they didn't even know Ma."

The next afternoon, Reverend Fisher preached Grandma's funeral. Willie and Daisy Lee and Lucy came home early from school so that they could go. I don't remember much of what Reverend Fisher said; I was too busy helping Papa hold Mama and wiping her face and patting her back. But I do remember him talking about the plantation, saying, "Where Sister Carrie Johnson's gone there ain't nomo' cotton to chop 'n' pick, nomo' weeds 'n' boll weevils to fight, nomo' comin' out in debt at settlement time, 'n' nomo' plantation owners to run away from in the night. Up there," he continued, "the Lawd owns the plantation 'n' evvybody on it. Don' nobody go hongry, don' nobody come up short, 'n' don' nobody work too hard, 'cause evvybody lives on flowery beds of ease. Sister Johnson done earned her place up there; her done sweated out life on the plantation; her done paid the price."

Those words brought the loudest scream from Mama I have ever heard, and everybody in the church seemed to say, "Have mercy, Jesus," and tired feet patted in a restless rhythm.

When Reverend Fisher had finished, they opened the casket and everybody walked past and look at Grandma. Willie had to hold Woodrow up so that she could see, and Papa held little Carrie Mae up high, while Mama stood staring and crying. It was a beautiful gray casket, lined with white silk that must have felt soft and smooth. I stood there wishing Grandma could see it.

That night, Reverend Fisher and his wife took us to the bus station. As we left their house, Willie, Daisy Lee, Lucy Mae, Addie Lou, and Woodrow stood at the gate, waving goodbye. At the station, we boarded the bus for Chicago. Up Sixty-One as we neared the turn-off to the Bend, Papa pressed his face against the window, trying to see the road. It was as if he knew he would never travel the road to the Bend again.